Adventures along the Star-Spangled Banner Trail

Library of Congress Cataloging-in-Publication Data
 Eshelman, Ralph E.
  In full glory reflected : discovering the War of 1812 in the Chesapeake / Ralph E.
Eshelman and Burton K. Kummerow ; foreword by Maryland Governor Martin
O'Malley ; introduction by Donald R. Hickey ; illustrations by Gerry Embleton,
Richard Schlecht, and Patrick O'Brien ; maps by Robert E. Pratt.
       p. cm.
  "Adventures along the Star-Spangled Banner Trail."
  Includes bibliographical references and index.
ISBN-13: 978-0-9842135-5-9 (hdbk. : alk. paper); ISBN-13: 978-0-9842135-4-2
(pbk. : alk. paper); ISBN-10: 0-9842135-5-4 (hdbk. : alk. paper) ; ISBN-10: 0-9842135-
4-6 (pbk. : alk. paper)
  1. United States—History—War of 1812. 2. Maryland—History—War of 1812.
3. Virginia—History—War of 1812. 4. Chesapeake Bay Region (Md. and Va.)—
History, Military—19th century. 5. Chesapeake Bay Region (Md. and Va.)—History,
Local. 6. Chesapeake Bay Region (Md. and Va.)—Guidebooks. 7. Historic sites—
Chesapeake Bay Region (Md. and Va.)—Guidebooks. 8. Historic sites—Maryland—
Guidebooks. 9. Historic sites—Virginia—Guidebooks. 10. Historic sites—Washing-
ton (D.C.)—Guidebooks. I. Kummerow, Burton K. (Burton Kent), 1940– II. Title.
  E355.1.C485E825 2012

  973.5′2—dc23   2012000943

Designed by Alex Castro, Castro/Arts LLC, Chestertown, Maryland
Printed by Walsworth Publishing Company, Inc., Marceline, Mo.

Preceding spread: The *Pride of Baltimore II* is a near replica of the
Baltimore clippers that operated successfully as privateers through
the War of 1812. Inspired by the famous privateer *Chasseur,* the *Pride II*
sails the oceans serving as an ambassador for Maryland and the City of
Baltimore in port cities around the world.

THIS BOOK IS DEDICATED
WITH LOVE TO
PATRICIA BROSNAHAN
KUMMEROW

"Time wastes too fast: every letter I trace
tells me with what rapidity Life follows my
Pen; the days and hours of it are flying over
our heads like light clouds of a windy day,
never to return more."

—*The Life and Opinions of Tristram Shandy,
Gentleman, 1759–67*, Laurence Sterne

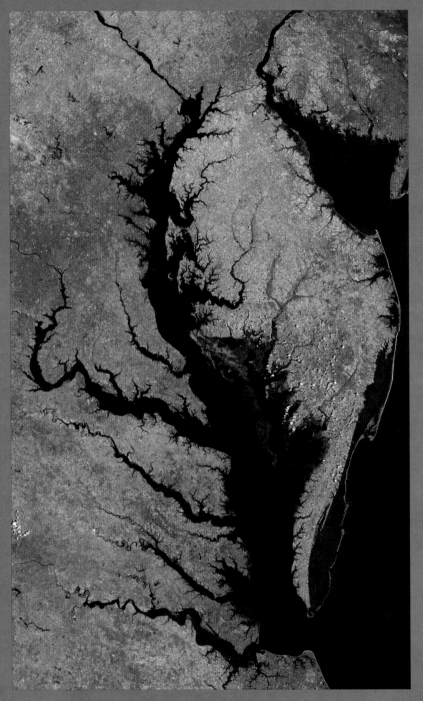

The Chesapeake Bay, shown here in satellite and map view, is approximately 200 miles long, nearly 30 miles wide at its widest point, with a total shoreline including its tributaries of 11,684 miles and a surface area including its major tributaries of 4,479 square miles. The British navy was able to freely use the Bay and its tidal waterways to attack and raid nearly at will, meeting only limited resistance from the Americans.

Contents

Circa 1814 view of the bombardment of Fort McHenry

FOREWORD

The Chesapeake Bay holds a special magic for all of us. As America's greatest estuary and gateway to a continent, it is famous throughout the world as the home of breathtaking vistas, succulent blue crabs, great sailing, and charming coastal villages. It has earned a celebrated reputation as the "land of pleasant living." Our nation's capital lies on the Potomac River, one of the Chesapeake's principal tributaries. The largest naval base in the world is near the Bay's mouth. The U.S. Naval Academy and great cities like Baltimore, Norfolk, and Annapolis grace its shores.

The Chesapeake's human history goes back thousands of years. As soon as the Bay was formed in the wake of the last ice age, American Indians settled here. Europeans and Africans arrived to what Captain John Smith found a matchless paradise. Four centuries later, that bounty has been tempered by challenges that test our resolve to preserve and protect. But the tapestry of a rich history, spanning multitudes of generations, has been woven into our collective memory and who we are today.

Perhaps the most dramatic moment in that history deserves more attention than it has been given. When the young United States declared war on Great Britain in 1812, the tragedy and triumph of the previous generation's revolution began anew. Over eighteen long months the superior British navy turned the Chesapeake into a landscape of terror and destruction. Public buildings in Washington, D.C., were burned. Only weeks later, Baltimore repelled the same invaders with a determined defense. It was a joyous moment of triumph that inspired our national anthem and created the Star-Spangled Banner, a flag that has become a treasured icon.

This book, *In Full Glory Reflected*, brings that nearly forgotten era vividly to life. A partnership of the Maryland War of 1812 Bicentennial Commission, the National Park Service, the Maryland Historical Trust, and the Maryland Historical Society has brought expert historians, illustrators, and travel writers together to paint a dynamic portrait of the colorful era often called "the second war for independence." On every page, you will find history and travel adventures to inspire your discovery of the places where the real war in the Chesapeake occurred.

The story is remarkable and the sights along the Star-Spangled Banner National Historic Trail are memorable. During these bicentennial years of remembrance and commemoration, discover tales of disgrace and honor, of despair and hope. Then explore a national trail of memory that turns back the clock. We invite you to enjoy this inspiring journey into the vigorous, gripping, and ongoing story of life in the Chesapeake.

Martin O'Malley, Governor of Maryland

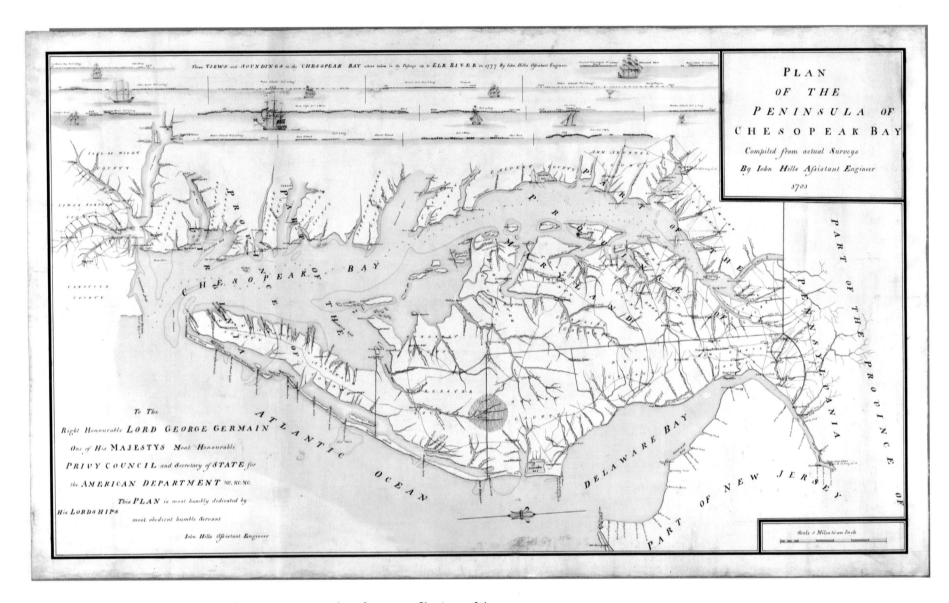

The 1781 John Hills manuscript chart, the first surviving example to feature profile views of the shoreline of the Chesapeake Bay and its rivers, was widely used for seventy-five years. It was probably used by the British during the Revolutionary War and possibly the War of 1812.

PREFACE

The title *In Full Glory Reflected,* a phrase from the second stanza of Francis Scott Key's lyrics for the "Star-Spangled Banner," points to one of the main reasons for this book. Just as people are unfamiliar with anything but the first of four stanzas, few people know much about the War of 1812, the dramatic event that provided the background for those words. However, we regularly hear and sing our national anthem and may know something about the giant flag that inspired it, now displayed in the Smithsonian Institution.

In 1814, the future of the young United States hung in the balance. During that hot, stormy summer, the British burned many public buildings in Washington and threatened Baltimore. When enemy ships bombarded Fort McHenry and enemy troops defeated Baltimore militia near North Point, the situation looked bleak. But the bombardment and a night naval flanking attack failed to capture the fort. Seeing the superior numbers of Baltimore defenders dug in with over a hundred cannon, the British called off their assault. The victorious moment became a lasting point of pride for a new country. That pride is still with us today as the Star-Spangled Banner, both the song and the flag.

Now, two centuries after those momentous events, the National Park Service has unveiled a Star-Spangled Banner National Historic Trail. The trail, as established by the U.S. Congress in 2008, is not only designed to tell the story of the dramatic events that produced our national anthem but also to place those events on the landscape where they took place. This book is designed as a popular companion piece to that important initiative.

In Full Glory Reflected: Discovering the War of 1812 in the Chesapeake will introduce you to this story, fought through the Chesapeake region over three years (1812–15), in exciting new ways. The lively historical narrative of Part I, tragic but also sometimes comic, is filled with the very human sacrifices, sufferings, failures, and achievements of a large cast of characters from both sides of the conflict. The engaging illustrations were produced by three internationally celebrated artists. They skillfully bring to life scenes that occurred before the advent of photography, and in doing so they amplify the visions of our imaginations.

By delving into Part II, potential travelers will be able to find, visit, and explore many of the War of 1812 sites along this historic trail. Our aim is to provide an illustrated popular account of the dramatic events and foster the preservation of the landscapes, historic buildings, archaeological sites, artifacts, and documents that keep these events alive for modern Americans. You can continue your exploration of places and programs related to the war in the Chesapeake through websites produced by the National Park Service for the Star-Spangled Banner National Historic Trail (www.nps.gov/stsp and www.starspangledtrail.net).

A brief introduction, contributed by Professor Donald R. Hickey, one of the best scholars of the era working today, follows this preface. It provides context for readers discovering how this historic drama unfolded. For those who want to continue exploring the War of 1812 in more depth, we provide a guide to the best of available further reading and websites.

In Full Glory Reflected will launch you into a fascinating world of free trade and sailors' rights, Federalists and Republicans, militia and Redcoats, rockets and bomb vessels, gun barges and ships-of-the-line, notorious villains and celebrated heroes. You are welcome to come back to the story again and again, discovering adventures that uncover a Chesapeake history you may have never known existed.

A Note about the Historical Illustrations

There was no photography during the era of the War of 1812, and contemporary illustrations are rare. With a commitment to bring the times to life and stimulate the imagination, we commissioned illustrations with a wide range of subjects, civilian as well as military, to complement a lively text and put readers into the shoes of the people who lived the War of 1812 in the Chesapeake.

Each and every piece of artwork has been researched to make the depiction as accurate as possible. Artists Gerry Embleton, Richard Schlecht, and Patrick O'Brien are experts in their own right on period clothing, ships rigging, etc. We went even further by engaging a whole range of authorities to review preliminary sketches. Still, none of us can totally recreate those lost days, and we will never know many of the details that made up the fabric of daily life. We made choices where certainty was impossible. For example, what color and shape was the pennant on Joshua Barney's flagship *Scorpion*? How many stars did it have? Did Barney's gun barges have leeboards and did the flotillamen stand or sit to row? These details may seem trivial to most, but our commitment to precision in recreating past events has been unwavering. The quest for all of us has often been frustrating and elusive but also fascinating and fun.

A Note about Sources and Terminology

Our aim has been to use the voices of the time as much as possible, and there are many contemporary quotes in this book's history sections. These quotes can bring more understanding to a complex political or military situation.

Many of these quotes, especially the comments of well-known figures like Presidents Jefferson and Madison or Admiral Cockburn and General Winder, are readily available in popular and scholarly histories of the war. The accessible and rich memoirs of lesser-known figures like Lieutenant Gleig are also sprinkled throughout the text. The newspapers and magazines of the era, especially the Baltimore *Niles' Weekly Register* and the Washington *National Intelligencer,* now largely available online, are an additional and rich source. Citations to direct quotes are provided in the notes section in the back of the book, keyed by page number.

Professor Donald Hickey has provided a bibliographic essay to give any reader who wants to delve more deeply into the subject a good beginning selection. One of the best collections of period quotes and their origins is the comprehensive resource guide *The War of 1812 in the Chesapeake: A Reference Guide to Historic Sites in Maryland, Virginia, and the District of Columbia,* by Ralph E. Eshelman, Scott S. Sheads, and Donald R. Hickey.

Definitions of words that might not be familiar to the reader are given in the glossary near the end of the book. Many words have more than one meaning and the definitions of words change over time. This glossary defines words as used in context during the War of 1812.

ACKNOWLEDGMENTS

In Full Glory Reflected is the result of cooperative efforts between the Maryland War of 1812 Bicentennial Commission, the National Park Service, the Maryland Historical Trust, and the Maryland Historical Society. Funding for the public/private partnership was provided by the Maryland Office of Tourism Development in part through a grant from the Federal Highway Administration, National Scenic Byways Program, the Chesapeake Bay Office of the United States National Park Service, and significant private donations by twenty-one friends and family in memory of Patricia B. Kummerow. This funding made it possible to assemble an extraordinary group of talented individuals, considered among the very best in their fields, to research; write; illustrate with specially commissioned artwork, photographs, and maps; and design the book.

THE WORKING TEAM

A core group from the various organizations worked together for almost two years to plan and produce this marriage of 1812 Chesapeake history and travel.

SUZANNE E. COPPING, Project Manager, Star-Spangled Banner National Historic Trail, National Park Service

PAULA A. DEGEN, Interpretive Specialist, National Park Service Chesapeake Bay Office

NICOLE A. DIEHLMANN, Chief, Office of Preservation Planning and Museum Programs, Maryland Historical Trust

RALPH E. ESHELMAN, Cultural Resource Consultant, Historian, Researcher, and Writer

BURTON K. KUMMEROW, President and CEO, Maryland Historical Society and President of Historyworks, Inc.

BILL PENCEK, Executive Director, Maryland 1812 Bicentennial Commission and Deputy Assistant Secretary, Maryland Division of Tourism, Film and the Arts, Maryland Department of Business and Economic Development

The working and creative teams would like to especially thank Maryland Governor Martin O'Malley, John Maounis, Superintendent NPS Chesapeake Bay Office, and the Maryland War of 1812 Bicentennial Commission for their support over the course of this project.

We are indebted to Donald R. Hickey, well-known War of 1812 scholar, for providing the introduction and bibliographic essay for this book, as well as a review of the historical text. Thanks also to Mary Lou Kenney for her critical support in editing the text. Elke Hautala provided needed assistance in chasing down the multitude of illustrations used throughout the book. Robert J. Brugger, Senior Editor, and Jack Holmes, Development Director, at the Johns Hopkins University Press were particularly helpful during the early stages of launching this project. The Maryland Historical Society staff, including Director of Publications and Library Services Pat Anderson, Photo and Digitization Coordinator Jenny Ferretti, and Collections and Exhibitions Manager Heather Haggstrom, provided quality assistance in accessing the Society's vast collection of artifacts and graphics.

Others who deserve acknowledgment for helping to make the book possible include: Lawrence Babits, Paul Berry, Michael Bosworth, Grace Mary Brady, Tim and Martha Brosnahan, Nancy Bramucci, Jeffrey Buchheit, Cindy Chance, W. Dickerson Charlton, Wayne E. Clark, Evie Cohen, Phil Deters, Christopher George, Mary Margaret Revell Goodwin, Scott Harmon, Miriam Hensley, David Hildebrand, Mark Hildebrand, Peter Himmelheber, Betty Hobgood, Elizabeth Hughes, Ross Kimmel, James Kochan, the late Patricia B. Kummerow, Nancy N. Kurtz, Susan Langley, J. Rodney Little, Kate Marks, Kent Mountford, Bernadette Pulley Pruitt, Linda Reno, Robert Reyes, Franklin Robinson, Scott S. Sheads, Donald G. Shomette, Michael A. Smolek, Blaine Taylor, Fran Taylor, Gay Vietzke, Steve Vogel, Anna von Lunz, Blaise Willig, and Harry Young.

The following individuals provided critical reviews of one or more illustrations specifically executed for this book: Lawrence Babits, Gerry Embleton, Christopher George, Chuck Ives, Ross Kimmel, James Kochan, Larry Leone, John McCavitt, Robert Reyes, Edward Seufert, Scott Sheads, Donald Shomette, Vince Vaise, and Glenn Williams.

On June 1, 1813, U.S. frigate *Chesapeake*, flying a large white flag proclaiming "Free Trade and Sailors' Rights," engaged with H. M. frigate *Shannon* several miles off Boston. After exchanging broadsides and small arms fire, Captain James Lawrence, commander of *Chesapeake*, was mortally wounded and taken below deck where he gave his final order "Don't give up the ship!" Although *Chesapeake* was forced to surrender, Lawrence's last words became an American naval battle cry.

Introduction

When the United States declared war on Great Britain on June 18, 1812, few residents of the Chesapeake Bay region anticipated what was in store for them. Although Federalists—the political party of George Washington—grumbled, most Republicans—the party of Thomas Jefferson—welcomed the news with smiles, handshakes, and public celebrations. At long last, there would be an accounting for British violations of American rights. The nation's honor would be vindicated, and its sovereignty confirmed. In the eyes of most Republicans, this was a long-overdue second war for independence. As they saw it, 1812 was a needed replay of 1776.

The United States went to war to force the British to give up some hated maritime policies. The "Orders-in-Council" (1807 and 1809) restricted American trade with the European Continent. Impressment was the Royal Navy practice of conscripting seamen from American merchant vessels. These policies were a direct outgrowth of the Napoleonic Wars that had raged in Europe since 1803. Although they had a significant impact on the United States, their main purpose was to further Britain's war effort against Napoleonic France.

Some Republicans hoped that a declaration of war by itself would win British concessions. The British would be so shocked by the decision that they would cave in to American demands. If there were fighting, the new nation could hardly challenge powerful Great Britain on the high seas so Canada would have to be the target. The loose group of British provinces to the north had a small and scattered population (only 500,000 compared to 7.7 million in the United States) and the loyalty of the people living in Canada was suspect. There was a French population in Lower Canada (now Quebec) as well as a large number of Americans who had migrated north after 1792 to take advantage of liberal land policies and low taxes.

Under these circumstances, the conquest of most of Canada was expected to be, in the words of Thomas Jefferson, "a mere matter of marching." Once the United States conquered Canada, the British would have to concede the maritime issues in order to get their territory back. If they refused, then Canada might be permanently annexed. There would be little that the British could do about it since they were busy fighting Napoleon in Europe.

Events, however, did not play out as Republicans had anticipated. The British repealed the Orders-in-Council, lifting the trade restrictions just as the United States was declaring war. However, Great Britain refused to make concessions on impressment. The United States launched a three-pronged invasion into Canada in 1812, but it ended in failure. A similar invasion in 1813 was successful in the West, a theater of operations so remote that the victories did not alter the course of the war.

In the spring of 1814, Britain and her allies on the Continent subdued France and compelled Napoleon to abdicate. Even before the European war ended, the British were cautiously redeploying men and ships to North America. Now they were clearly in the driver's seat in the American war. But waging offensive war in North America proved no easier for the British in 1814 than it had been for the Americans earlier in Canada. By 1815, the warring parties agreed in the Treaty of Ghent (negotiated in what today is Belgium) to restore all conquered territory and return to the *status quo ante bellum* (the state that existed before the war).

Although the British had been on the defensive early in the war, they used their naval power to conduct predatory raids on the Atlantic Coast. Their aim was to draw off American regular troops from the Canadian invasions and bring the war home to Americans. While they failed to force the redeployment of any American soldiers from Canada, Britain showed Americans on the eastern seaboard the perils of waging war against the mighty Mistress of the Seas.

The principal theater for British raids in 1813 and again in 1814 was the Chesapeake Bay region. This was a target-rich environment that was home

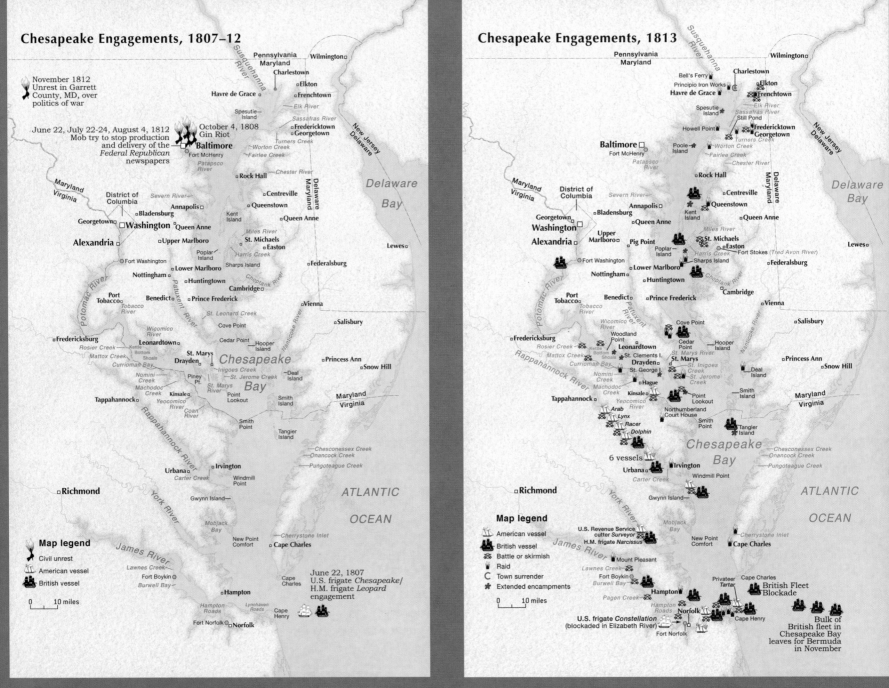

This series of maps demonstrates the escalating tension between the United States and Britain (1807–12) and the massive number of engagements that occurred in the Chesapeake region throughout 1813 and 1814.

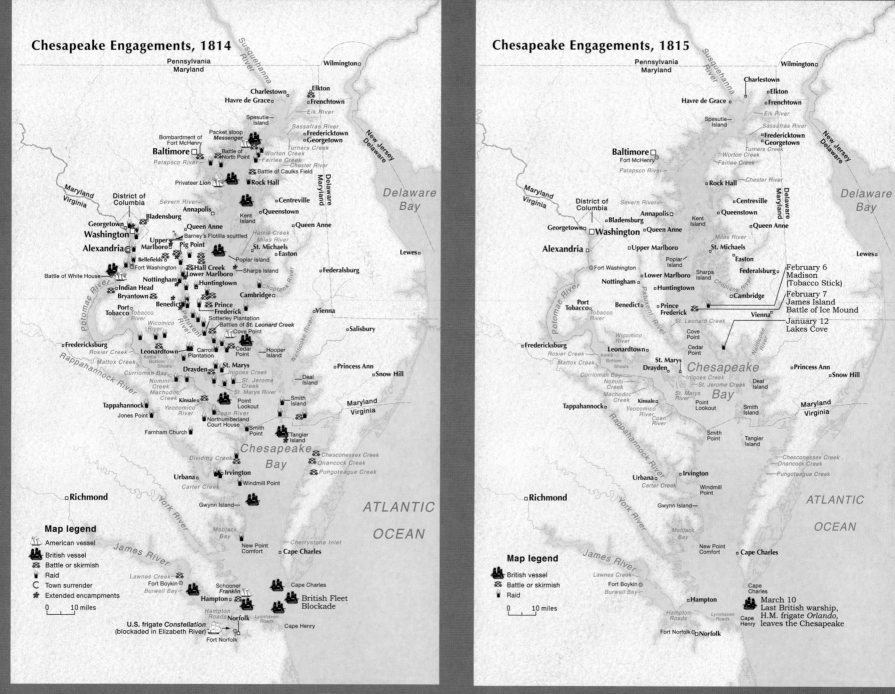

Chesapeake Engagements, 1814

Pennsylvania
Maryland

Wilmington

Charlestown
Havre de Grace
Elkton
Frenchtown
Elk River

Spesutie Island
Packet sloop *Messenger*
Sassafras River
Fredericktown
Georgetown
Turners Creek

Bombardment of Fort McHenry
Baltimore
Battle of North Point
Worton Creek
Fairlee Creek
Chester River
Patapsco River
Battle of Caulks Field

Privateer *Lion*
Rock Hall

Maryland
Virginia
District of Columbia
Bladensburg
Annapolis
Severn River
Centreville
Queenstown
Queen Anne
Kent Island

Georgetown
Washington
Queen Anne
Harris Creek
Miles River
Barney's Flotilla scuttled
St. Michaels
Easton

Alexandria
Upper Marlboro
Pig Point
Bellefields
Fort Washington
Poplar Island
Sharps Island

Battle of White House
Hall Creek
Lower Marlboro
Choptank River
Federalsburg

Indian Head
Nottingham
Huntingtown
Cambridge

Bryantown
Prince Frederick
Port Tobacco
Tobacco River
Benedict
Sotterley Plantation
Battles of *St. Leonard Creek*
Cove Point
Vienna

Fredericksburg
Rosier Creek
Mattox Creek
Leonardtown
Carroll Plantation
Cedar Point
Hooper Island
Salisbury

Drayden
St. Marys
Inigoes Creek
Deal Island
Princess Ann
Snow Hill

Currioman Bay
Nomini Creek
Machodoc Creek
Kinsale
St. Jerome Creek
St. Marys River
Smith Island

Tappahannock
Yeocomico River
Point Lookout
Maryland
Virginia

Jones Point
Coan River
Northumberland Court House
Smith Point

Farnham Church
Tangier Island

Dividing Creek
Chesapeake Bay
Chesconessex Creek
Onancock Creek
Pungoteague Creek

Urbana
Irvington
Windmill Point

Richmond
Carter Creek

ATLANTIC OCEAN

Gwynn Island

Mobjack Bay
New Point Comfort
Cherrystone Inlet
Cape Charles

Map legend
- American vessel
- British vessel
- Battle or skirmish
- Raid
- C Town surrender
- Extended encampments

0 ___ 10 miles

Lawnes Creek
Fort Boykin
Burwell Bay
Schooner *Franklin*
Hampton
Cape Charles

British Fleet Blockade

Hampton Roads
Norfolk
Lynnhaven Roads
Cape Henry

U.S. frigate *Constellation* (blockaded in Elizabeth River)
Fort Norfolk

Chesapeake Engagements, 1815

Pennsylvania
Maryland

Wilmington

Charlestown
Havre de Grace
Elkton
Frenchtown
Elk River

Spesutie Island
Sassafras River
Fredericktown
Georgetown
Turners Creek

Baltimore
Fort McHenry
Worton Creek
Fairlee Creek
Chester River
Patapsco River

Rock Hall

Maryland
Virginia
District of Columbia
Bladensburg
Annapolis
Severn River
Centreville
Queenstown
Queen Anne
Kent Island

Georgetown
Washington
Queen Anne
Miles River
St. Michaels
Easton

Alexandria
Upper Marlboro
Poplar Island
Sharps Island

Fort Washington
Federalsburg

Nottingham
Lower Marlboro
Huntingtown

February 6
Madison (Tobacco Stick)

Port Tobacco
Tobacco River
Benedict
Prince Frederick
St. Leonard Creek
Vienna

February 7
James Island
Battle of Ice Mound

Cambridge

January 12
Lakes Cove

Fredericksburg
Rosier Creek
Mattox Creek
Leonardtown
Cedar Point
Cove Point

Drayden
St. Marys
Inigoes Creek
Deal Island
Princess Ann
Snow Hill

Currioman Bay
Nomini Creek
Machodoc Creek
Kinsale
St. Jerome Creek
St. Marys River
Point Lookout
Chesapeake Bay
Smith Island

Tappahannock
Yeocomico River
Coan River
Smith Point
Tangier Island
Maryland
Virginia

Chesconessex Creek
Onancock Creek
Pungoteague Creek

Urbana
Irvington
Windmill Point

Richmond
Carter Creek

ATLANTIC OCEAN

Gwynn Island

Mobjack Bay
New Point Comfort
Cape Charles

Map legend
- British vessel
- Battle or skirmish
- Raid

0 ___ 10 miles

Lawnes Creek
Fort Boykin
Burwell Bay

Hampton

March 10
Last British warship, H.M. frigate *Orlando*, leaves the Chesapeake

Hampton Roads
Lynnhaven Roads
Cape Charles
Cape Henry
Fort Norfolk
Norfolk

New Jersey
Delaware

Delaware Bay

Lewes

Delaware Maryland

The Chesapeake suffered more raids, skirmishes, and battles than any other theater in the War of 1812. By March 1815 the British had withdrawn completely from the region.

to Baltimore and Washington as well as millions of dollars in shipping fleets, tobacco, and other valuable commodities. British raiding parties in the Chesapeake usually adhered to the international rules of war—or at least how the raiders understood those rules. They paid cash for provisions and other supplies that they needed, although sometimes at grossly undervalued prices. They confiscated or destroyed whole fleets of ships and boats as well as any commodities or other property they found in warehouses. But more alarming, they burned unoccupied private homes or, if they met with resistance, whole towns. The inexperienced American militia called up to fight them often arrived late or were quickly overpowered by the invaders.

In the summer of 1814, the British continued their raids but also undertook major operations, targeting both Washington and Baltimore. Although they briefly occupied the national capital and burned its public buildings, they were rebuffed in Baltimore. The Royal Navy could not soften up the formidable city defenses to help the British land attack. British bomb and rocket ships were unable to get close enough to batter Fort McHenry into submission. The successful defense of the fort by the Americans so moved Francis Scott Key that he wrote the lyrics to a song we know today as "The Star-Spangled Banner."

People living in the Chesapeake did not soon forget the British depredations. No theater of operations was hit harder by the war, and the region was slow to rebuild and recover. Oft-repeated tales of British misdeeds kept the embers of hatred alive for decades. Even today, there are some families with long memories who are still angry about the looting and burning that occurred. The only real winners in the conflict were several thousand runaway slaves who found sanctuary in British camps or on British ships and then made new lives for themselves in Canada, the West Indies, or elsewhere in the British Empire. The loss of these slaves only added to the economic misery of the region (although, long after the war was over, the British provided reparations to some property owners).

If the British war in the Chesapeake left much hard feeling, it also contributed to the progress of the young United States. "The Star-Spangled Banner" became a popular patriotic tune that Congress finally proclaimed the national anthem in 1931. The huge garrison flag that flew over Fort McHenry in 1814 gradually emerged as one of our most venerable relics from the war; it is one of the most sought-out objects in the entire collection now on display in the Smithsonian Institution. These symbols along with other icons produced by the war (General and later President Andrew Jackson, the Kentucky rifle, "Old Ironsides," and "Uncle Sam") began to forge a new national identity. The War of 1812 may not have been a second war for independence, but it certainly helped Americans better understand who they were and where their nation was headed.

PROFESSOR DONALD R. HICKEY
Wayne State College
Wayne, Nebraska

British troops withdrawing from Washington City hauling wounded in wagon behind.

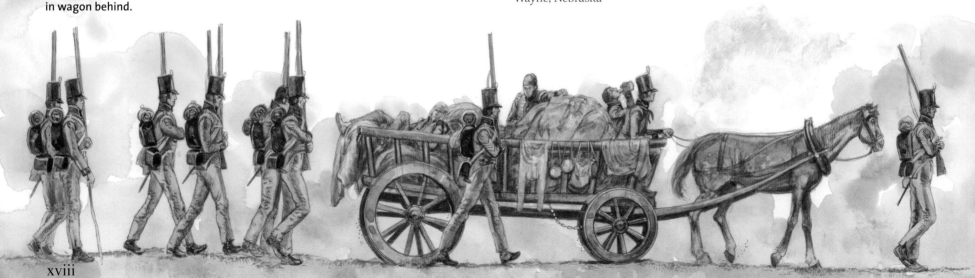

PART I

War in the Chesapeake, 1812–1815

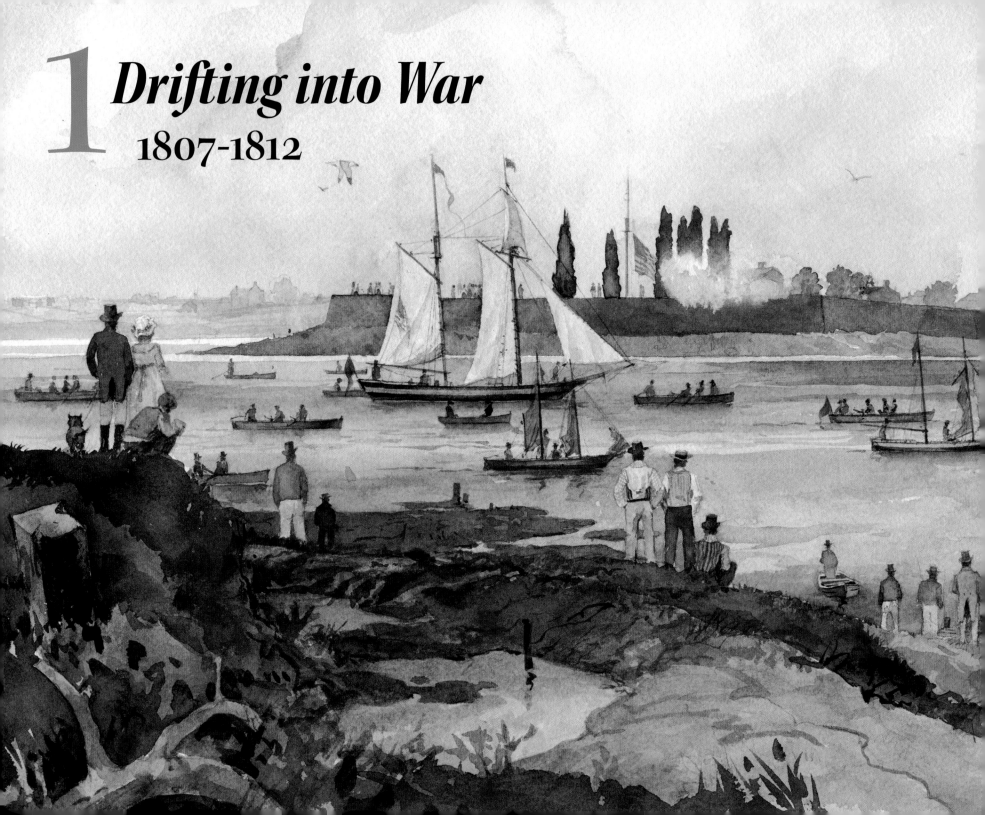

1 *Drifting into War*
1807-1812

Furious Americans

"Never since the Battle of Lexington have I seen the country in such a state of exasperation."

—President Thomas Jefferson, 1807

The crew rowed with slow and careful precision. Gliding across the wide expanse of the Elizabeth River, they were headed from Portsmouth Naval Hospital to the Norfolk docks, where thousands waited. American ships and small boats anchored in this important port of call lowered their flying colors to half mast. Minute guns broke the somber stillness. An ordinary seaman was being honored with an extraordinary funeral. The date was June 27, 1807.

The casket on board that small ferry contained the remains of Robert MacDonald. Mortally wounded five days earlier by a British broadside about nine miles off the coast of Virginia, MacDonald had lingered for several days in the hospital before succumbing to his injuries. He was the last of four sailors lost in a brief but sharp and one-sided sea battle that had also wounded eighteen Americans.

The 38-gun U.S. frigate *Chesapeake,* her deck piled high with supplies yet to be stowed, had sailed from Norfolk on June 22, 1807. She was headed across the Atlantic to relieve the U.S. frigate *Constitution,* then patrolling for pirates with a Mediterranean squadron. The eight-year-old *Chesapeake,* one of six

frigates authorized for the U.S. Navy during George Washington's administration, was the flagship of Commodore James Barron, a rising naval star who had spent twenty-eight of his thirty-nine years at sea. Both *Chesapeake* and Barron were well known in Virginia waters. Barron was born and raised in Portsmouth, and the frigate was built at the town's Gosport Navy Yard.

Conditions aboard Royal Navy vessels were deplorable for the lowly seaman, and desertion was common among sailors. British ships routinely stopped American merchant ships to search for and seize such deserters and sometimes to force unwilling American seamen to fill the ranks. Needless to say, this practice of impressment became a first-class irritant over decades for the Yankees.

As *Chesapeake* passed through the Thimble Shoals Channel, she entered the Atlantic with the Cape Henry Lighthouse off her starboard beam. There was no thought of British harassment. Several hours later, however, the 56-gun H.M. frigate *Leopard* hailed *Chesapeake.* When a junior British officer boarded the American ship, he handed Commodore Barron a demand to allow the British to search his vessel for deserters.

Barron politely declined. *Leopard* then signaled *Chesapeake,* and the American commander either ignored or misunderstood the message. *Leopard* fired a warning shot across *Chesapeake*'s bow, followed by a devastating broadside. *Chesapeake* was caught totally unprepared. Her confused, smoking decks were littered with rigging, sails, luggage, splintered boxes and barrels, and moaning wounded sailors. Having fired only one gun and taken twenty-one shots to their frigate's hull, the Americans struck their colors, giving up

---

Preceding spread: A large, somber, and angry crowd in Norfolk harbor watched as the remains of ordinary seaman Robert MacDonald were rowed to their final resting place. The attack by the British H.M. frigate *Leopard* on the U.S. frigate *Chesapeake* on June 22, 1807, resulted in the deaths of MacDonald and three other seamen—and created a major international crisis for President Jefferson. Five years later, the United States was at war for a second time with Great Britain.

Commodore Stephen Decatur

Commodore James Barron

James Barron (1768–1851) was a product of Virginia's tidewater maritime culture. When not yet a teenager, he joined his father in the struggle to defend local waters during the American Revolution. Decades of experience with the merchant service followed before Barron joined the fledgling U.S. Navy as a lieutenant in 1798.

When Commodore Barron sailed from Norfolk aboard *Chesapeake* in 1807, his nine years of distinguished service placed him among the navy's most-experienced leaders. Within days of his defeat off the Virginia Capes, dark clouds descended over Barron's career. A court martial, convened on board *Chesapeake* the next winter, found the commodore guilty of sailing unprepared into harm's way. He was suspended without pay for five years and spent much of the next decade in Europe as his country and navy faced a full-scale war with England.

Barron sought a return to active duty with the navy in 1818. He was still resentful of members of his

An Ill-Starred Commodore

"For neglecting on the probability of an engagement to clear his ship for action."

—U.S. Navy Court Martial Charge, February 8, 1808

court martial board. Notable among Barron's critics was Maryland-born naval hero Stephen Decatur (1779–1820), who blocked the commodore from any command because of his failure during the 1807 *Chesapeake* affair. An exchange of hostile letters between Barron and Decatur led to a duel on March 22, 1820. The two men met at the traditional east Washington dueling ground, ironically on a piece of land where the Battle of Bladensburg had taken place. Standing only eight paces apart, both men fired on the count of "two." When the pistol smoke cleared, it was revealed that Barron was wounded in the hip and Decatur in the abdomen. Decatur died in agony that evening at his Lafayette Square home that still stands today near the White House.

Remembered for his role in two memorable but dreadful events, James Barron later commanded several navy yards and outlived his fellow officers, dying at age eighty-three as the senior officer of the U.S. Navy.

Impressed Chesapeake Sailors

"We consider a neutral flag, on the high seas, as a safeguard to those sailing under it. Great Britain, on the contrary, asserts a right to search for, and seize, her own subjects . . ."

—Secretary of State James Monroe, February 5, 1806

H.M. *Leopard*'s commander accused four Americans of desertion. Daniel Martin, John Strachan, and William Ware had run from H.M. frigate *Melampus*; and Jenkin Ratford had run from H.M. sloop *Halifax*.

Of the four, only Ratford was British born and a true deserter. The other three sailors were American citizens who claimed they had been pressed into Royal Navy service. There is some evidence, however, that one or more may have actually volunteered. Two of the men were Marylanders: John Strachan, from Queen Anne's County, and William Ware, an African-American from Pipe's Creek, Frederick County (now Carroll County)—although one report claims he was from Allegany County. Daniel Martin, from Massachusetts, was also a man of color.

Leopard carried the men to Halifax, Nova Scotia, for trial. The British citizen, Ratford, was sentenced to death and hanged from the yardarm on August 31, 1807. The three Americans were sentenced to five hundred lashes each, but the sentence was later suspended. Ware died in an English prison. Strachan and Martin, who remained in Halifax, were eventually released under a flag of truce back to *Chesapeake* at Boston harbor in July of 1812.

For decades, no American seaman was safe from British impressments on the high seas. The fate of an unlucky impressed seaman was forced service with the Royal Navy under terrible conditions.

four suspected deserters to the British. Three of the four were Americans who had been impressed into British service.

The *Chesapeake* crew was mortified and humiliated as they sailed their stricken ship back to Norfolk. As news of the incident spread, Americans were infuriated. How could such a blatant act against an American warship take place just off the U.S. coast?

Norfolk residents were outraged. Many sought revenge; some wanted war. Local meetings led to threats; mobs destroyed water casks meant for British ships. The home of His Majesty's local consul was spared only owing to the consul's popularity. The Virginia governor called out the state militia, and decaying forts, built during the Revolutionary War, were hastily repaired and improved. Lookouts scanned the watery horizon, searching for British sails at a post called Pleasure House (near the south end of the present-day Chesapeake Bay Bridge Tunnel).

Thomas Jefferson, in the sixth year of his presidency, suddenly had a full-scale international crisis on his hands. He ordered British ships out of American waters, called home his Mediterranean squadron, and sent an envoy to England to demand that all impressment cease. Negotiations went nowhere.

Launched in 1799, U.S. frigate *Chesapeake* was badly damaged in the 1807 encounter with the H.M. frigate *Leopard* and then soundly defeated and captured by H.M. frigate *Shannon* in 1813. Shown here, *Shannon* brings *Chesapeake* into Halifax harbor as a prize, *Chesapeake*'s ensign being flown below the English ensign on *Shannon*. *Chesapeake*'s career with the Royal Navy ended when she was dismantled in 1819 and her timbers became framing for a grist mill in Wickham, England.

"Don't Give Up the Ship!"

—The Last Order of Captain James Lawrence, June 1, 1813

The frigate named after the Chesapeake Bay was not a lucky ship. Repaired after the *Chesapeake-Leopard* affair, *Chesapeake* was commanded by James Lawrence (1781–1813) when she engaged H.M. frigate *Shannon* on June 1, 1813. Two full broadsides were fired during the first six minutes of the fight. *Chesapeake* was struck by 362 shots, while *Shannon* was hit by 258. *Chesapeake* had its wheel shot away and lost maneuverability.

Lawrence was mortally wounded and carried below deck while his crew fought to carry out his last order. The battle lasted just thirteen minutes, killing or wounding 252 men before the Americans gave up the *Chesapeake*. She and her crew were taken to Halifax, Nova Scotia, where they were held as prisoners of war.

Because of *Chesapeake*'s ill-fated encounters with *Leopard* and *Shannon*, as well as several accidental deaths of crewmen onboard, some superstitious sailors regarded her as cursed. *Chesapeake*'s blood-stained and bullet-ridden American flag resides in the National Maritime Museum in Greenwich, England. Her ultimate fate was undignified. She was sold and her timbers used to frame a mill in Wickham, England. In 1996, a timber fragment from the appropriately named "Chesapeake Mill" was returned to the United States and is on display at the Hampton Roads Naval Museum in Norfolk.

Avoiding War

"Our trade is the most powerful weapon we can use in our defence."

—Boston *Independent Chronicle,* December 11, 1805

Thomas Jefferson (1743–1826), the third U.S. president, had been one of the brilliant architects of American independence. He was intensely private, troubled by family tragedy, personally charming, and, like most of his contemporaries, surprisingly thin-skinned. The bitter party politics that vexed a new nation tested his patience as much as the challenges imported from Europe.

Much of Jefferson's second term in office was spent struggling over his young country's trading policies with European nations at war. From the beginning, the lifeblood of the United States was its vigorous trade. American ships appeared in every port between China, Africa, and South America. Fast-growing cities like Baltimore soon boasted neighborhoods with names such as Canton, proclaiming their lucrative commerce with ports on the other side of the world. Carrying cargo between warring nations mixed large profits with even greater risks. American vessels sailed through a gauntlet of harassment as France and England, wrapped in a hundred-year war for world domination, regularly seized American merchant ships and their cargoes.

The 1807 *Chesapeake-Leopard* affair, only one in a string of incidents on the high seas, created a particular dilemma for President Jefferson. Americans were furious and wanted "free trade and sailors' rights." But Jefferson had all but abandoned the effort to build a strong navy, believing instead in the utility of a small gunboat fleet protecting American coasts. He was convinced that he could avoid war by imposing trade restrictions.

The president focused on locking down American ports. He pushed an Embargo Act through Congress at the close of 1807—effectively cutting off

Responding to the British attack on the U.S. frigate *Chesapeake* in 1807, President Jefferson declared an embargo on trade with the world power. Cartoonists had a field day—depicting the United States as a turtle drawing into its shell and reversing embargo to spell "O-grab-me." By the time Jefferson abandoned his disastrous policy, the United States was in a full-blown depression.

trade. Law-abiding seamen and merchants dependent on foreign trade lost their livelihood. Commodity prices suffered as farmers could not ship their produce to foreign markets. Smugglers ruled the day—the quest to stop them apparently hopeless. Soon, New England was talking of secession. Seaports were all but deserted. Everyone was attacking the "Dambargo."

Jefferson responded by digging in his heels. He contended that New England commerce with foreign powers had put America at risk, "trying to convert this great agricultural country into a city of Amsterdam." His next attempt to enforce the embargo was a new law. Known as the Force Act, it was a thinly disguised attack on civil rights that gave government officials new powers. Many states refused to obey the edicts and "Indians," reminiscent of the Boston Tea Party, took matters into their own hands, seizing a ship under federal "arrest." The strife engendered by the embargo almost created a home-grown civil war in place of the foreign conflict.

How were the English and French responding to this American "coercion"? Reports from France were far from encouraging. "Here it is not felt, and in England . . . forgotten." The European targets of Jefferson's misguided embargo efforts soon discovered other sources for obtaining the unavailable American goods. John Bull (a national personification of Great Britain, similar to Uncle Sam in the United States) in particular was proving to be an all-but-invincible economic rival.

Brother Jonathan, John Bull, and Uncle Sam

"A plain, downright matter of fact fellow, with much less poetry about him than rich prose."

—A description of John Bull in *The Sketch Book,* by Washington Irving, 1819–20

Both Americans and British have been fond of personifying their nations with down-to-earth, everyday characters. Three of these characters came together during the War of 1812.

Yankee Doodle and Brother Jonathan were vying for the honor of representing the American Revolutionary War patriots. The British and their loyalist supporters in America were fond of portraying Continental soldiers as unkempt hay seeds. But the American citizen-soldiers enjoyed that unmilitary and slightly unruly image. Brother Jonathan survived until the Civil War with the song "Johnny Comes Marching Home" and the term "Johnny Rebs" for Confederate troops.

Columbia, representing the United States, and Napoleon, representing France, teach John Bull, representing Great Britain, a lesson of respect in this 1813 cartoon.

The term "Uncle Sam" first appeared at the end of the War of 1812 and by the 1840s he appeared as a grandfatherly and serious man dressed in red, white, and blue and sporting a top hat and a white goatee. He was popular during the Civil War but came into his own during World War I recruiting campaigns as he pointed his finger directly at young male viewers, calling on them to show their patriotism by joining up.

The British John Bull was a mature, jolly, stout man you might see plying his trade as a coachman on the streets of London. When Mr. Bull came to America in 1814, he took on the traits of an actual bull, cloven hooves and all, as he led British soldiers during a raid on Alexandria, Virginia.

Gin Riots and an Infamous Tribute

"Liberty of the Seas, Huzza!"

—A slogan popular during the Gin Riots

It was hardly a riot. The events labeled the "Gin Riots" in Baltimore on October 4, 1808, looked more like a grand day of celebration. A giant afternoon procession snaked through the bustling seaport. It was early America at its flamboyant best. A beautiful barge on wheels led the parade. Manned by some ships' captains, the vessel was adorned with flags and streamers floating in the rigging decorated with patriotic messages: "No Stamp Act," "Bunker Hill Forever," and "No Tribute." A large banner, proclaiming "God Speed the Plow," was followed by a trumpeter who blared out the arrival of thirteen hundred horsemen.

Behind them came four hundred sailors carrying an American flag and a white flag announcing, "A proof that all the American seamen have not gone to Halifax," a reference to the four crewmen taken by the British from *Chesapeake* in 1807. A wagon bristling with national mottoes led five hundred citizens in platoons as wide as the street. Another wagon carried a brightly decorated ship followed by more swarms of citizens singing "Yankee Doodle" as they marched.

All of the hubbub was caused by 720 gallons of Dutch gin. The crowd was determined to destroy the whole lot. It seems a Baltimore-based brig, the *Sophia*, under the command of Samuel Carman, had sailed with the gin from Rotterdam, only to be stopped at sea by the British. The Americans were ordered to England where they were required to pay a duty on each gallon of gin or face seizure of their whole cargo. Carman paid his duty and sailed on to Baltimore, earning public wrath because he had paid "an infamous tribute." A town meeting passed its verdict on the newly arrived barrels of gin.

The giant parade wound its way up Hampstead Hill (now Patterson Park) on Baltimore's eastern edge. In the gathering dusk, bonfires, torches, candles, and lamps illuminated the thirteen hundred horsemen. The now-famous barrels of "tributary" gin hung on a homemade gallows surrounded by bundles of sticks. The fagots were set ablaze, the gin was consumed in a great burst of fire, cannons boomed and echoed in the night, and fifteen thousand

---

The Baltimore-based ship *Sophia* was forced to pay British duties on a cargo of Dutch gin. Baltimoreans condemned the cargo as a victim of an "infamous tribute." Amidst parades and celebrations called a "Gin Riot," thousands cheered as the 720 gallons of gin were "condemned to the flames" in protest on October 4, 1808.

Baltimoreans cheered. One suspects that some of the condemned gin had been consumed before its "execution."

At the height of the squabble over Jefferson's hated embargo, the message of Baltimore's spectacular "riot" was clear. Honest Americans were suffering and the British were benefitting when smugglers escaped the U.S. government's grip.

With exports down a fifth of what they had been a year before, the country was in a full-blown depression. The president and Congress finally gave in after fifteen months of national trauma. Trade was now banned only with France, England, and their colonies. American ships again sailed to foreign ports. Jefferson's experiment in economic cold war had been a catastrophe for U.S. interests.

The young United States was trying to face off against a growing empire that would soon control one quarter of the world's land and people. Although Americans were trading all over the globe, England had thousands of merchant vessels and warships that overwhelmed their competition. Britannia literally ruled the waves.

During the first decade of the nineteenth century, as Great Britain fought fierce naval battles with France and its allies, the need for seamen was critical. Stopping American ships to look for British subjects became a regular routine on the high seas. Between 1803 and 1812, an estimated four hundred American ships were stopped. Along with their cargoes, the merchant fleet lost approximately six thousand American citizens, impressed into the British navy.

When *Leopard* attacked *Chesapeake* in 1807, Americans had seen enough British arrogance. Great Britain, however, now mixed up in a high-stakes trade war with Napoleonic France, continued to bully merchant traders. It soon issued the "Orders-in-Council," a series of restrictions aimed at stifling trade on the European continent. France responded with its own decrees and, over the next five years, Americans lost nine hundred ships, seized by the two warring nations and their allies.

Violent wars were consuming Europe. Trade continued in fits and starts but no compromise or policy seemed to work. After Americans barred all British ships and goods in 1811, the Republican party of Thomas Jefferson and James Madison began to talk openly of war. The question was, would it be war with Great Britain, France, or both?

A War against the Odds

"The time is come to humble the overgrown monsters [the British]—and to cause our republic to be respected at home and abroad."

—Republican A. McLane to Peter B. Porter, February 28, 1812

In 1809, Thomas Jefferson left the presidency to his handpicked successor, another founding father named James Madison (1751–1836). The fourth U.S. president was a small, unassuming man with a great mind. His influence on the U.S. Constitution was legendary, but he was a far from confident public figure. Trembling and pale at the inaugural ceremony, he labored to project his voice to the audience straining to hear his address. It was up to his spirited, attractive wife, Dolley (1768–1849), a pioneering first lady, to give the new administration some vim and vigor.

President Madison promised peace with honor, but he was faced with the same challenges that had all but brought down his predecessor. Like Jefferson, he believed that "no nation can preserve its freedom in the midst of continual warfare." But France and England remained intractable. The cautious, often indecisive, new president was no match for Napoleon Bonaparte and cagey, duplicitous British foreign ministers. The young U.S. republic was the ball in a game of diplomatic ping pong, bouncing from one frustration to another.

As the United States and Great Britain drifted toward war, tensions increased dramatically with incidents on the high seas. The 44-gun U.S. frigate *President* chased the 20-gun H.M. sloop *Little Belt*. Hails and counter hails were followed by a confused fight after dark on May 16, 1811. In the end, the *President* wrecked the much smaller *Little Belt* and left behind thirty-two British casualties.

13

To make matters worse, Madison had an ineffective secretary of state in Marylander Robert Smith (1757–1842). When the president replaced Smith with James Monroe (1758–1831), relations with Great Britain continued to worsen. In mid-1811, another incident at sea had British newspapers calling for revenge for "the blood of our murdered countrymen." The 44-gun U.S. frigate *President*, commanded by Marylander John Rodgers, had fired at night on the smaller H.M. sloop-of-war *Little Belt*, leaving behind thirty-two casualties.

Americans began to wonder if submission or war were the only alternatives available. In 1811, a year filled with ominous events—including a major Midwestern earthquake and the appearance of a comet—religious groups were predicting the end of the world while newspapers and political speeches were preaching war. "By war," stated Vice President Elbridge Gerry (1744–1814), a signer of the Declaration of Independence, "we should be purified, as by fire."

The War Hawks, a growing group of younger politicians, put aside the lingering memories of a dearly bought war for independence. They wanted to mobilize the president and the country in defense of American rights. The newly created nation was still more idea than reality, and bowing to foreign domination could easily destroy the fragile union. President Madison reluctantly agreed. After two years of disappointing diplomacy, he called for war preparations and stated that giving in to the British would "sacrifice the neutral guaranty of an Independent flag."

The Eleventh U.S. Congress, forever known as the "War Congress," marched slowly toward war throughout the winter and spring of 1812. When the June 18 declaration passed 19–13 in the Senate and 79–49 in the House, it was the closest war vote in American history. Many were concerned about taking on the might of the British. The reality of seventeen American warships against five hundred British warships did not inspire confidence. The president had glossed over this disparity, noting that "a well-regulated militia, composed of the body of the people, trained in arms, is the best, most natural defense of a free country." Others wondered if citizen-soldiers (militia) could stand up against professional soldiers (regulars). There were also persistent questions about how prepared the country was for war and how it would pay the cost. Soon, President Madison would discover that this war against the odds would belong to him alone.

Territorial Pursuits and American Indians Stir the War Hawks!

"When the regular troops of this House [the U.S. House of Representatives] . . . are inactive in their posts, it becomes the duty of its raw militia [new U.S. Representatives] . . . to step forth in defense of the honor and independence of the country."

—Henry Clay calls for war, February 22, 1810

Henry Clay

Henry Clay (1777–1852) was a young leader in the new political generation that included Daniel Webster and John Calhoun. Clay was a great orator, superb on the stump. He was so impressive that the U.S. House of Representatives elected him Speaker the first day he served in 1811. Henry Clay soon became a leader among the congressmen, known as "War Hawks," who were pressing for war with Britain.

Clay imported issues from the frontier where the lingering effects of the American Revolution were still plaguing the region. A nasty struggle to defeat and displace American Indians had consumed the region called the Old Northwest for half a century. British troops had never completely abandoned their Indian allies after the Revolution. Another obstacle was the presence of a great leader among the Shawnee nation named Tecumseh who dreamed of a united Indian nation that could repel the American invaders.

The "War Hawks" insisted that war with the British must lead to the conquest of Canada. Annexation of the British colony would add as much land to the United States as the Louisiana Purchase.

First Shots

June 23, 1812

*"And Rodgers with his gallant crew . . .
crush old Albion's pride."*

—Columbian Naval Melody, 1813

While Americans clashed over going to war, the U.S. Navy wasted no time looking for trouble on the high seas. Commodore John Rodgers (1772–1838) sailed from New York harbor with a squadron of five ships only three days after war was declared.

Two days later, Rodgers and his crew aboard the U.S. frigate *President* were chasing a British frigate in the early morning light. The commodore himself touched off a carefully aimed bow chaser cannon. It was the first shot of what would later be called the War of 1812.

That first American shot crashed through the rudder of H.M. frigate *Belvidera* and smashed into its gun room. The Yankees smelled a quickly won victory, but their fourth shot brought disaster. One of the large cast iron guns burst on the deck right below the commodore, killing or wounding sixteen seamen. The blast threw Rodgers to the deck with enough force to break his leg.

In the ensuing confusion, the *Belvidera* fired her stern chaser guns, killing six more American crewmen. Undaunted by these bloody setbacks, Commodore Rodgers pressed the pursuit. Desperate to escape, the crew of the *Belvidera* cut loose her anchors and boats and pumped drinking water overboard to lighten her load and increase speed. After an eight-hour chase, the British frigate was distancing herself from the *President,* so Rodgers abandoned the hunt. *Belvidera* sailed directly to Halifax, Nova Scotia, delivering the news that Great Britain was at war.

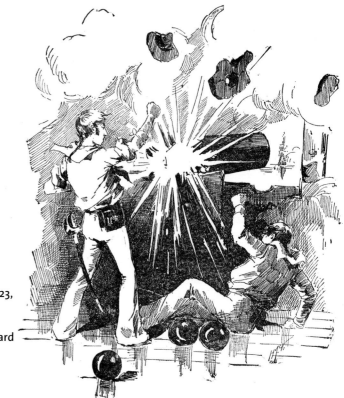

Above: Escape of H.M. frigate *Belvidera* June 23, 1812

Right: Explosion onboard U.S. frigate *President*

Maryland's Naval Hero

Commodore John Rodgers

A native Marylander, Commodore John Rodgers reportedly fired the first shot of the War of 1812 and went on to become an essential leader in establishing the 1814 land and harbor defense of Baltimore. Much honored for his service, Rodgers was the first of four generations of naval heroes in the Rodgers family.

"Hated and feared by the enemy . . . revered and beloved by his countrymen."

—A toast from Baltimore Mayor Edward Johnson, March 1814

From the start, intrepid John Rodgers, hailing from Havre de Grace, Maryland, was a star in the young American navy. As a 26-year-old second lieutenant, he was assigned to the new U.S. frigate *Constellation*. Just a year later, Rodgers was a captain in command of the 36-gun U.S. sloop *Maryland*. Promotions came quickly to young, bold officers bravely fighting the French in an undeclared "Quasi-War" (1798–1800) and then Barbary pirates in the Mediterranean (1801–1805).

Commodore Rodgers was senior naval officer on active duty when war broke out with the British in 1812. After a bloody engagement on the high seas, Rodgers won more fame on land in 1814. Taking charge of the naval aspects of Baltimore's defense, he commanded one of the key bastions along the well-prepared mile long defenses centered on Hampstead Hill (now Patterson Park).

With his illustrious fighting years behind him, John Rodgers served for decades as the head of the newly created U.S. Board of Navy Commissioners. The Commodore's family became a U.S. Navy dynasty as his son commanded ironclads during the Civil War; his grandson was an admiral in World War I and his great grandson a naval aviator. Sion Hill, the Federal-style home still privately owned by descendants of the Rodgers family, stands on a hill overlooking the Chesapeake Bay.

Americans were sharply divided for and against the war, but nowhere more so than in Baltimore. After a mob destroyed the offices of the Baltimore *Federal Republican*, a virulent antiwar newspaper, editor Alexander Contee Hanson plotted a return. A new inflammatory edition, released in July 1814, ignited two nights of vicious rioting that resulted in maiming, and even death, of Federalist newspaper supporters.

The Baltimore Riots

"We'll feather and tar every d——d British Tory.
And this is the way for American glory."

—A song of the Baltimore Mob, July 1812

Party politics were alive and well in America. The Federalist Party of Washington and Hamilton was solidly against war with the British. It believed in a strong defense but thought the Jeffersonian Republicans had first ruined the American economy with an ill-advised embargo and then launched a dangerous war against the world's mightiest nation.

Nowhere was the difference between the Federalists and the Republicans more pronounced than in Maryland. Republicans, with their base in the bustling port of Baltimore, had controlled state government for a decade.

Federalists, strong in the plantation world of Southern and Eastern Shore Maryland, hated Republican immigration policies. They complained about Baltimore's vulgar Irish who brought their "savage hatred" of England with them to the United States. The tough, brawling city, at sixty thousand souls and growing very quickly, was over 80 percent foreign born.

The Federalists had a vigorous champion in *Federal Republican* editor Alexander Contee Hanson (1786–1819). Heir to Maryland patriots, including his grandfather, John Hanson, who was the first president of the Congress of

Privateers Make Their Mark

"By licensing private armed vessels the whole naval force of the nation is truly brought to bear on the foe."

—Baltimore *Niles' Weekly Register,* August 1, 1812

The young United States, with its tiny navy of frigates, had one sea-bound advantage. Its growing fleet of privately owned vessels was sent out with government licenses called "Letters of Marque." Authorized to carry guns, the ships preyed on defenseless British carriers. It was a lucrative business although captured prizes were subject to the customary import taxes. The U.S. government issued 1,100 commissions to privateers between 1812 and 1815. The self-styled marauders were a serious annoyance for British commerce and drove up insurance rates. Merchants demanded government protection. Cruising around shipping lanes in the West Indies, the Gulf of St. Lawrence, and near the British Isles, American privateers forced many British carriers to sail in armed convoys.

Baltimore had a leg up on the rest of the maritime community. In their search for speed under sail, local ship builders and owners had developed a topsail schooner known as the Baltimore clipper. Heavy with sail, they were the majestic, sleekly designed thoroughbreds of their day. Clippers were known to taunt their competition by flying pennants that announced "catch me if you can."

Baltimore privateers garnered 122 letters of marque from the U.S. government. After a British blockade closed in on the Chesapeake and American warships were trapped or closed out, swift-sailing clippers were still able to occasionally slip out to sea, especially

Privateer *Patapsco* of Baltimore escaping from an 18-gun brig after receiving three broadsides off Lanzarote, Canary Islands, September 21, 1814.

when the weather closed in and visibility was limited. As early as 1812, legendary skipper Joshua Barney, commanding the clipper *Rossie,* set a high standard by capturing 18 British prizes valued at $1,500,000. In 1814, Thomas Boyle, at the helm of the *Chasseur,* displayed Baltimore's own brand of bravado by proclaiming a mock one-ship blockade of the entire British Isles.

After defeating the H.M. schooner *St. Lawrence* near Cuba in early 1815, Boyle returned to his home port in triumph, winning the title "Pride of Baltimore" for his plucky vessel. The *Pride of Baltimore II,* a modern-day reproduction of a Baltimore clipper, serves as a world ambassador for Baltimore and is named for Boyle's famous privateer.

the Confederation in 1781, Hanson was unrepentant and unrelenting in his editorial attacks on Republican policies. When the United States declared war on Great Britain in June of 1812, the passion of party politics collided with a vicious Baltimore mob. Future president John Quincy Adams had warned, "the worst of these parties . . . uses its triumph with all the unprincipled fury of a faction."

The trouble began when a Republican-inspired mob sacked the Baltimore offices of the *Federal Republican* four days after war was declared on June 18. Far from folding his tent, Alexander Hanson retreated to Georgetown, District of Columbia, and plotted his return. By July 26, Hanson was back in town and spoiling for a fight with a new edition of his inflammatory newspaper. With little regard for the consequences, he and more than a score of his armed Federalist colleagues moved into a house in the very center of Republican Baltimore.

Two nights of terror ensued as a loud, menacing, and ever-growing crowd surrounded the Charles Street residence. Alexander Hanson had brought along "Light Horse" Harry Lee (1756–1818), a Revolutionary war hero and the father of Robert E. Lee, who had volunteered to instill some military order in the face of ugly threats of violence. Soon rocks were flying and windows were shattered. When the intruders broke through the front door of the house, the beleaguered defenders fired muskets, killing one assailant, wounding several others, and escalating the wicked mood of the thousand protesters raging in the night. A cannon was rolled up to blast the house, but a small force of militia, finally brought in to restore order after hours of trouble, talked the mob out of another devastating assault on the Federalist stronghold.

After a night of dithering, the mostly Republican local authorities, including the mayor, convinced the defenders to abandon the house. A mile-long march to a "safe haven" at the local jail ensued as the howling mob seethed around a hollow square of militia inching its way, covering the cowering Federalists.

Alexander Hanson and his chastened colleagues spent the day in an empty jail cell dreading the night ahead. They were deserted by friends and protectors alike. As darkness again descended, the mob fury returned. Swarming through heavy wooden doors suspiciously left unlocked, the rabble searched the cells with torches in hand. Finally, face to face with their prey, they hesitated, peering through the dim light. A melee followed as the desperate men tried to claw their way to freedom.

Hysterically clubbing, stabbing, slashing, and beating their victims, the rioters could not have been "more joyful at a dance, than they were at the abuse of the murdered." After hours of frenzied bloodletting, a sympathetic local doctor came to the rescue, persuading the mob that he wanted the bodies for his dissection studies. As bands continued to roam the streets looking for trouble, the entire militia brigade was finally called up. They scattered the rioters after the mob had done its worst.

Miraculously, only one man died, a sixty-year-old Revolutionary War veteran begging for his life. Light Horse Harry Lee was terribly beaten and bloodied and never totally recovered. Alexander Hanson, whose serious injuries led to his premature death five years later, became a Federalist hero and was elected to Congress the next year. During the summer of 1812, democracy failed and law vanished on the mean streets of Baltimore. It was a tragedy that became headline news throughout the young U.S. Republic.

A Nation Struggles to Prepare for Its Own War

"Since war is the word, let us strain every nerve
To save our America, her glory increase . . .
The hotter the war, boys, the quicker the peace."

—Boston *Republican Broadside,* June 1812

In spite of brave catchphrases, Americans were slow to commit to harm's way. There were close to 750,000 militiamen on the U.S. government's books. Virginia was number three among the states with 76,000 militiamen. Maryland was thirteenth with 32,000, while the tiny District of Columbia was dead last with a little over 2,000. With only a few exceptions, none of the militia units was at full strength or properly equipped and trained for all-out war with hardened British veterans.

Congress passed resolutions that offered "bounties" (signing bonuses) for enlistees in the small regular army and called for 50,000 one-year volunteers. Hundreds of Maryland and Virginia recruits marched off to beef up American attempts to invade Canada and defend the western frontier. Except for the action of a few privateers bringing prizes to Chesapeake ports, the region remained ominously calm through the end of 1812. His Majesty's schooner *Whiting,* quietly anchored near Hampton, Virginia, was seized in July. When her captain announced that he was unaware there was a war going on, he and his vessel were ordered "to quit the waters of the United States with all possible speed."

In November, the British turned their attentions to the U.S. mainland. Worried about American forces being poured into a one-front campaign against Canada, Royal Navy Admiral Sir John Borlase Warren (1753–1822), commanding the North American Station, ordered raids against ports along the Atlantic and Gulf coasts. The order came to blockade the Chesapeake just after Christmas. On a cold and blustery February 4, 1813, a British squadron suddenly appeared at the mouth of the Bay. The U.S. frigate *Constellation,* unable to reach the open seas before the blockade closed in, remained bottled up on the Elizabeth River for the rest of the war. Once the necessary proclamations of a blockade were issued on February 5 and 6, the Royal Navy set out to prove it meant business. Two days later, the first American casualty, a privateer named *Lottery,* was taken in Lynnhaven Roads near the mouth of the Chesapeake. A frightening and destructive terror would descend on the region for the next two years.

A Frontier Hero

General Zebulon Pike was mortally wounded at York (present-day Toronto, then capital of British Upper Canada) on April 30, 1813. Pikesville, Maryland, is named after this war hero, as is the Pikesville Armory, begun in 1816 as a result of the war.

Along with his disappointments, President Thomas Jefferson had some spectacular successes. In 1803, he took advantage of Emperor Napoleon's financial woes and purchased millions of acres of wild land, then known as Louisiana, at a bargain price. In one stroke of the pen, the United States, a fragile republic of eight million souls, was doubled in size.

Meriwether Lewis and William Clark get the lion's share of attention for their famous trek into the largely unexplored Northwest. Another fearless American explorer, however, took the Stars and Stripes into the southwest part of the Louisiana Territory.

Zebulon Montgomery Pike, Jr. (1779–1813), the son of a Revolutionary War officer, was raised on frontier military posts. After leading a military force that searched unsuccessfully for the headwaters of the Mississippi River, Pike went southwest in 1806 to find the source of the Arkansas and Red Rivers. During a year of hardship, danger, and many discoveries, he and his soldiers tried to climb the 14,000-foot peak that now bears his name. Pike journeyed on, spending some time in Santa Fe as a prisoner of the Spanish who were also claiming what became known as the Great American Desert.

Pike's career during the War of 1812 is less known. By 1813, the now-famous explorer was a brigadier general leading an army into Canada to fight the British. During a successful attack on York (present-day Toronto), Pike was mortally wounded by flying debris when an ammunition magazine exploded. John Beckett of Maryland's Calvert County, a captain in the 14th U.S. Infantry, carried the dying general from harm's way. Zebulon Pike was dead at thirty-four but this frontier hero is remembered today by Pike's Peak, counties in ten states, and Pikesville, Maryland.

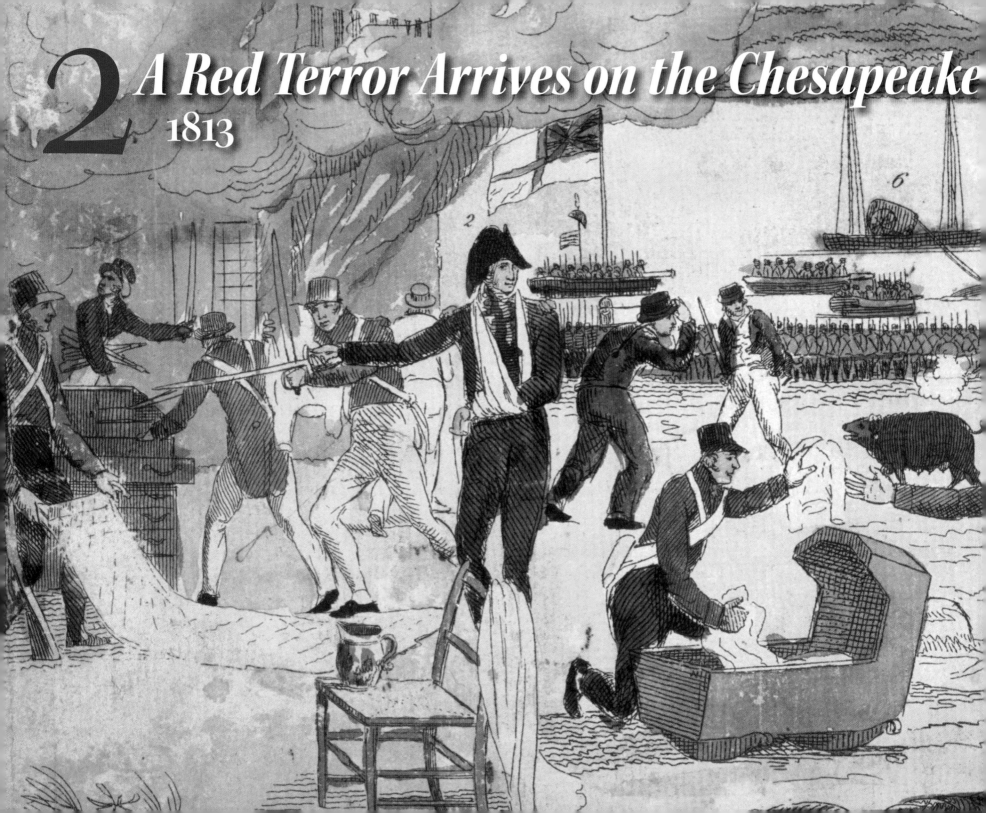

2 *A Red Terror Arrives on the Chesapeake*
1813

Shock and Awe at Dawn

"The enemy robbed every house of everything valuable that could be carried away."

—American eyewitness account of the Havre de Grace raid, May 7, 1813

Rear Admiral George Cockburn (1772–1853) (pronounced "Coeburn" in the Scottish/English manner) was pleased with himself. As second in command of the British navy's North American Station (behind Vice Admiral Sir John Borlase Warren), it was his job to oversee the Royal Navy on the Chesapeake and teach the Americans a lesson. Havre de Grace, with a name inspired by the Marquis de Lafayette, was a Maryland village at the mouth of the Susquehanna River. It was proving to be a perfect target for that lesson.

The town's militiamen had been guilty of a foolhardy blunder in late April of 1813. Running up their flag and firing their cannon at some distant British, they succeeded only in attracting the admiral's attention. Writing to his commander, Cockburn commented that "this of course gave to the Place an Importance which I had not before attached to it."

And now, early on this May morning, the admiral had the bit in his teeth. He was personally leading nineteen row barges laden with four hundred

---

In full uniform, the hated British Rear Admiral George Cockburn stands before his proud handiwork, an embellished version of the burning of Washington in 1814. The admiral was a competent as well as ruthless Royal Navy officer, symbolizing the world-class forces brought to punish the Americans during the War of 1812.

Preceding spread: After a major British raid destroyed most of Havre de Grace, Maryland, on May 3, 1813, an American printed this broadside, complaining of enemy atrocities. The villainous Rear Admiral George Cockburn stands triumphantly in the center as Royal Marines shoot, steal, and burn in the background. A barge carries off a coach, Cockburn's gift for his wife. A rocket vessel, introducing a new terror weapon, is close by.

British troops and his intended victim was a sleeping Havre de Grace. The townspeople were rudely awakened by the boom of cannons and the unsettling shriek of Congreve rockets, the British terror weapon. The streets were soon filled with "distressed people, women and children half naked; children enquiring for their parents, parents for their children, and wives for their husbands."

British marines and sailors easily overran the two earthen forts placed at the water's edge to protect the town. They next fired the Yankees' own cannons on the village. The hastily assembled and frightened local militia mounted a feeble defense. Admiral Cockburn reported that the citizen-soldiers quickly abandoned a "manly and open resistance," commencing "a teasing and irritating fire from behind their Houses, Walls, Trees &c." When pressed further, the militia fled to the nearby woods, abandoning Havre de Grace to its fate as fifty British troops pressed their pursuit.

The fleeing Americans were able to muster only one local hero. Militia-man Second Lieutenant John O'Neill (1768–1838), an Irish immigrant who found some prosperity on the banks of the Chesapeake, was awakened by a call to action and rushed to his gun battery on the waterfront. He and a handful of companions touched off a few cannon rounds but O'Neill suddenly found himself the sole defender as the others skedaddled. "The grape-shot flew very thick about me. I loaded the gun myself . . . and fired her, when she recoiled over my thigh. I retreated to town and . . . with a musket fired on the barges . . . and then retreated to the common, where I kept waving my hat to the militia who had run away . . . but they proved cowardly and wouldn't come back."

The brave but hopelessly overmatched O'Neill was soon caught with two muskets in hand and carried off to a British frigate. As the resistance evaporated, the British marched to the central square, divided up into thirty-man platoons, then methodically burned and plundered the all-but-abandoned town. Some hysterical local women pled with Admiral Cockburn to spare St. John's Episcopal Church and some nearby homes. As the flaming torches found targets elsewhere, the marauders "shew[ed] their respect for religion" by "magnanimously attack[ing] the [church] windows with brick-bats and stones, and demolishing them."

During the devastating morning attack on Havre de Grace on May 3, 1813, John O'Neill was captured by overwhelming British forces but was later released and became a town hero.

The British knew that Havre de Grace was the home of the notorious Commodore John Rodgers, their sworn naval enemy then at sea. Mrs. Rodgers evidently convinced Cockburn to leave the family house, Sion Hill, intact, but the admiral couldn't resist pilfering some of its contents. Rumors flew that Cockburn had Rodgers's desk and pianoforte shipped to Halifax. From another owner Cockburn took a fancy carriage as a gift for his wife.

When the nightmare morning raid was over, two-thirds of Havre de Grace's sixty buildings were in flames. The smoke was visible in Elkton, sixteen miles away. American newspapers ranted about the "wanton barbarity among civilized people." In an unusual public gesture, the Maryland government voted $1,000 to aid the devastated town.

Casualties, amazingly, were light. One fleeing militiaman, a Mr. Webster, was obliterated by a Congreve rocket. He was one of only three known victims killed in the Chesapeake by one of these noisy but largely ineffectual weapons of terror.

For their part, the British invaders wasted no time going on to new, vulnerable targets. After busting open a barrel of whiskey and burning a warehouse at Bell's Susquehanna Ferry, they crossed the river and soon were destroying an important nearby landmark, the almost century-old Principio Iron Furnace and cannon foundry. By razing the extensive complex and spiking forty-five guns, including twenty-eight naval 32 pounders bound for the American forts and fleet, they returned to their ships confident that they had dealt a strategic blow to the American war effort. Admiral Cockburn reportedly quipped that the Yankees were better at making guns than using them.

After destroying Havre de Grace, British raiders crossed the Susquehanna River and attacked the old Cecil Furnace, later called the Principio Iron Furnace. Royal Marines spiked forty-five cannons and burned the mill complex. An enormous fire lit up the sky and terrified Americans for miles around.

A Hometown Hero

" . . . an English officer on horseback followed by the marines, rode up and took me."

—John O'Neill's account of the engagement, reprinted in Baltimore *Niles' Weekly Register,* May 15, 1813

On the morning of May 3, 1813, militiaman John O'Neill found himself in a heap of trouble. After his spirited but nearly solitary defense of Havre de Grace, O'Neill was a prisoner of war, clapped in irons aboard H.M. frigate *Maidstone.* His prospects looked bleak, but a plea, remembered in local lore, won his freedom.

Mr. O'Neill had a 15-year-old daughter named Matilda. It appears that Miss O'Neill gained access to a town flag-of-truce delegation that rowed out to the British ship seeking a parole for their new-found hero. Whatever actually transpired, John O'Neill was paroled after only three days of captivity. The story goes that Matilda so impressed Admiral Cockburn that he not only released her father but also gave her a gold-mounted, tortoise shell box. That box, with its story of family loyalty and love, is now one of the War of 1812 treasures preserved at the Maryland Historical Society.

Celebrated for his bravery, John O'Neill was appointed lighthouse keeper at Concord Point in 1827 by President John Quincy Adams. He devotedly served the beacon until his death in 1838. The lighthouse still stands today only a short distance from a monument to him, but ironically not near the location of the gun battery where John O'Neill won immortality defending his adopted town of Havre de Grace.

This sword was presented to the "gallant [John] O'Neill" for his bravery defending Havre de Grace. The tortoise shell box reportedly was given to 15-year-old Matilda O'Neill by British Admiral Cockburn when she helped negotiate her father's release.

A Notorious Incendiary and Infamous Scoundrel

"Childe Cockburn carries in his hand
A rocket and a burning brand,
And waving o'er his august head
The red-cross standard proudly spread . . ."

—"The Lay of Scottish Fiddle: A Tale of Havre de Grace," by American satirist James Kirke Paulding, best known for "Peter Piper picked a peck of pickled peppers"

Launching its second war against Great Britain in a generation, the United States found a perfect villain in Admiral George Cockburn. As his hated raids in the Chesapeake region continued unchecked throughout 1813 and 1814, American newspapers printed venomous attacks. Cockburn was the "Great Bandit" and the "Leader of a Host of Barbarians." Baltimore *Niles' Weekly Register* published notice of a reward by a Virginian "naturalized Irishman" named James O. Boyle, who offered one thousand dollars for the head of the "violator of all laws, human [and] divine," or "five hundred dollars for each of his ears, on delivery."

In reality, Admiral Cockburn was an impressive and commanding flesh-and-blood counterpart of the Royal Navy's famous fictional contemporary heroes Jack Aubrey and Horatio Hornblower. Born to a London baronet, he was at sea as a midshipman while still a boy. He was fearless, capable, and coldblooded, a combination that served him well in the fighting navy of Admiral Horatio Nelson. By the time he sailed to America in 1813 as a rear admiral, Cockburn was a seasoned veteran who had won the praise of the British House of Commons.

Americans never came close to collecting Admiral Cockburn's head or his ears, although he was shot at by snipers near the U.S. Capitol. After his Chesapeake service, he was chosen to transport Napoleon to his final exile on St. Helena in 1815. He capped his career as Admiral of the British Fleet.

War and Victualing

"We do not intend this to be a mere paper blockade, but as a complete stop to all trade & intercourse by Sea with those Ports . . ."

—First Lord of the Admiralty Viscount Robert Saunders Dundas Melville to Vice Admiral Sir John Borlase Warren, March 26, 1813

Americans ridiculed an early British raid on the Cape Henry Lighthouse in February of 1813. The only "victims" were meats taken from the smokehouse to supplement the raiders' bland rations.

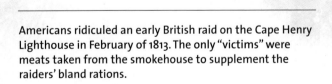

The first recorded British Chesapeake raid, February 14, 1813, gave little indication of what was to come. Attacking the Cape Henry Lighthouse, the raiders made a beeline for the keeper's smokehouse and pantry. A Wilmington newspaper pointed out that "with the most undaunted heroism [they] captured his hams, mince pies and sausages, leaving not a link behind!—after they effected their retreat in the greatest order . . . with flying colors, without the loss of a ham! So much for British heroism and discipline."

Americans might have thought these "victualing" expeditions were unnecessary acts of harassment, but the British navy, far from home, needed fresh supplies. It was a six hundred–mile sail to Bermuda and seven hundred miles to Halifax, Nova Scotia, the closest secure English naval bases. London was three thousand miles across the Atlantic, and the four- to six-week sail, even longer in bad weather, was always a challenge with no guarantee of a safe arrival. Enemy marauders in time of war made a crossing even more perilous. Local supplies were a necessity, and the Cape Henry hams, pies, and sausages were undoubtedly consumed with gusto.

There was tension in the British high command over how to take the war to Americans in the Chesapeake. For the Board of Admiralty, in command from London, war meant bringing a blockade that would strangle commerce. Admirals with the fleet, like George Cockburn, saw the "victualing" that helped feed the navy as an opportunity to take the war directly to towns and plantations. The result was raiding on weaker civilian and military targets. But admirals were instructed not to lose sight of their prime objective. "You must be content with blockading its [the Chesapeake Bay's] entrance & sending in occasionally your cruisers for the purpose of harassing & annoyance." By June of 1813, British sea power was overwhelming the mouth of the Chesapeake. Much of the North American Squadron—scores of ships including ships-of-the-line, frigates, and sloops—was anchored in Hampton Roads.

Privateers were still sneaking through this British gauntlet and risking capture, but Americans had few options to defend themselves. The one important warship in the region, the U.S. frigate *Constellation,* was bottled up near Norfolk. There were several attempts to attack the British fleet with predecessors of the "IED" (the Improvised Explosive Device). The U.S. Congress was intent on rewarding enterprising souls for finding ways to blow up His Majesty's ships. During June and July of 1813, British seamen were fishing up floating "powder machines," kegs of gunpowder rigged to explode on impact. Daring one-man attacks, carrying powder machines into the enemy fleet with rowboats, almost succeeded. Officers, led by Admiral Cockburn, were appalled by the American disregard for the rules of war.

The biggest war prize in the neighborhood was tantalizingly close to the British blockade. Capture of the trapped U.S. frigate *Constellation* was a high priority. Admiral Cockburn launched three waterborne March forays against the frigate without success before most of the fleet sailed up the Bay in April looking for easier prey. As the enemy warships appeared off Annapolis, the Maryland capital reacted with increasing panic. Wagons were piled high with books and papers as an official caravan lumbered south. They stacked the precious state records for safekeeping in spare buildings at Upper Marlboro. No one imagined then that the Prince George's County seat would become a British target the very next year.

Raiding wherever they sailed, the English were using merciless and frightening tactics. Encountering little or no resistance, they had a free hand to terrorize the whole region. It was a controlled intimidation as Cockburn sought to destroy only military targets, pay for supplies, and generally punish Americans only when they resisted. Yet, one of the British captains later described the true nature of the raids. "The more you ruin in a war, the more you hurt the nation at large . . . the hue and cry always was—'Respect private property, pay for what you take but take care to take all you can,' and under this wholesome legislation we burnt and destroyed right and left . . . If the Americans . . . do not entail upon their posterities the deepest hatred and loudest curses upon England and her marauders, why, they must possess more Christian charity than I have given them credit for."

What would you do if you suddenly had dozens of Royal Marines swarming over your property in the darkness before dawn? There were only bad choices. You could defend yourself and face the burning of your home or cooperate with the enemy and be considered a traitor by other Americans. Marylander Jacob Gibson, an odd sort of man who strongly supported the war, owned Sharps Island, now eroded away but then a 450-acre plot near the mouth of the Choptank River. The British took all his cattle roaming on the island and paid him $225. Gibson donated the money to both the state and federal governments but nevertheless was accused of trading with the enemy.

Raiding the Head of the Bay

"These People . . . have more to hope for from our Generosity than from erecting [gun] *Batteries and opposing us by the Means within their Power."*

—Admiral George Cockburn, May 1813

Facing little or no opposition, the British took their time sailing up the Chesapeake in April 1813. All the panicked Americans could do was watch helplessly as a dozen or so enemy warships anchored in their neighborhoods. No untrained and ill-equipped local militia could offer much of a defense. Even worse, the British high command was setting up a safe haven on Tangier Island. The new base had ready access to the tributaries in the middle Bay and shortened their sailing time to the upper Bay. Slaves began to flee from plantations, lured by hopes of freedom. Some were taken to Tangier to be trained and readied to take up arms against their former owners.

Admiral Cockburn kept sailing north with his small fleet, raiding as he went with four hundred fifty veteran Royal Marines. The head of the Bay was familiar territory. A fifteen thousand–man British Army had landed near Head of Elk (now Elkton) in 1777. It had marched on to capture Philadelphia during some of the American Revolution's darkest days.

Several local rivers—the source of the Chesapeake, the Susquehanna River, as well as the Elk, Northeast, Bohemia, and Sassafras Rivers—were convenient highways for the British raids. The Elk River was the strategic prize. Many travelers between Baltimore and Philadelphia took packet boats across the Bay up the Elk to the warehouses, stables, and tavern of Frenchtown, where they continued their journey by bumpy stagecoach ride to Philadelphia. Well aware that they would be a British target, two hundred Elkton residents met and pledged $1,000 for construction of three earthen forts and placement of a large chain across the river.

Only weeks later, Frenchtown became the first victim in the area. With one hundred fifty Royal Marines rowing out of the darkness on April 29, a motley assortment of fifteen militia, stage-drivers, and wagoners touched off some cannons in a recently built log gun battery and fled for their lives. Spiking the cannons and putting torches to storehouses and boats at the wharves, the British destroyed about $30,000 in government supplies and equipment. Leaving behind a wall of flames licking at the early morning light, they headed upriver toward Elkton.

The marines soon rowed into a much stouter defense. The thirteen barges rounded a bend in the river and faced persistent fire from two new earthen forts, Frederick and Defiance. A chain stretched across the river made them sitting ducks for the American cannons, so they turned tail with "considerable precipitation." Easier targets beckoned, and the May 3 raid on Havre de Grace—the town that had foolishly attracted Admiral Cockburn's attention—raised the destruction to a new level.

By May 6, the terror had sailed to the Sassafras River, what Cockburn called the "Last Place of Shelter" from British ravages. With H.M. frigate *Maidstone* looming at the river's mouth, the admiral unleashed his barges and tenders packed with Royal Marines. By dawn, they were still rowing hard to get to their goal, the twin hamlets of Fredericktown and Georgetown, several miles upriver. Two Maryland watermen out on the river at dawn had the surprise of their lives and a story for their grandchildren. Suddenly surrounded by four hundred heavily armed Royal Marines and Royal Artillerymen bobbing about in their barges, they were lectured by the admiral, who sent them ahead of the assault with instructions to "warn their Countrymen against acting in the same rash manner as the People of Havre-de-Grace."

Only a mile further on, the invading flotilla received its answer, heavy musketry and cannon fire from Fort Duffy and Pearce Point Fort on opposite sides of the river. The British answered with a barrage of "grape, canister, slugs, rockets and musketry" and landed marines with three cheers to meet the threat. Half the American militia had already run at the "terrible noise" of the barrage, but the half remaining returned the Englishmen's three cheers and put up a stiff resistance for a time before also running away.

This 1806 watercolor depicts Frenchtown as seen from the wharf where a gun battery was established to defend the town in 1813.

31

Elkton prepared its defenses with three earthwork forts and a double chain across the Elk River. British invaders were repelled in 1813 and 1814, making Elkton one of two communities that successfully defended themselves twice. This conjectural view at Elk Landing looks downriver from Fort Hollingsworth toward Forts Frederick and Defiance.

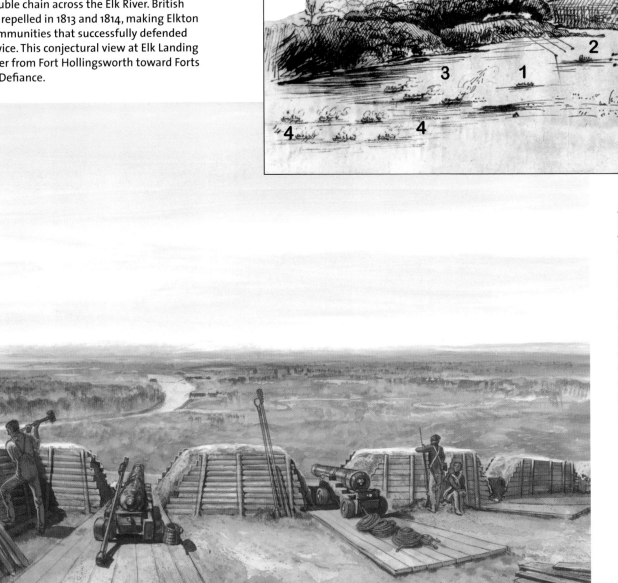

A rare 1813 British sketch, drawn by Royal Navy Lieutenant Henry Crease, depicts the May 6 raid on Fredericktown and Georgetown. The key identifies: *(1)* Rear Admiral George Cockburn's boat; *(2)* Captain Henry D. Byng's boat with First Lieutenant Frederick Robertson; *(3)* Launches fitted with Congreve rockets; *(4)* Boats with Royal Marines; *(A)* Fort Duffy; *(B)* Georgetown; *(C)* Fredericktown (note that *B* and *C* are reversed, Georgetown is to the extreme right and Fredericktown to the left of it). Americans are firing at the invaders from Fort Duffy and the Pearce Point Fort. North is to the left.

Admiral Cockburn and his barges arrived at their destination in no mood for compromise. They "threw several rockets in the town [Fredericktown] and reduced the whole place to ashes." Of the town's twenty-two structures, only a tavern and seven houses survived the conflagration. "The ruin complete, the savages crossed to Georgetown . . . where they, in a like manner, destroyed that place . . . The property destroyed is estimated at seventy to eighty thousand dollars." About ten buildings survived in Georgetown.

Undoubtedly delighted with his success, Cockburn stopped at another hamlet called Turner's Creek on his return to the *Maidstone*. When the chastened inhabitants pledged that there would be no opposition, the admiral re-embarked "leaving the People of this Place well pleased with the wisdom of their Determination on their mode of receiving us."

The town fathers of Charlestown, a nearby village on the Northeast River, fearful from the news of the destruction of their neighboring towns, decided to surrender even though the British had not entered the river. Admiral Cockburn haughtily reported to his commander that Charlestown "is considered by them as at your Mercy, and that neither Guns nor Militia Men shall be suffered there . . . and as there is now neither Public Property, Vessels, nor Warlike Stores remaining in this Neighborhood, I propose returning to you with the light Squadron."

Charlestown, Maryland, officials, although never threatened, were alarmed by the destructive British raids all around them. By promising to avoid any resistance in exchange for civility and peace, Charlestown became the only Maryland town to officially surrender to the enemy.

A Legendary Lady

"She saved several families from being made homeless and friendless by the fire and sword . . ."

—Kitty Knight's obituary, November 22, 1855

Tall and graceful, Catharine Knight (circa 1775–1855) was recalled as a most beautiful and accomplished woman. Attending a ball in Philadelphia during a session of Congress, she reportedly was asked to dance by President George Washington himself.

For much of her life, Kitty Knight, who never married, was a resident of tiny Georgetown, Maryland. She was renting the brick William Henry House when the British pounced on Georgetown and its sister community, Fredericktown, on May 6, 1813. With both towns in flames, Miss Kitty is said to have stamped out fires in her home twice. The story goes that she confronted Admiral Cockburn in person and argued that by destroying her house the British would be putting a sick and elderly lady lying in the adjoining house in mortal danger. Perhaps because of her beauty and charm, she convinced the admiral to spare the dwellings. (These two brick structures survived and have since been combined into the Kitty Knight Inn.)

In 1836, Kitty Knight was able to purchase the house that she had saved. After she died in that home in 1855, she was buried several miles north, at the Old Bohemia Church. Following her wishes, her tombstone reads simply, "Miss Catharine Knight."

While Fredericktown and Georgetown burned around her during a British raid on May 6, 1813, local resident Kitty Knight is said to have talked Admiral Cockburn out of burning her rented house, and next door neighbors' house, pointing out that an elderly lady was living there. Both houses still stand today as the Kitty Knight Inn.

A British Defeat and Atrocity

"Officers of the [U.S. frigate] Constellation fired their 18 pounder more like riflemen than Artillerists, I never saw such shooting and seriously believe they saved [Craney] Island yesterday."

—Captain John Cassin to Secretary of the Navy William Jones, June 23, 1813

June 1813 would not be a good month for the British cause in the Chesapeake. Admiral Cockburn had rejoined the main fleet at the mouth of the Bay in early May from his self-proclaimed triumph at its head. Casualties had been low on both sides but American property damage had been high during raids. Yankee newspapers were chattering about Cockburn's savagery. The Washington *Daily National Intelligencer* declared the Englishmen "so much inured to villainy and destruction, that there is no mercy in their composition."

Cockburn's boss, Vice Admiral Warren, sailed forty recently captured American vessels to Halifax. His fleet at Virginia's Hampton Roads now

A British attack of at least fifty barges took place near Norfolk at Craney Island on June 22, 1813. Led by Captain John Hanchett with umbrella in hand aboard the commanding admiral's barge *Centipede,* the barges got stuck in shallow mudflats. Americans poured cannon and musket fire into several trapped barges, causing the enemy to retreat.

included eight 74-gun ships-of-the-line and twelve frigates. It was a sea of sails that awed nearby Norfolk's anxious citizens. Within days, it became obvious that the British were still intent on grabbing the big Chesapeake prize, the *Constellation*, bottled up in the local navy shipyard.

The Americans had prepared defenses to protect Norfolk, their crucial Gosport naval shipyard, and the *Constellation*, all on the Elizabeth River. Existing forts were strengthened, gunboats stationed at the mouth of the river, and sunken vessels and booms deployed. The English, confident after recent successes, decided to take the defenses straight on.

The assault began on June 22. Long lines of enemy-laden row barges aimed at a small island called Craney. The forty-acre parcel of land stood in the way of any attack on Norfolk. Over five hundred Yankees, including one hundred fifty seamen borrowed from the *Constellation* crew, waited on the island with three large cannon and four 6-pound field guns at their disposal.

As the Craney Island defenders watched, twenty-five hundred Englishmen landed to the west, intending to attack their left flank. The main attack, fifty barges strong, came straight at the Americans from the Hampton Roads in late morning. Captain John Hanchett, said to be the illegitimate son of King George III and skipper of H.M. ship-of-the-line *Diadem*, commanded the charge reportedly holding an umbrella to block a hot sun. He sat majestically in the lead barge, the admiral's personal bright green, 24-oar boat called *Centipede*.

The arrogant British commanders hadn't done their homework. Rockets, as usual, were loud but ineffective as grapeshot and canister from the Craney Island artillery poured into the approaching assault. The *Centipede* was hit by a round shot side on and Captain Hanchett was seriously wounded. Worse yet, the attackers hadn't considered the outgoing tide, and five of the barges were soon stuck in mud only a hundred yards from gathering militiamen. The British ordered a ragged retreat while some defenders waded out to the mired barges and collected sixty prisoners, including a terrier mascot standing unhurt on *Centipede*'s bow gun. The flank attack retreated as well, leaving behind forty deserters.

The British had lost eighty-one men and the Americans none, although after the attack a guard foolishly smoking his pipe around a gunpowder magazine lost his life. The resulting explosion sent new alarms through Norfolk, but the city, *Constellation*, and the shipyard remained safe for the rest of the war.

Muskets, Canister, and Hot Shot: 1812 Weapons

Small Arms

The standard infantry weapon during the war was the muzzle-loaded smooth-bore flintlock musket. The United States musket typically fired a .69 caliber and the British a .75 caliber soft-lead ball. Muskets weighed approximately eleven pounds and were able to mount a detachable fourteen- to sixteen-inch triangular-shaped bayonet. Some light infantry carried rifles, so named for the grooves or rifling on the inside of the barrel. Rifles were much more accurate and had a greater range than the smooth-bore musket, but they were slower to reload and took more training to use efficiently. The musket had an accurate range of about 100 yards and the rifle a range of at least 200 yards. Infantrymen typically carried a leather cartridge box hanging from a sling on their right side. The cartridge box contained twenty to sixty pre-wrapped cartridges, each with a measured amount of gunpowder and a soft-lead ball. After constant training, infantrymen were expected to automatically go through the many steps of loading and firing. Since the weapons were so inaccurate, armies lined up and maneuvered shoulder-to-shoulder so they could intimidate the opposing line with maximum firepower.

Artillery

Cannon, typically cast iron and often referred to as guns, were used both onboard ships and on land. Naval cannon typically consisted of long guns and carronades. Long guns were larger and heavier and usually were carried on the lower gun decks of ships. Carronades were short, lighter guns usually carried on the upper gun decks. Naval long guns were mounted on wooden truck carriages with small iron-rimmed solid wooden wheels. Carronades were most often mounted on sliding carriages. Naval and fort guns were large and heavy and did not need to be transported once in place. They typically ranged from 18 to 32 pounders. The number in the cannons' name refers to the weight of the cannonball that it fired. Field cannon were guns mounted on wooden field carriages with large diameter, spoked, iron-rimmed wheels. Field artillery, typically ranging from 3 to 12 pounders, was lighter because it often needed to travel long distances towed by draft animals or, sometimes, men.

Ammunition

In addition to solid shot, cannon could fire grapeshot or canister, consisting of multiple smaller-sized lead balls fired at one time. Grapeshot was used to disable ship's sails and rigging. Canister shot was similar to the naval grapeshot, but fired smaller and more numerous balls packed in a can. This type of shot was the equivalent of a giant shotgun, causing severe harm to massed troops on land and sailors onboard ships. Some Americans used bits of iron, glass, and other debris with effect. Bar or chain shot was two balls connected by a chain or a bar fired into the rigging and sails of enemy ships. When cannonballs hit the wooden hulls of ships they created a great shower of splinters that often did more damage to crew than the cannonball itself. Hot shot, a cannonball heated in a furnace (some were portable), was fired on land and sea to cause a fire wherever it landed.

Bombs and Rockets

During the bombardment of Fort McHenry, the British used cast-iron mortar shells fired from specially designed bomb ships. The bombs, fired from large mortars, measured ten and thirteen inches in diameter and weighed up to 190 pounds. Depending on the quickness of the fuse, some shells exploded over the fort, spreading lethal shrapnel. The "bombs bursting in air," words from Francis Scott Key's lyrics that became our national anthem, refer to these high explosive mortar shells. The "rockets' red glare" refers to Congreve rockets, discussed in chapter three.

Armament: *(upper left)* Congreve rocket showing exterior and interior cross-section views. A long wooden pole served as a stabilizer during flight; *(upper right)* a naval long gun being loaded and then hauled forward ready for firing; *(middle left)* a Maryland gun crew loading a small-caliber field cannon (note man at rear holding a linstock [a lighted slow match] to fire gun); *(middle right)* tools used by the gun crew included a combination ram and sponge rod, wad hook (also called a wormer), gunner's haversack, and a staff with a fork at one end to hold a linstock. The cross-section of a cannon tube shows the gunpowder charge bag, cannonball, and wad in place ready to fire; *(lower left)* various size cannonballs including one grapeshot, chain shot, gunpowder charge bag, wad, and grapeshot bag; *(lower right)* carronade.

Redcoats, Militia, and Regulars: 1812 Troops Fighting in the Chesapeake

British Soldiers, Sailors, and Marines

In the Chesapeake theater, the British used troops representing the Royal Navy, Royal Marines, and British Army. Because of their red jackets, British Army troops were often called Redcoats or, pejoratively, Lobsterbacks. During the British march against Washington and Baltimore, there were elements of four regiments, the 4th, 21st, 44th, and 85th Regiments of Foot, all veterans of fierce fighting against Napoleon in Spain. The invading army had nearly 5,000 men, including soldiers, Royal Marines, and sailors. The British also trained about 550 escaped African-American slaves, called the Colonial Corps or Colonial Marines, who fought valiantly in the 1814 campaign and found freedom after the war in the British Empire. During the 1813 battles of Craney Island and Hampton, Virginia, the British used over 100 French deserters and prisoners of war who agreed to serve as Independent Foreigners. They behaved disgracefully in the battles and were sent back to Europe.

British uniforms: *(from left)* a private soldier in caped great coat and waterproof cover for his cap; a corporal of grenadiers, 44th Regiment of Foot, showing winter uniform; a private in the 21st Regiment of Foot wearing summer uniform and a pre-1812–style cap (as regiments that came directly from Spain probably hadn't received the new regulation caps). He is carrying a .75-caliber muzzle-loaded smooth-bore flintlock musket; officer, grenadier of the 44th Regiment of Foot, wearing a practical low version of the cocked hat, his waist sash low on his hips carries a captured French curved saber rather than the regulation straight sword; a private from the light company, 21st Regiment of Foot; a Royal marine; a midshipman, Royal Navy; a seaman in a landing party, carrying a boarding ax.

American Soldiers, Sailors, and Marines

In 1812, the United States had a relatively small number of professional soldiers in the still-young U.S. Army. The U.S. Navy, also only a few decades old, had both sailors and marines serving in its fleet of frigates and smaller vessels. Members of the Revenue Cutter Service, predecessor of the U.S. Coast Guard, were placed under the command of the U.S. Navy during the war. At the beginning of the war there were about 7,000 U.S. Army troops. By war's end, that number had increased to about 35,800.

The Chesapeake Flotilla, a gunboat unit of the U.S. Navy raised during the war to protect coastal areas, had about 1,000 sailors. Just over 100 U.S. Marines are known to have fought in the Battle of Bladensburg. The total number of regulars stationed in the Chesapeake theater during the war fluctuated but was never more than a few thousand.

The bulk of the defense was placed on the shoulders of part-time militia, citizen-soldiers with limited training and usually no combat experience. The militia, often under the direction of inexperienced officers, lacked many of the maneuver and weapon-coordination skills of professional troops on the battlefield. In some engagements, they had the benefit of experienced and insightful leadership and they were sometimes effective, especially in defensive positions. Local militia also sometimes had the advantage of knowing the land better than the enemy. An 1836 audit reported that the total number of United States troops during the War of 1812 was 528,000, including 458,000 militiamen. Of this total, Virginia reported 88,584, Maryland, 52,416, and the District of Columbia, 4,029. Virginia ranked first in the number of troops. Maryland ranked third, and the District of Columbia, not a state and very small in size, ranked sixteenth.

American uniforms: *(top, from left)* a U.S. regular infantry senior officer wearing the plain and practical uniform that was favored as the war progressed; a Maryland militia rifleman; a flotillaman, armed with typical cutlass, cartridge box, and a pistol clipped to his cutlass belt (his uniform and armaments are almost identical to his British counterpart); a private and drummer, 5th Maryland Regiment infantry militia. American equipment: *(bottom, from left)* a bayonet was positioned on the left hip, a cartridge box on the right, the shoulder belts crossed on the soldier's breast. This combination was worn by most infantrymen of the period, the American and British versions only varying in small details; *(bottom center)* a U.S. model 1803 rifle. The spiral grooves inside the barrel sent the ball spinning on its way further and more accurately than the smooth-bore musket. The U.S. model 1795 .69-caliber muzzle-loaded smooth-bore flintlock musket was very similar to its British counterpart, although it had a slightly smaller caliber. Well-trained troops were capable of firing three or more times a minute and would often follow with a charge with fixed bayonets. The soldier on the extreme lower right wears a typical uniform of a regular U.S. Army soldier.

Typical uniform of mounted U.S. Light Dragoon including saber and helmet with horsehair plume.

British Mounts

The British had no regular cavalry in America during the War of 1812. They brought perhaps half a dozen horses on their ships to serve as mounts for their senior officers who led the invasion force that landed at Benedict in August 1814. Major General Robert Ross brought his prized Arabian horse that he had used during the previous Iberian Peninsula Campaign. Horses were loaded and offloaded on ships with canvas slings attached to rigging and pulleys operated by windlasses. To supplement the horses they brought with them, the British paid for or took horses from Americans as needed. A few dozen artillery drivers were converted to horsemen for scouting purposes. About forty horses were rounded up in and near Washington and harnessed to wagons, carts, and carriage to transport wounded men and supplies back to their ships. During the attack on Baltimore, the small contingent of British artillery was fully mounted.

American Mounted Troops

At the start of the war, the United States's regular army had two regiments of cavalry, called dragoons, that were largely assigned to the Canadian front. An estimated 315 cavalry were present at the Battle of Bladensburg, including part of a squadron of the 1st U.S. Dragoons, five troops of Maryland militia cavalry, three troops of District of Columbia militia cavalry, and a troop of Virginia militia cavalry. These and other militia cavalry troops, some from Pennsylvania, served at the Battle for Baltimore. During the British withdrawal back to North Point, the American cavalrymen were the only troops who followed and harassed the enemy.

During the war, Maryland had some fifty-two troops in eleven regiments called cavalry districts. Most Maryland cavalry regiments had two squadrons with two troops in each squadron. Troops, with a total of four officers, four sergeants, four corporals, and nearly fifty mounted dragoons, were commanded by a captain. Prior to 1812, militia cavalry troops assembled twice a year for training, generally in the spring and late summer. In 1812, the war conditions caused Maryland to increase its training tempo to ten drills per year. Sessions included individual equestrian training, mounted evolutions in formation, and instruction in the use of a curved saber and the muzzle-loaded pistol. All riding was done with only the left hand on the reins, so the right hand remained free to manage weapons.

Admiral Warren played down the setback and the embarrassing failures of his command. He wasted no time ordering another foray, this time aimed at Hampton, a less-significant target on the north side of Hampton Roads.

The June 25 predawn raid had all the usual earmarks. The British landed from two directions with overwhelming force. The four hundred fifty hastily assembled American militia stood up for a time with significant casualties on both sides, including a British lieutenant colonel. After the inevitable flight of defenders to save life and limb, raiders spent three days sacking the thousand-person town. But these latest ravages took on a new and more sinister turn.

Hampton was stripped of everything: knives, forks, private drawers, even the sail cloth on windmills. Beyond that, the locals were brutalized; there were reports of rape and even killings in what was described as "deeds of infamy and barbarity." The Virginia militia commander, Brigadier General Robert B. Taylor, officially complained about the excesses and the British blamed the trouble on two companies of French recruited in war-torn Spain who "could not be restrained." The mercenaries were sent packing to Halifax but the ugliness continued. Eight destructive raids during the next two weeks spread the terror as far as Williamsburg.

British troops accidentally shot and killed Mr. Kirby and wounded his wife while chasing a dog into the Pembrooke Mansion, shown here as it appeared in 1853. American newspapers sensationalized the incident as a British atrocity.

The Heart-Rending Death of Mr. Kirby

"Expect No Quarter!"

—Comment from a British officer at Hampton, Virginia, according to the Washington *Daily National Intelligencer*, July 2, 1813.

British atrocities, real and fanciful, made good copy for the newspapers. One old Hampton man named Kirby, said to have been murdered on his deathbed, quickly became a front-page story. "Remember Hampton" became a rallying cry for beleaguered Americans.

The Washington *Daily National Intelligencer* reported that Kirby "was dying in his house in the arms of his wife, when the British troops approached and one of them coolly pulled out his pistol, shot poor Kirby and the ball lodged in the hip of his wife." The Baltimore *Patriot* echoed the story a couple of weeks later. "Kirby, who for seven weeks or more had been confined to his bed, and whose death the savages only a little hastened, was shot in the arms of his wife . . . Go to his wounded wife and hear her heart-rendering tale."

Another version of the story was collected from an interview with Mrs. Kirby herself in 1853. "With vengeful feelings, the soldiers chased an ugly dog into the house, which ran under Mr. Kirby's chair, in which he was sitting, and, in their eagerness to shoot the dog, shot the aged invalid, the bullet grazing the hip of Mrs. Kirby. [She] always considered the shooting of her husband an accident."

The Town That Fooled the British

St. Michaels residents proudly retell the story of some quick-thinking townspeople who fooled the British attackers in the early morning of August 10, 1813. As the British approached, the citizens reportedly placed lanterns high in the trees, on ships' mastheads, and on the roofs of buildings so that the enemy would be fooled into firing over the town.

There are at least three problems with the story. First, it was a British surprise attack. How did the villagers have time to hang lanterns? Second, it was already light, even if overcast, during the cannonading that morning, and the village was clearly visible. Third, when H.M. sloop *Conflict* fired its cannons, it scored several hits. The commander of the American forces commented in his report that several houses were damaged. One round shot plunged through the Merchant House, forever after earning that structure the name Cannonball House.

St. Michaels claims it was "the town that fooled the British" into shooting high over the buildings. Several structures, however, including shipwright William Merchant's 1805 Cannonball House, were damaged by enemy cannon fire. A cannonball reportedly crashed through the roof, rolled across the attic, and bounced in front of Mrs. Merchant carrying her young daughter.

Raid upon Raid

"From the face of things they could have had no other view than to completely destroy the whole of the property."

—Father Francis Neale, St. Inigoes Manor, writing to Georgetown College about the devastation on St. George Island, November 22, 1813

An 1814 Chesapeake map pinpoints Kent Island, now the eastern end of the Chesapeake Bay Bridge, at the mid-Bay's narrowest crossing. Approximately two thousand British raiders set up camp on the island during the summer of 1813, terrorizing local citizens.

Undeterred by their checkered record in June, the British continued their relentless Chesapeake raids through the summer of 1813. The next target was the Potomac River in July.

Every set of raids was a new source of trouble for the beset American defenses. Most of the dawn sorties went unopposed, and locals could only flee or stand by helplessly while livestock, produce, belongings, and slaves disappeared. The U.S. schooner *Asp* was chased into the Yeocomico River and, after a sharp fight that killed her commander, Midshipman James Sigourney, she was captured. On the Potomac River at Woodland Point, one hundred forty militiamen, many unarmed or without ammunition, fought off a nighttime foray. An anxious Secretary of State James Monroe participated there with some Washington horsemen. Monroe would become an important presence in Southern Maryland in 1814.

The greatest concern was two thousand Englishmen who set up camp at Point Lookout near the end of July to launch raids. A local militia captain put out the call. "The situation is extremely critical . . . Several of our most respectable inhabitants have been taken by the enemy. . . . Many negroes have also been taken. . . . What will be their next movement I know not."

In August, the crisis moved up the Bay to strategic Kent Island. Here, the narrow part of the Bay was a main ferry crossing on trips east and north. With the island firmly in their grasp, the British could launch raids against "some of the finest and best stocked farms in the state." During the two-week occupation, English troops set up camp in what they called a "beautiful spot resembling a gentleman's park." Fresh food and supplies were so abundant

that the camp "evinced that we had fallen on the land of milk and honey." Pressed American militia, chased off the island, could only march and countermarch their forces in view of British lookouts, trying to convince their enemy that their fighting men were there in large numbers.

August 10 brought another unpleasant surprise for Maryland's Eastern Shore. A dozen war barges were rowing into the Miles River headed for St. Michaels, a boat-building community known for launching at least

four successful privateers. In the predawn darkness the British overran an American battery and spiked the cannons after shots had been fired by the defenders alerting the town. With their surprise lost and militia gathering, the British decided to withdraw and let their sloop *Conflict* fire some rounds, damaging several local homes.

After crossing the Bay and again giving Annapolis citizens reason to worry, some of His Majesty's ships took soundings in the Severn River but did not attack. The next raid was launched due east from Kent Island during the night of August 13. The target was a large number of militia said to be encamped at Queenstown. Colonel Sir Thomas Sidney Beckwith led three hundred men with two cannons while a battalion of marines shadowed the column in barges to trap any opposition. While the marines missed their

During the night of August 13, 1813, British troops launched a raid on American militia camped at Queenstown. At a rise in the road called Slippery Hill about twenty American pickets fired on the column, causing some panic among the invaders. In order to calm the men, officers ordered their accompanying military band to play.

Governor Wright Defends His Plantation

Robert Wright (1752–1826) had every reason to be terrified. On the night of August 13, 1813, hundreds of Royal Marines were landing at his Blakeford Plantation near Queenstown, Maryland. He could not know that the marines, lost in the dark night, would soon withdraw. What he suspected was that, as a former governor (1806–1809), he was a target who would soon lose his property and possibly his life.

Governor Wright quickly loaded his wife and daughter into a carriage and hurried them to safety. He saddled up his favorite mount, Pocahontas, and galloped bravely about while his loyal slave ran to the shore and fired haplessly at the Royal Marines as they rowed away. Wright was so shaken by the scare that he auctioned off his horses and cattle that fall to avoid their possible loss to another raid.

During the August 13, 1813, attack on Queenstown, three hundred enemy troops mistakenly landed in barges at former Maryland Governor Robert Wright's home. Sending his family to safety, the spry Revolutionary War veteran mounted his horse and ordered his bewildered slave to take a rifle and fire at the withdrawing enemy barges.

landing point in the darkness, some American pickets fired on Beckwith's men. A British captain described the chaotic scene: "the men, seeing the road suddenly lighted up by the firing . . . were panic-stricken, and . . . fired right and left, shooting each other." Colonel Beckwith brought up the regimental band to settle the men down and was rewarded by having his horse shot from under him as the troops advanced.

Twenty Americans, firing in the darkness, had caused all the consternation known today as the Battle of Slippery Hill. In the meantime, the commander of the Queen Anne's County militia received word of the marine landing and, fearing they would be trapped, ordered his men to march north out of harm's way, leaving the enemy free to sack the town.

At the end of August, the British were probing the defenses of St. Michaels again, this time with twenty-one hundred men in sixty barges. The large force landed about six miles from town and sent three hundred men to attack a nearby militia camp. More troops, sailing up the Miles River, alerted locals that if they stayed in their homes no trouble would come their way. About one and one-half miles from St. Michaels, eighteen hundred attackers collided with five hundred determined Americans supported by cavalry and artillery. The largest Eastern Shore battle of the war lasted only a few volleys as the English quickly withdrew. The relieved citizens of St. Michaels had repelled the invaders twice in a month.

After November 1, the British spent another ten devastating days on St. George Island in the Potomac. Cutting down all the large oaks and burning every house, they also took away about one hundred seventy slaves. Two months earlier, most of His Majesty's North American Squadron had all but finished inflicting its special brand of Chesapeake terror. Leaving behind a small blockade at the mouth of the Bay and a few ships in Tangier Sound, the fleet sailed to the Halifax and Bermuda safe havens with seventy-two American merchant ships captured in just four months.

One British lieutenant colonel, Charles James Napier, questioned what had been accomplished. "Nothing was done with method, all was hurry, confusion and long orders. We have done nothing but commit blunders." Angry and frustrated Americans in the Chesapeake had their own concerns with a powerful enemy that could not be stopped. There was every reason to believe that 1814 would bring much more death and destruction.

About eighteen hundred British troops attacked St. Michaels on August 26, 1813. At a narrows northwest of town, five hundred militiamen traded a few shots with the English raiders in the largest yet possibly shortest engagement of the war on Maryland's Eastern Shore. St. Michaels and Elkton residents share the distinction of twice repelling British attacks on their community.

A RED TERROR ARRIVES ON THE CHESAPEAKE, 1813   47

Richard Schlecht
2011

3 A Fateful Year Begins
1814

David Meets Goliath

"I then made the signal 'for Patuxent,' and was followed by a 74, the three schooners and Seven Barges, with a fresh wind."

—Commodore Joshua Barney to Secretary of the Navy William Jones, June 3, 1814

The gasping, rain-soaked seamen sat at their oars nervously eyeing the squalls rolling in from the west. Menacing thunderstorms had turned the vast mouth of the Patuxent River and the Chesapeake Bay beyond into quite an afternoon spectacle.

These five hundred or so Yankee flotillamen, with muscles aching after hours of hard rowing occasioned by sailing only when the contrary winds cooperated, had other things on their minds. An assortment of British vessels, including a 74-gun ship-of-the-line named *Dragon,* had been chasing the flotilla for most of the day. Now, as they watched, the Americans were at the receiving end of a barrage of smoking Congreve rockets that screamed into the firmament.

The flotillamen were committed to protecting the Chesapeake from a naval world power. Part of a "mosquito fleet," a collection of small, hastily built barges designed to harass the vastly superior resources of the enemy, they knew the odds of success were long. Some would call it a fool's errand, but the Chesapeake defenders had to do something.

Commodore Joshua Barney, commander of America's eighteen-vessel mosquito flotilla, was taking stock after several hours of challenges. Barney, a celebrated man of action, had spent many of his fifty-five years at sea. Rarely had he faced such a daunting set of difficulties. Two of his largely untested and low-slung barges were now taking on water during this stormy weather. His first foray against the enemy had become a race to escape. It seemed a game of cat and mouse. Buying time to somehow blunt the sharp British raids was the only available strategy.

The idea of a fast-moving but lightly armed barge fleet to meet the "fury of the enemy" was hatched by Revolutionary War hero Barney, who on July 4, 1813, had presented a plan to Secretary of the Navy William Jones for the "Defence of the Chesapeake Bay." He made a convincing case for a "flying squadron" of inexpensive barges, expertly rowed and sailed by veteran mariners in shallow waters with the support of nearby land forces. Constantly pestering their muscle-bound enemy, this mosquito fleet might make the British pay dearly for their attacks.

Secretary Jones bought the idea, Congress put up $250,000, and Barney found himself acting master commandant of the "distinct and separate" U.S. Chesapeake Flotilla. With rivals and enemies from his past close at hand, the new acting master commandant soon fought a duel and severely wounded one Lemuel Taylor, who had called him "an abandoned rascal."

Having attended to his personal matters, Barney went to work tirelessly in Washington, Baltimore, and St. Michaels on building and assembling his flotilla. He found capable subordinates but had trouble competing with privateers for experienced seamen. Racing to prepare for the 1814 campaigns and struggling with micromanagement by Secretary Jones, the commandant created a fleet of gun barges. Besides the banks of oars, the first-class 75-foot versions had two sails and the second-class 50 footers had one. Built for shallow draft speed, they had to be reinforced to support heavy iron cannons. At the stern, long guns fired either 12-, 18-, or 24-pound cannonballs; at the bow, stubby carronades fired 24-, 32-, or 42-pound cannonballs. Firing these large cannons could stress the small vessels. One of Barney's biggest dilemmas was the older, "heavy sailing," and slow support vessels used for command and supplies. His flagship, a block sloop called *Scorpion,* was seaworthy enough, but two clumsy old gunboats, named *No. 137* and *No. 138,* could not keep up with the fast-rowing flotilla.

After some shakedown forays down the Bay, the Chesapeake Flotilla finally headed south from Baltimore on May 24, 1814. Its target was the British base on Tangier Island, near the center of the Bay, where Barney hoped

Preceding spread: The U.S. Chesapeake Flotilla is being chased by a vastly superior British squadron. Off the mouth of the Patuxent River during an afternoon squall, the 75-foot two-masted and the 50-foot one-masted gun barges have dropped their sails and have come about to support two slow supply gunboats. Commodore Joshua Barney, aboard his flagship *Scorpion,* distinguished by its square sail, pennant, and signal flags, is followed by the slow gunboats just visible behind the flagship. All are in danger of being overtaken by enemy vessels firing cannons and rockets in the far distance.

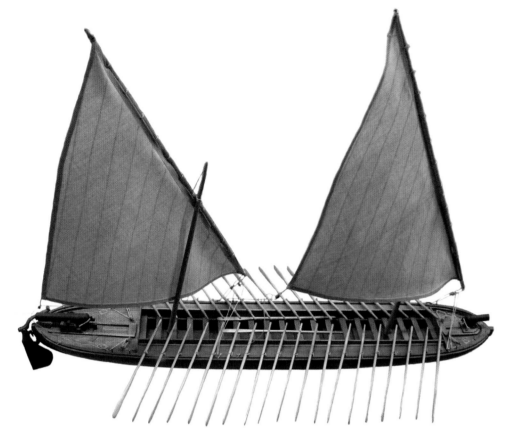

Scale model of U.S. Chesapeake Flotilla 75-foot gun barge. Note the stubby carronade in the bow and the long gun in the stern, seats for flotillamen to row from, and the unusual triangular-shaped lateen sails. Other than higher gunnels and square stern shown on Barney's original plan, the gun barges show a strong resemblance to his design. After sea trials, washboards were added to heighten the gunnels. The rudder may have been a yoke rudder as shown in the illustration introducing this chapter to allow the long gun to fire over it.

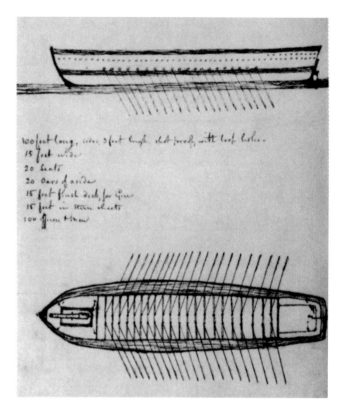

On July 4, 1813, Joshua Barney included this sketch of a gun barge with his plan for a "mosquito fleet" to harass the British blockaders. The U.S. Navy Department, desperate to find a way to defend the Chesapeake from the overwhelming enemy presence, gave Barney authorization to build a Chesapeake Flotilla.

lightning attacks could vex and trouble enemy interests. Barney received Secretary Jones's worried message, "Your force is our principal shield, and all eyes will be upon you." He answered simply, "I am anxious to be at them."

And now, a week later, sitting with his eighteen-vessel flotilla in the mouth of the Patuxent River, Commodore Barney was considering his next move. The fighting on June 1, later called the Battle of Cedar Point, was an inauspicious beginning. The British were led by another tough Napoleonic War veteran, Captain Robert Barrie (1774–1841), who had orders to "do any mischief on either side of the Potomac . . . within your power." They were raiding north of Point Lookout when they spotted many sails closing fast. The strange vessels had lateen sails like some Middle Eastern pirate squadron. Hundreds of oars were slapping in unison across the water. Barrie frantically gathered his scattered force and called for reinforcements, including his flagship, the 74-gun H.M. ship-of-the-line *Dragon*.

With the command "sails and oars," Barney and the flotilla were headed at flank speed for their British prey. Suddenly, the giant ship *Dragon*, sails billowing, rushed in their direction. Just as quickly the wind shifted against them amidst a series of squalls. They turned tail, rowing for all they were worth toward some security in the mouth of the Patuxent River. One old gunboat, *No. 137*, laden with supplies, could not keep up. With the British in hot pursuit, Barney ordered his gun barges to reverse direction and assist in towing *No. 137* away from the approaching enemy. Despite the firing of cannon and rockets, the Yankees were able to rescue the gunboat and, for the moment, seek safety near Somervell's Island (Solomons). But the flotilla was now trapped in the river by an enemy blockade.

Commodore Barney worried about these strange new British rockets and complained to Washington about his "miserable tools." Barney also now realized the gunboats were such poor sailing vessels his provisions could not be trusted in them. He therefore pleaded for a "vessel to carry provisions, such as will not be the means of disaster and disgrace."

The Prince of Privateers and Adventurers

Joshua Barney was one of the great naval heroes of early America. A highly respected Revolutionary War veteran, Barney headed to sea as a successful privateer during the early days of the War of 1812. In the summer of 1814, he and his U.S. Chesapeake Flotilla were the backbone of a checkered American defense on Maryland waters.

"To content himself with following the plough . . . while the blast of war was blowing in his ears, would have been . . . altogether contrary to his nature."

—Mary Barney, *A Biographical Memoir of the Late Commodore Joshua Barney*, 1832

Joshua Barney rarely sat still for long. From the time he first went to sea at age thirteen, the Baltimore native was a magnet for adventure on the high seas.

At sixteen, he commanded a ship that was caught up in a Spanish campaign against Algiers. His experiences during the Revolution, while he was still in his teens, made Barney an American hero. Captured three times, he was held on a notorious prison ship and escaped his captors twice. As the war ended, he fought and won a spirited sea battle, then carried secret messages to and from France during the peace negotiations. The French were so impressed with Barney, they hired him to run their West Indies Squadron in the 1790s.

Retired from the sea, and after years of success as a Baltimore merchant trader, the veteran mariner launched his most important adventure. As another war began in 1812, Barney was at sea again, commanding the legendary Baltimore privateer *Rossie* and preying on British shipping. During the summer of 1814, Barney, now commodore of the U.S. Chesapeake Flotilla, bravely engaged the mighty Royal Navy. Scuttling their gun barges in the face of overwhelming odds, Barney and his flotillamen marched to Bladensburg and won British respect with their determined defense of the road to the Federal City. Seriously wounded at the battle, the commodore was headed for new adventures in Kentucky when he finally succumbed to the Bladensburg wound in 1818, thus ending his remarkable life.

Barney's posthumous portrait, depicting him as an honored 1812 defender, reveals an active gentleman with tousled hair and a ruddy complexion. He confidently grasps his side sword and proudly wears his Society of Cincinnati Medal, marking him as a decorated veteran of the Revolution. Early America had only a handful of heroes who measure up to the bold achievements of Commodore Joshua Barney.

Facing "the Rockets' Red Glare"

"The enemy advanced a barge which threw Rockets, but as they cannot be directed with any certainty they did no Execution . . ."

—Commodore Joshua Barney to U.S. Secretary of the Navy William Jones, June 3, 1814

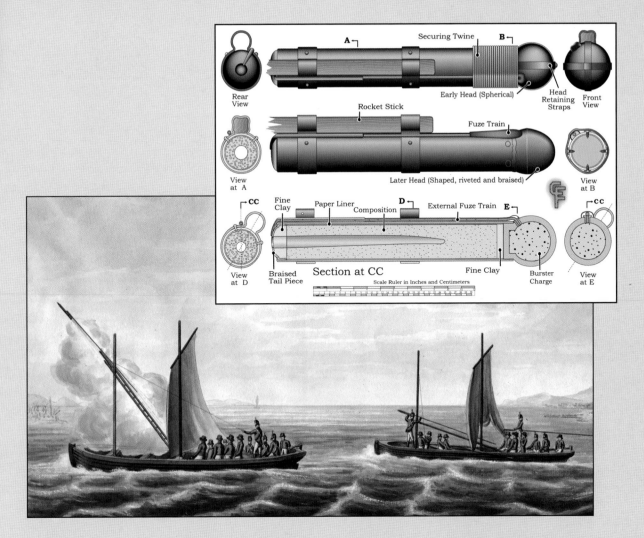

An eccentric British colonel named George Hanger, the Fourth Baron of Coleraine, famously said in 1814, "no man was ever killed at 200 yards by a common musket, by the person who aimed at him."

The same could be said of the Congreve rocket. Accuracy wasn't the point. In the days when whole armies could see each other, and showy uniforms and close-order drill were important, intimidation could put your adversary at a serious disadvantage. It was a bonus if a rocket, screaming through the sky, hit something of interest. What was more important was that a barrage of rockets could stampede frightened enemies. Only three Americans were killed by rockets during the war in the Chesapeake, but few who saw them in action soon forgot them.

The British Army discovered the power of rockets when it was on the receiving end of terrifying attacks in India. Some captured Indian rockets were delivered to the Woolwich Royal Arsenal in 1801, and a resident inventor named William Congreve went quickly to work in creating a facsimile. By 1804, Congreve had a working prototype for the army. A strong iron tube was filled with gunpowder and attached by three rings to a long stabilizing wooden pole. When set at an angle in a simple frame and touched off, a 12-pound rocket, pole and all, could travel about a mile and a half, shrieking all the way. This was about twice the range of light field ordnance. When mounted with an exploding warhead, it spread shrapnel and could start fires where it landed.

Rushed to Napoleonic battlefields, the new weapon appeared at Boulogne in 1806 and would remain a part of the English arsenal until the 1850s.

When Francis Scott Key watched the bombardment of Fort McHenry unfold, it was the bomb ships and rocket boats spreading their terror at the city's defenses that led him to write of "the rockets' red glare, the bombs bursting in air."

Above: The diagram details the construction of a British 12-pound Congreve shell rocket. Rockets ranged in size from 6 pounds to 42 pounds. The 12 pounder was commonly used by land troops owing to its relatively light weight and effectiveness.

Below: The elevation of the Congreve rocket launching ramp could be adjusted to account for the distance to the target and the desired trajectory. Rockets launched on land used a similarly adjustable tripod.

The Raids Begin Anew

"I have it much in my heart to give them a complete drubbing before peace is made."

—Vice Admiral Sir Alexander Cochrane taking command against the Americans, 1814

Yet another British admiral who had no love for Americans now took command. Sir Alexander Forrester Inglis Cochrane (1758–1832), one of the hard-edged British naval officers of the era, had fought in the American Revolution, lost a brother at Yorktown, and had his hat blown off by a cannonball in the 1806 Battle of San Domingo. Now a vice admiral, he was replacing the lackluster Admiral Sir John B. Warren as commander of the North American Squadron. With only three weeks in April to plan an 1814 campaign, Admiral Cochrane was eager to take the war to Americans in the Chesapeake region, in part because of their well-known privateering activities.

Cochrane's second in command, the hated Rear Admiral George Cockburn, was back for another campaign season with orders to plant a naval base on a suitable Chesapeake island. Rumors were flying that Cockburn, still itching to capture the bottled up U.S. frigate *Constellation,* had been personally reconnoitering American defenses at Norfolk disguised as a common sailor and a fisherman.

It soon looked as if 1814 would become a repeat of 1813. As early as February, British landing parties captured the New Point Comfort Lighthouse, a valuable observation post and watering place on the western shore north of Norfolk. Throughout the spring months, damaging and costly raids continued in the Chesapeake tidewater region. British barges loaded with marines rowed up ancient rivers with Indian names—Annemessex, Yeocomico, Rappahannock, and Pungoteague. The intruders carted off slaves, livestock, and produce, regularly burning property when owners resisted.

And occasionally local militiamen did resist, resulting in some successes. When the British returned to New Point Comfort on March 17 to fetch needed fresh water, they were soon in a fifteen-minute fire fight with waiting locals. Retreating to the shelter of some sand hills, they called in a barge armed with a 12-pound cannon and exchanged shots with a Yankee 6 pounder. The only casualty was the militia captain's horse, hit and killed by a cannonball as the British withdrew.

Two months later, the enemy aboard H.M. brig *Jaseur* went after a vessel in Somerset County's Annemessex River. The owner, one George Davey, was not intimidated. With his boat burning in the river, he gathered up some neighbors and is said to have instructed his slaves to march around with shouldered sticks so the distant enemy would think militia was mustering. He approached the *Jaseur* with his own small fleet of four locally made log canoe workboats, firing a "salute" at the raiders as they gathered their landing party and departed. Davey saved the day and his vessel with his homegrown bravado.

On the late afternoon of May 29, just days before the war moved decisively up to Maryland's Patuxent River, the 74-gun H.M. ship-of-the-line *Albion,* Admiral Cockburn's flagship, with "a great number of elegant colors" flying, anchored at the mouth of Pungoteague Creek on Virginia's Eastern Shore. Local militia, expecting trouble, had prepared a skimpy defense near West Point. Two crude, 20-foot square pine plank barracks were defended by a rusty and worn Revolutionary War 4-pound cannon.

The British announced their intentions with a salute gun in the early evening. By sunrise, five hundred Royal Marines had landed near the home of a John Smith with their rockets and cannons blazing from barges on the river. Seventy or so 2nd Virginia Regiment militiamen were forced into the woods by the cheering raiders. The old cannon was spiked, the barracks burned, and Mr. Smith's house plundered. Suddenly, a thousand new Yankee militiamen entered the fray and the British beat a hasty retreat, losing six killed in the fracas. The Battle of Pungoteague (or Rumley's Gut) was the largest Virginia Eastern Shore fire fight of the war. The Americans had prevailed for a change.

The important new factor in this all-too-familiar raid and skirmish was the presence for the first time of the Colonial Corps of Marines (black marines whom the British often called "Ethiopians"). These recently trained escaped slaves were in the forefront of the fighting. Admiral Cockburn reported that the thirty new marines "behaved to the admiration of every Body."

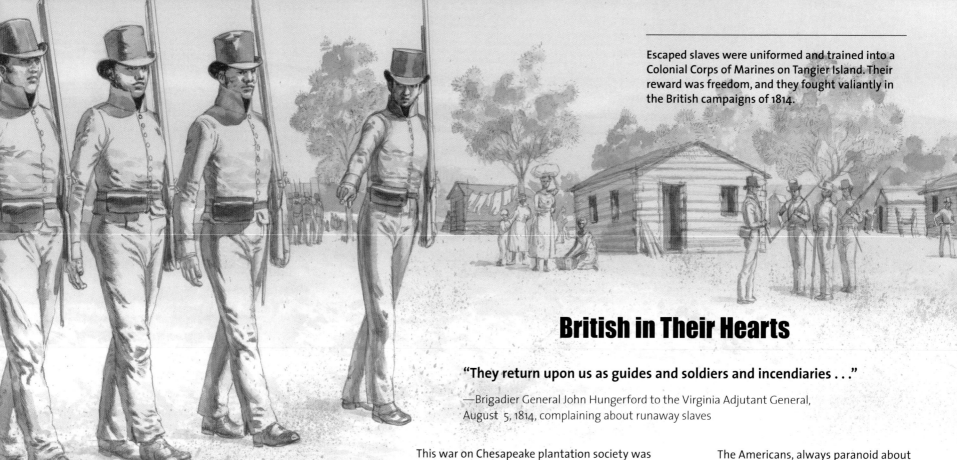

Escaped slaves were uniformed and trained into a Colonial Corps of Marines on Tangier Island. Their reward was freedom, and they fought valiantly in the British campaigns of 1814.

British in Their Hearts

"They return upon us as guides and soldiers and incendiaries . . ."

—Brigadier General John Hungerford to the Virginia Adjutant General, August 5, 1814, complaining about runaway slaves

This war on Chesapeake plantation society was creating an opportunity for the British and a challenge for Americans. Some royal officials claimed that American slaves were really "British in their hearts." At the urging of the blockading Royal fleet, slaves were stealing away from plantations in ever-increasing numbers. One hundred "Negroes" were reported to be onboard H.M. ship-of-the-line *Dragon* at the end of April in 1814. Admiral Cochrane had seized the opportunity and issued an April 2 proclamation offering slaves or free blacks service in His Majesty's armed forces or free passage to settle in nearby colonies.

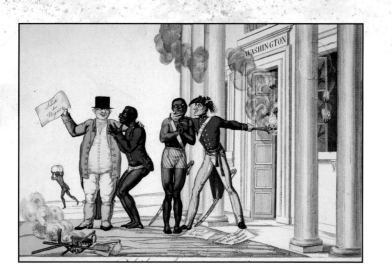

Circa 1814 cartoon of British officer and politician encouraging American slaves to escape to the British in exchange for freedom.

The Americans, always paranoid about slave rebellions, were both angry and frightened. They were in danger of losing their primary plantation labor force. Worse yet, some of the slaves were being converted into "troops, vindictive and capricious with a most reliable knowledge of every bye path . . ."

Something was indeed happening that plantation owners could hardly imagine. Slaves were not only running away into the arms of the British, they were coming back to attack their former owners. At least seven hundred slaves—men, women, and children—were given shelter on Tangier Island. As many as two hundred were being trained and issued arms to fight side by side with the British troops as a Colonial Corps of Marines.

A Fort and Mosquitoes on Tangier Island

"I consider . . . that Tangier Island . . . though not perhaps without its inconveniences, is far better adapted for the purposes you contemplated than any other in the Chesapeake. . ."

—Admiral Cockburn to Admiral Cochrane, May 9, 1814

Tangier Island, actually a collection of several islands and marshes located near the center of the lower Chesapeake Bay at its widest expanse, is twelve miles from the nearest mainland. Shallows surrounding the island afford protection, but one deep anchorage on the south end gave large British ships-of-the-line access. Admiral Cockburn commented on one serious consideration: "though I have no doubt Moschettos [mosquitoes] will be numerous in the Summer time, yet I do not think it probable they will be much worse here than at the other islands." Pondering sources of fresh water, the admiral happily reported that his parties "readily found [drinking water] in every part we have dug for it."

On April 14, 1814, island watermen, suddenly caught between a rock and a hard place, became the neighbors of two hundred enemy troops who began building a substantial British base of operations. Cockburn named it Fort Albion, not only echoing his flagship but also the ancient name for the English island. It was soon obvious the interlopers planned to stay awhile. The British built barracks to accommodate a thousand persons, a hospital for a hundred, a church, twenty dwellings laid out in streets, and storage sheds for plunder, all protected by timber and earthen 250-yard-long walls and two redoubts with large cannons.

It was far from a healthy setting for a fort. Despite Cockburn's pronouncement, deserters complained of bad, brackish water and plagues of dysentery. The seven hundred escaped slaves brought to the island, mostly women and children, became a worrisome drain on scarce resources. Still, this bold stroke, building a fort in hostile territory, gave British leaders the security to launch large attacks on important American targets in all directions on the mainland.

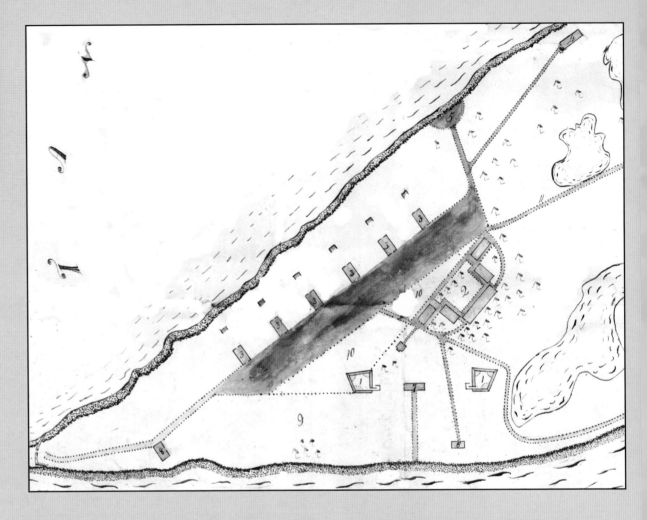

Map of the British base at Tangier Island, Virginia, circa 1814. Key: (1) two trapezoidal redoubts of Fort Albion; (2) officers' barracks; (3) privates' barracks (possibly used by the Colonial Corps, six in total, with doors on each end) and three-sided cookhouses; (4) hospital; (5) fish market; (6) garrison barracks; (7) garrison storehouse; (8) guard house; (9) parade grounds; (10) gardens.

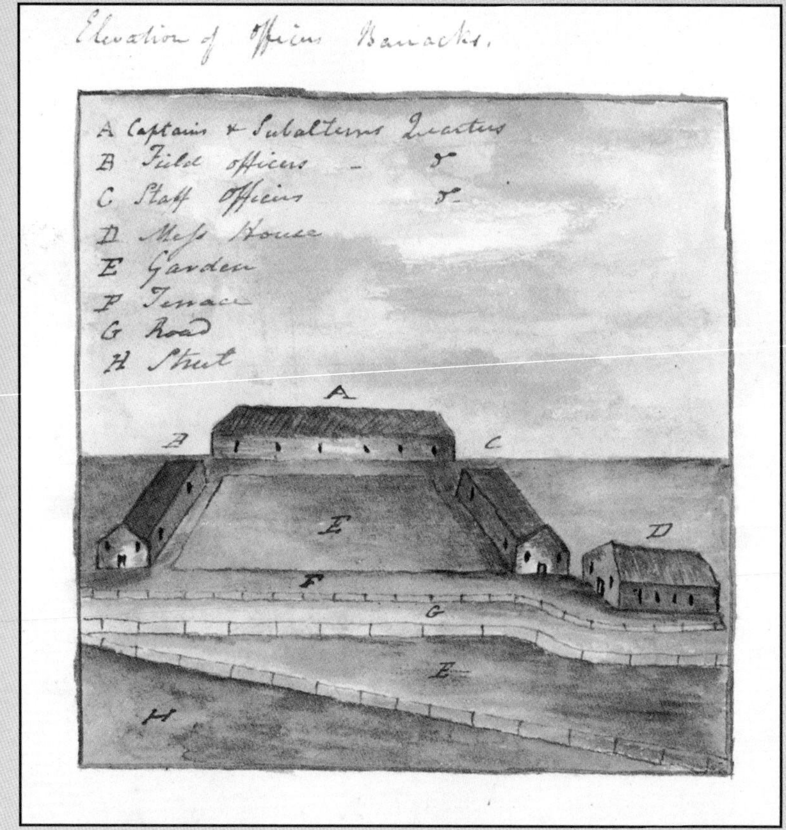
Elevation of Officers Barracks.
A Captains & Subalterns Quarters
B Field officers do
C Staff Officers do
D Mess House
E Garden
F Terrace
G Road
H Street

This circa early 1815 British sketch shows the officers' barracks, number 2 on the illustration to left.

The First Battle of St. Leonard Creek

June 8–10, 1814

"This kind of fighting is much against us as they can reach us when we can't reach them."

—Joshua Barney to Secretary of the Navy Jones, June 9, 1814

Captain Joshua Barney peered through his telescope, searching for enemies in the rising heat and humidity. Barney, self-styled commodore of the Chesapeake Flotilla, was surrounded by hundreds of oarsmen and gunners, all at the ready in the gunboats and gun barges arrayed across the cove. To a man, they were staring down the creek at the empty water and green bluffs. They were braced for a British assault that would soon shatter the charged stillness.

During this midday, Wednesday, June 8, Barney was playing for time. It had been a week since he and his flotillamen, outgunned and outmanned, had boldly sailed and rowed into the teeth of the British threat on the Chesapeake Bay. The subsequent retreat up the Patuxent River may have sealed their fate. They were now bottled up in the temporary sanctuary of St. Leonard Creek, but the old sea dog Commodore Barney had been in tight squeezes before. He was determined to go down fighting, making the British pay for every inch of advantage they sought. He was prepared to sacrifice his tiny fleet, giving leaders in Washington City time to cobble together their defense.

Suddenly the enemy appeared, battle flags flying. A hodgepodge of small barges was warily approaching through the twists and turns of the tidal creek. Larger vessels, a sloop, schooner, and a frigate with a lower profile called a razee, were miles away, backing them up. With long decks of menacing iron guns, these warships hovered like specters in the Patuxent River west of the

During the June 8, 1814, Battle of St. Leonard Creek, a rocket struck a gun barge, killing a flotillaman and exploding gunpowder onboard. As the crew abandoned the burning boat, Sailing Master William Barney, Commodore Joshua Barney's son, jumped aboard. The young Barney heroically bailed water into the boat and rocked it about onto the flames, singlehandedly extinguishing the fire and saving the vessel.

creek's shallow mouth. Captain Robert Barrie, with his flagship, the 74-gun ship-of-the-line *Dragon*, now anchored seven miles downriver, had boarded a barge to personally lead the attack.

At first, the British kept their distance. They were carefully probing for trouble from land as well as water in the narrow creek. One of their barges launched Congreve rockets that screamed toward the flotilla. Barney ordered his oarsmen to the fight, legions of calloused hands rowing quickly in practiced unison to engage the enemy. The barges' curious lateen sails were raised to urge the vessels on. Gunners stood at the bows of their boats, burning portfires at the ready to touch off a first volley of up to eighteen guns. The British turned tail and disappeared.

The contest continued later that afternoon. A slightly larger squadron of British barges rowed even closer, taunting the Yankee tars with more rockets. Suddenly, the unthinkable happened. One of the terrifying but notoriously inaccurate rockets scored a direct hit. Screaming into one of Barney's barges, it eradicated an unfortunate flotillaman, exploded a barrel of powder, and severely burned another sailor. Faced with a menacing fire, the crew quickly abandoned ship, jumping overboard without ceremony. The Americans prepared to watch helplessly as one of their hard-bought vessels blew to smithereens.

Sailing Master William Barney, son of the commander and leader of one of the flotilla's three divisions, quickly hailed his father for permission and, alone, bravely boarded the flaming vessel. With hundreds of breathless spectators looking on, the younger Barney, "by dint of active labor," pitched buckets of water into the hold and briskly rocked the boat, sloshing the fire into submission. The boat was saved, much to "the very great delight and astonishment of the commodore."

The English were back the next day. Commodore Barney, regularly reporting to Secretary of the Navy Jones in Washington, was frustrated. "This kind of fighting is much against us . . . when we pursue [the British] their light boats fly before us." He decided on a different ploy.

Twice on June 9, Captain Barrie again launched forays into the upper reaches of the creek. The second, a twenty-barge force, was accompanied by more firepower. The 18-gun H.M. schooner *St. Lawrence* was carefully sailing through tricky narrow waters, sounding as she came upstream. The flotilla, in turn, retreated behind a log boom stretched across the creek. With cannon batteries and musket men threatening from the bluffs on both sides of the narrow passage, the Americans dared their adversaries to come on. They were locked in, over three miles up St. Leonard Creek, but secure for the moment. Barney was certain that they had "little to fear from an attack by boats, no matter how numerous."

In the early morning of June 10, American infantry reinforcements quietly attempted to cross the river from Sotterley Plantation, but the nearby blockading ships quickly brought their progress to a halt. While British raiding parties were sent out to chase the Yankees and harass the local residents, Barney again changed gears. He had the masts and sails removed from all but his three slowest vessels. Three columns, fifteen barges arranged in red, white, and blue divisions, rowed doggedly down the creek looking for a fight.

After four forays in two days, the English had also decided to go for the jugular. Up to seven hundred men, armed to the teeth in twenty-one barges, towed two schooners into battle. Following an eccentric custom of the age, a band of musicians, possibly including pairs of woodwinds, horns, bass "serpents," and "jingling johnnies," played marches by the likes of Mozart and Haydn amidst the sweating oarsmen.

This time, when the Chesapeake Flotilla came charging down the creek, the English "seemed determined to do something decisive." The noisy "smart action" captured the attention of the British fleet, miles away at the mouth of the Patuxent. Trading blows like prizefighters, the two small flotillas faced off in an hours-long collision of shrieking rockets and 18-, 24-, even 32-pound iron shot. A shot smacked into an American barge below the waterline and it soon sank. Barney's flotilla, however, kept up a withering fire. When the Englishmen finally retreated, the Americans "pursued them down the creek."

Captain Robert Barrie was optimistic. Perhaps he could finally lure the enemy barges into his trap. Surely the heavy guns in the square-riggers just beyond the mouth of the creek would turn the tide.

Commodore Barney and his barges pressed on, bow guns sending shot in all directions. Navigating the narrow mouth of the creek just ahead of the charging flotilla, the British schooner *St. Lawrence* was suddenly grounded in the sand. The Americans moved in like a swarm of yellowjackets, pouring at least four rounds into the schooner's hull as the crew scrambled ashore. During the melee, Captain Barrie's own barge was almost cut in two and the vexing rocket boat was hit full on.

Now faced with broadsides from the river, Barney's barges rowed to shelter in a nearby cove. British spotters high in the rigging of the larger ships began to direct fire into the refuge. Enemy marine snipers were landed on bluffs overlooking the flotilla. The exhausted Americans, after six hours of maneuver and combat without a single casualty, quietly withdrew up the creek.

The hard-fighting Chesapeake Flotilla had almost bested a vastly superior English force. Joshua Barney was convinced that the Americans "must have done them considerable damage." On June 11, the British pulled their stranded and damaged schooner off the sand bar and began repairs. They also committed several lost seamen to the river's embrace. The Americans, in turn, had managed to refloat their barge sunk in the fray.

The First Battle of St. Leonard Creek had changed nothing—the flotilla was still bottled up in the creek. But it had bought the anxious Americans a little more time to prepare their tidewater defenses. Captain Barrie and the other enemy leaders, still waiting for reinforcements, decided to leave Barney alone for the moment. The local countryside, however, would feel the full sting of their presence in the weeks to come.

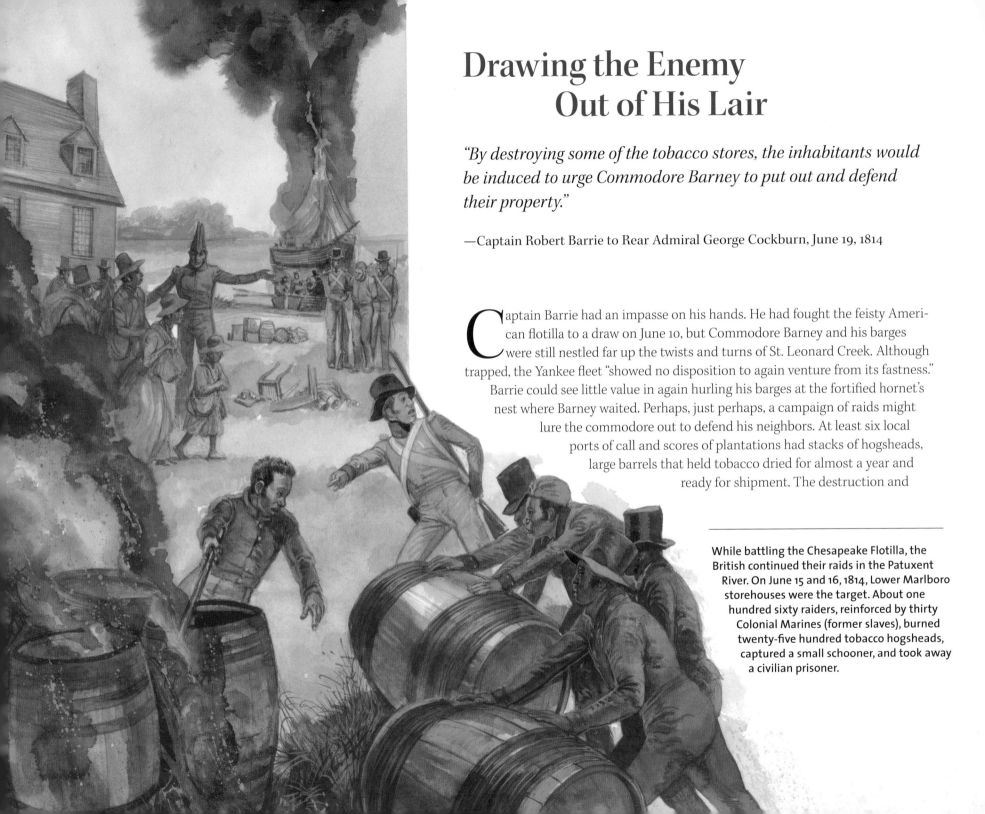

Drawing the Enemy Out of His Lair

"By destroying some of the tobacco stores, the inhabitants would be induced to urge Commodore Barney to put out and defend their property."

—Captain Robert Barrie to Rear Admiral George Cockburn, June 19, 1814

Captain Barrie had an impasse on his hands. He had fought the feisty American flotilla to a draw on June 10, but Commodore Barney and his barges were still nestled far up the twists and turns of St. Leonard Creek. Although trapped, the Yankee fleet "showed no disposition to again venture from its fastness." Barrie could see little value in again hurling his barges at the fortified hornet's nest where Barney waited. Perhaps, just perhaps, a campaign of raids might lure the commodore out to defend his neighbors. At least six local ports of call and scores of plantations had stacks of hogsheads, large barrels that held tobacco dried for almost a year and ready for shipment. The destruction and

While battling the Chesapeake Flotilla, the British continued their raids in the Patuxent River. On June 15 and 16, 1814, Lower Marlboro storehouses were the target. About one hundred sixty raiders, reinforced by thirty Colonial Marines (former slaves), burned twenty-five hundred tobacco hogsheads, captured a small schooner, and took away a civilian prisoner.

capture of those hogsheads would strike at the very marrow of the local economy.

Navigable for nearly fifty miles into the center of Maryland, the Patuxent River was an efficient thoroughfare for the damaging British attacks. Throughout June, the incursions went on like drum beats up and down the river. It was a campaign of terror that local inhabitants would remember for generations. John Broome, a local militia captain, lost his house at Broomes Island. Across the river, Sotterley Plantation, a local landmark, lost thirty-nine slaves, carried away while a tobacco warehouse burned. Upriver, the destruction escalated: 360 hogsheads burned at Benedict; 1,100 at Magruders Landing; and 2,500 at Lower Marlboro as hundreds of militia and townsfolk fled for their lives.

Local residents were stunned but not totally helpless in the face of the onslaught. While the 36th U.S. Infantry headed to reinforce Commodore Barney's flotilla, they drove off marauding British and saved a defenseless Nottingham from destruction. An American attempt at ambushing enemy barges from Hollands Cliffs was foiled when escaped slaves warned the British. Royal Marines landed, chased off the militia, and burned a barn and more tobacco. A second skirmish on Benedict met with a surprising response by hundreds of American cavalry and infantry from Washington's Georgetown Volunteers supported by four cannons. A brave and determined British sergeant fighting a lonely holding action was killed and several others captured during the fracas. The notoriously unreliable citizen-soldiers called up for the emergency were loudly applauded for a rare victory in a sea of bad news.

While the Chesapeake Flotilla lurked amidst the wooded bluffs of St. Leonard Creek, enemy raiding parties went after nearby plantations. James John Pattison lost his house and a tobacco barn before the intruders were chased off trying to burn down another barn. John Stuart Skinner, Barney's purser and a local planter, was another victim of the slash-and-burn tactics. Skinner was the American agent for prisoner exchange who would play an important role during the British invasion. For the moment, the Royal Marines were making Skinner's life miserable, taking sheep and burning his property located near the creek.

Commodore Barney had other challenges besides the British fleet. A gentleman named John Parran, who lived near the mouth of St. Leonard Creek, told the flotillamen that he and his brother had been grabbed by the enemy but both were released with a message; "If [the Americans] remained

This August 1814 sketch by Commodore Joshua Barney shows the British blockade at the mouth of the Patuxent River off Drum Point. From left to right are the H.M. frigate *Brune,* two gunboats, H.M. frigate *Severn* and H.M. brig *Manly.* Somervell (Somerville) Island is known as Solomons Island today. The Dr. William D. Somervell house, the Nicholas Sewall house, and the Carroll house were all raided by the British. Barney's sketch shows three British schooners and eight gun barges raiding the Carroll Plantation.

at home quietly, they should not be molested. But if on landing [the British commander] found their houses deserted, he would burn them all. . . ." A suspicious Barney arrested Parran when he let slip that he was returning to the enemy fleet. Fearing local unrest, federal superiors in Washington, communicating via express riders, ordered Barney to release his captive.

Many locals, steadfastly opposed to Mr. Madison's war, wanted Barney and his troubled mosquito fleet to go away. Mr. Thomas B. King was blunt in a July letter from a besieged Calvert County: "I tell you the mischief the British have done it will be enough to make you and every man abuse [President] Jim Madison and old Barney in Hell." The spunky American commander may have thought he was already in hell, but he was now part of a bold plot to escape from his predicament.

The Second Battle of
St. Leonard Creek

June 26, 1814

"... thanks to hot and cold shot, the blockade is raised."

—Joshua Barney, quoted in *American and Commercial Daily Advertiser,*
June 29, 1814

Both of the 1814 protagonists were struggling with their own special challenges during the hot, humid, and moody Chesapeake summer. An ill British Admiral Cockburn, complaining that the weather "has tried our constitutions a little," ordered Captain Barrie and his flagship *Dragon,* loaded with tobacco and escaped slaves, back down the Patuxent River to help protect Tangier Island. Americans had lost over $1 million in goods and property during the recent month of raids. But Cockburn, used to little or no opposition to his forays, was frankly worried about the Chesapeake Flotilla, writing to Admiral Cochrane, "How sharply and unexpectedly [Brother] Jonathan [the U.S.] has exerted himself in putting forth his marine armaments in this bay."

Commodore Barney, literally up a creek with his flotilla since early June, was struggling with meddling from the Federal City. Secretary of the Navy William Jones couldn't decide what to do with his trapped defenders. First Jones wanted Barney to roll his barges overland across the Calvert peninsula to the Bay and freedom. Next he decided the commodore should take everything of

---

Cannons and infantry on the St. Leonard Creek bluffs supported the Chesapeake Flotilla in a predawn attack on June 26. The plan ended in confusion, but Barney's barges rowed down the creek with cannons blazing. When the British blockade withdrew to repair damage, Barney's flotilla temporarily escaped up the Patuxent River. The barge shown here depicts Barney's original design but the barges were probably built as shown in the Battle of Cedar Point illustration introducing chapter 3.

value off the vessels and scuttle the fleet. While a reluctant, frustrated, and depressed Barney was trying to follow orders, preparing to do the unthinkable, word arrived that reinforcements were coming with heavy artillery.

The reprieve came in the person of Colonel Decius Wadsworth (1768–1821), a respected and competent engineering officer. Wadsworth arrived on June 24 with portions of the U.S. 36th Infantry, two 18-pound cannons, some smaller field pieces, and a portable furnace to heat up some hot shot. A hundred-man company of marines with more field guns, led by a fighting captain named Samuel Miller, had been at the creek as an independent command for a couple of weeks. The 2nd Battalion of the U.S. 38th Infantry from Baltimore would arrive bone-tired after a forced march on the evening of June 25. Wadsworth brought the plan that could put new pressure on the British and spring the flotilla: command the high ground around the mouth of the creek, place some cannons, and blast the blockaders while Barney's barges rowed headlong down the creek with guns blazing.

The British force—two frigates, a schooner, and barges now commanded by Captain Thomas Brown—could easily figure out what was going on. They had access to local newspapers that printed a running account of the American troop movements for all to see. They had local spies everywhere in the largely antiwar neighborhood. Yet, without a large force to seize and hold land around the creek, they sat plugging the creek's mouth and waited.

Morale was sky high as the flotilla gun barges, stripped of their masts and sails, rowed quietly down St. Leonard Creek and into position about a mile from the British on the night of June 25. Barney had loaned his trusted and brave sailing master John Geoghegan and seventeen of his men to the land forces. Colonel Wadsworth desperately needed muscle and experienced gunners. Surrounded by exhausted soldiers who refused to help, Geoghegan and the flotillamen spent a tense and tiring night with the marines working nearby trying to quietly carve out usable gun emplacements. Wadsworth was

War Crimes?

"The full bottles created a painful suspicion that the wine and liquor might be poisoned."

—British Captain James Scott, autobiography, 1834

During the dramatic summers of 1813 and 1814, the beleaguered residents of the Chesapeake tidewater region must have been sorely tempted to leave a malicious calling card for their British invaders. On a couple of occasions, British officers were convinced that locals were trying to poison their troops.

While raiding the Nomini Ferry landing on the Northern Neck of Virginia in July of 1814, British Captain James Scott and his men discovered a suspicious table setting at a house of one Mrs. Thompson. "The House had evidently been [the local militia] headquarters . . . The . . . largest room on the ground floor appeared as if it had been the scene of a carousing party, from the number of glasses, bottles of liquor, &c. that graced the whole length of the table . . . I fortunately observed that the glasses had not been used . . ." Suspecting poison, Captain Scott sent the full bottle's contents to the surgeon of Admiral Cockburn's flagship. According to Scott, the bottle was "found to contain a very large quantity of arsenic."

Americans, of course, disputed the claim. Lieutenant Colonel Richard Elliott Parker of the Virginia militia claimed "he had drunk of the spirits but a few moments before the British came up, and that it was impossible it could have been poisoned." A similar incident, reported at Benedict a couple of months earlier, also produced contrary claims and no casualties.

little help. After telling the men to "place [the cannons] where you please," he later ordered them to move to a "safer" position behind the brow of the hill, wasting hours of hard work. A message was sent to Barney informing him the batteries might not be ready as planned.

Miraculously, in spite of the confusion, the guns began firing hot and cold shot at 4 in the morning, much to the surprise of both Barney and the British. As often happens in the fog of war, the chance for a coordinated attack was lost, but the British, caught sleeping, were at the mercy of American cannon until they brought their shipboard guns to bear. Although the American fire from the bluffs was slow and often too high, the flotilla gun barges, rowing at flank speed downstream, finally entered the fray and pounded their enemy. Brown's flagship, H.M. frigate *Loire*, took fifteen shots to her hull and lost some of her rigging.

Then, suddenly, Barney's support from the bluffs all but ceased. The British had sent some barges with rockets up the Patuxent to flank the Americans. When some American cannon were redeployed to meet this new threat, the militia thought they were withdrawing and this misunderstanding led to a disgraceful American retreat. The beset flotillamen could only man one gun on the bluff, and Barney's force was left exposed to the full fury of British grape and canister. The commodore ordered a withdrawal up the creek thinking his opportunity to escape was again lost.

Two hours into the fight, with the sun just rising, British Captain Brown inexplicably decided to withdraw his force, licking its wounds, downriver. *Loire*'s pumps were hard at work as she was in some danger of sinking. It took no time for Commodore Barney to seize the opportunity. Brown later wrote, "I had the mortification to observe [the flotilla] rowing down the creek, and up the river." Leaving behind the old and slow gunboats *No. 137* and *No. 138*, the Chesapeake Flotilla had finally burst into freedom from St. Leonard Creek, rowing for all they were worth up the Patuxent.

Taking his frustration out on the locals with more raids, Captain Brown had some explaining to do. In his terse and short after-action report, he was happy to report only one casualty, a boatswain who had lost a leg. He avoided detail about the real result. In spite of serious battle mismanagement on both sides, old Commodore Barney had escaped to fight another day.

Propaganda during Wartime

"Here they made a furious attack on every window, door, and pane of glass in the village, not one was left in the whole . . . "

—Baltimore *Niles' Weekly Register,* August 14, 1814, reported an account of the British July 30, 1814, raid on Chaptico, Maryland

War produces distorted views, each side trying to gain an advantage in the public arena. American newspapers had an audience eager to hear of every enemy atrocity. The same event could sound completely different when described by British officers carefully crafting reports to their superiors. The July 30, 1814, raid on the tiny community of Chaptico near the Potomac River produced strikingly different accounts.

First Admiral Cockburn, the leader of the raid, described it this way:

> We marched to [Chaptico] and took possession without opposition. I remained all day quietly at Chaptico whilst the boats shipped off the Tobacco . . . and at night I re-embarked without molestation. I visited many Houses in different parts of the County we passed through, the owners of which were living quietly with their Families and seeming to consider themselves and the whole Neighborhood as being entirely at my disposal, I caused no further Inconvenience to [them] than obliging them to furnish Supplies of Cattle and Stock for the use of the Forces under my orders.

American newspapers painted quite a different picture:

> They [the British] got about 30 hhds. [hogsheads] of tobacco and other plunder, the inhabitants having moved all their property out of their grasp. Yet here they made a most furious attack . . . They picked their stolen geese

in the church, dashed the pipes of the church organ on the pavement, opened a family vault in the churchyard, broke open the coffins, stirred the bones about with their hands in search of hidden treasure.

Whom to believe! There probably is some truth in both accounts.

Propagandists lost no time putting their own spin on events after raids and skirmishes. In American newspapers, the enemy was painted as a bloodthirsty and ruthless foe committing atrocities on defenseless civilians. The British reports characterized their raids as harmless visits to their Yankee brothers and sisters.

The Last Cocked Hat

Called "The Last Cocked Hat," James Monroe was the final member of the Revolutionary War generation to serve in high U.S. government positions. During the first decades of the nineteenth century, the unflappable and capable Monroe filled the important roles of secretary of state and secretary of war. After the war he was elected president.

"National honor is the national property of the highest value."

—President James Monroe, March 14, 1817

U.S. Secretary of State James Monroe became a self-styled scout for the American forces. He and a detachment of dragoons searched for a British fleet reported to have entered the Bay. From a height about three miles from Benedict, Maryland, he spotted the enemy landing more than four thousand soldiers, sailors, and marines.

James Monroe was the last U.S. president who actually fought in the American Revolution. He was a member of that old guard instrumental in founding the country, the fourth Virginian of the first five presidents. At eighteen, he had been at General Washington's side, wounded at the Battle of Trenton.

An admiring lady described him as "tall and well formed . . . quiet and dignified." Thomas Jefferson said,

"Monroe [is] so honest if you turned his soul inside out there would not be a spot on it." His successful presidency (1817–25) was called the "era of good feelings."

Lured regularly into public service, Monroe was drafted by President Madison to serve as secretary of state during America's run-up to war in 1812. He was an unusual secretary, choosing to personally scout the

British movements as they invaded the Chesapeake tidewater region in 1814. At the Battle of Bladensburg, he countermanded his own military commanders, redeploying the confused militia and weakening the American position. The president rewarded him by making him secretary of war. Thus, James Monroe became the only government official to hold the positions of state and war at the same time.

Various Rumors Prove True

"Now that the tyrant Bonaparte has been consigned to infamy, there is no public feeling in this country stronger than that of indignation against the Americans."

—The London *Times*, April 15, 1814

The unsettling booming of cannons at 4 in the morning put the Patuxent River Valley on alert. Late in the afternoon of June 26, the citizens of Benedict, raided twice in one month, nervously watched more barges rowing upriver in their direction. They suddenly realized that, by some miracle, the American Chesapeake defenders were still in fighting trim.

The intrepid flotilla sailing master John Geoghegan, left on a St. Leonard Creek bluff watching his commodore and his barges disappear up the Patuxent, went immediately to work. Dodging British raiding parties all around, he was able to scuttle gunboats *No. 137* and *No. 138* and salvage the flotilla sails, spars, and supplies, quickly rejoining Barney while complaining that the St. Leonard's locals were "more anxious to plunder the property of the U.S. than to defend their own."

Reinforced by Captain Joseph Nourse with the 56-gun H.M. frigate *Severn*, British forces unleashed more terror on the Patuxent River. Throughout July and early August, daily raids plundered and destroyed the rich resources of the valley. The first order of business was raining destruction and vengeance on St. Leonard Town, the Chesapeake Flotilla haven throughout June. From there, the usual frightening pattern—tobacco hogsheads burned or stolen, slaves confiscated, and buildings put to the flame—continued with

The British naval movement up and down the Bay was monitored by Major William Barney from the dome of the Maryland State House.

little resistance in Calverton, Sheridan Point, Hallowing Point, Gods Grace, and as far up the river as Huntingtown, which was totally destroyed by a raging fire.

July 19 became a notably dark day for Southern Maryland. Prince Frederick, Calvert County's seat of government and a supply base for Barney's flotilla, was attacked, the jail and courthouse destroyed. To the southwest, Rear Admiral George Cockburn personally returned to the campaign trail, leading fifteen hundred troops on a raid that descended on the St. Mary's County seat in Leonardtown. The raid destroyed $1,500 in local merchandise and some militia muskets that were declared "broke to pieces [and] only fit to stick frogs with." America's favorite villain was back to his old tricks. Cockburn, cruising in his flagship *Albion*, spent late July and early August raiding at will on both sides of the lower Potomac Valley.

Although Southern Maryland suffered most during this time, British raiders did not spare the rest of the Bay. Virginia's Eastern Shore saw its last major attack, a night raid, burning and plundering public stores and chasing local militia at Chesconessex on June 25.

The entire Chesapeake region was in a state of panic. President James Madison called a cabinet meeting on June 27 to discuss the emergency. Washington, D.C., loomed large on British maps as a target, but cabinet members thought Baltimore or Annapolis might be likelier candidates for invasion. Secretary of War John Armstrong was distracted by repeated American invasions of Canada that were going nowhere. Secretary of the Navy Jones summoned Commodore Barney to Washington, but the brave defender with his tiny flotilla could offer few words of encouragement.

Captain Nourse wrote to his superiors that the "black refugees increase so fast that I begin to be somewhat puzzled about them." Asked to help stem the slave stampede to the British, Barney, having just spent a month trying to defend antiwar plantation owners, could only say, "Altho Calvert [County] deserves nothing from us, yet I conceive it a duty we owe our country." With few options to meet the British threat, President Madison could only hope for the best.

Unfortunately, there was no best in that long hot summer, except for a small victory near the head of the Bay. The British again probed Elkton's defenses on July 12. Thomas Marsh Forman, the local militia general, wrote his wife that "We gave them in all eleven guns, so well directed, that they hastily put about and retreated down the river."

On August 2, Admiral Cochrane sailed into the Chesapeake aboard his impressive 80-gun flagship, H.M. ship-of-the-line *Tonnant*, captured from the French in the Battle of the Nile. The admiral was leading a new large task force arriving to punish the Americans. Rumors flew up the Bay ahead of the enemy fleet. On August 17, Thomas Swann, forward observer at Point Lookout, sent an urgent message to Washington verifying the rumors. Rear Admiral Cockburn had already met with Admiral Cochrane and the newly arrived army commander, Major General Robert Ross. After weeks of raiding, Cockburn reported that "[t]his country is in general in a horrible state. It only requires a little firm and steady conduct to have it completely at our mercy."

But where was this menacing fleet headed? On August 20, Secretary of State James Monroe was peering through the morning haze just three miles from the tiny hamlet of Benedict. The self-styled scout, attended by about thirty District of Columbia Georgetown dragoons could see that a large fleet was landing many troops. Monroe reported that, "[t]he general idea . . . is, that Washington is their objective." A late edition of the Annapolis *Maryland Republican* printed the distressing news that "There were forty six sail in the bay, amongst which we understood there were several transports, bearing a large number of troops." Despite Secretary of War John Armstrong's strong belief that Washington was not a likely military target, he failed to realize the demoralizing effect the capture of the capital city would have on the nation. As were nearly all the towns and cities in the Chesapeake region, Washington was vulnerable to attack.

4 *Invasion!*
August 1814

Cool Intrepidity and a High State of Discipline

"Your force on this occasion is of immense importance and is relied upon with the utmost confidence."

—Secretary of the Navy William Jones to Commodore Joshua Barney, August 20, 1814

Commodore Joshua Barney mounted his horse in the hot midday sun of this Wednesday, August 24. He was bracing for the fight as the deafening sounds of disorder increased around him. Surrounded by about four hundred of his flotillamen, one hundred fourteen U.S. Marines, hundreds of militia, and supported by several cannon, he stood on the brow of a hill on Bladensburg Road awaiting the advancing British. After two American lines of defenders had been routed, his was the third and last line between the enemy and the Federal City. How had this veteran mariner and his rawhide-tough seamen ended up defending a ridge miles from his flotilla boats?

Events had begun spiraling out of control just five days earlier. Barney's gallant Chesapeake Flotilla, the fleet of armed barges escorted by his command sloop *Scorpion*, was trapped in the Patuxent River. With scores of British vessels suddenly beating their way up the river, the besieged American defenders had nowhere to go but into the shallow narrow waters further upriver. Secretary of the Navy William Jones recognized this could be an end game. Writing to Barney as the British were landing troops in Benedict on August

19, Jones made his orders clear: "should [the British] advance upon you, with an overwhelming force, you will effectually destroy the flotilla by fire." The following day Jones cautioned, "in the event of the enemy advancing upon the flotilla in force to destroy the whole effectually . . . you [then] will retire before the enemy toward this place [Washington] opposing his progress . . . [and] presenting every . . . possible obstacle to his march."

By the next day the infamous Rear Admiral George Cockburn was personally leading his own flotilla upriver following as near as the narrowing river would allow while at the same time offering support and protection to the British land forces' right flank as they marched northward to attack Washington. Cockburn was intent on destroying the pesky American barges.

Retreating from the British as they entered the port town of Nottingham, Barney and his tiny flotilla reached Pig Point, said to be named for the iron pigs that were shipped downriver on flatboats from the Patuxent Iron Works and then loaded onto merchant vessels. His orders were clear. The months of preparation and hard rowing into harm's way would soon end.

Barney, the obedient naval commander, acted quickly. Selecting four hundred flotillamen and passing out three days' rations, he left a hundred men behind with the sick, wounded, and most of the supplies. He ordered his young lieutenant, Solomon Frazier, to prepare explosives and destroy the flotilla should the British attempt to seize their boats and cannon. Taking his leave without ceremony, the commodore led his men to join the American army encamped about eight miles to the west.

On August 22, Admiral Cockburn rounded Pig Point and glimpsed the abandoned sloop *Scorpion* with pennant still flying. The elusive flotilla was all there, stretched in a long line behind *Scorpion* up the river. Cockburn later reported, "[o]n nearing them we observed the Sloop bearing Broad Pendant to be on fire, and she very soon afterwards blew up. I now Saw clearly that they were all abandoned and on Fire with Trains to their Magaz[ines], and out of the Seventeen Vessels which composed this formidable and So much Vaunted Flotilla, Sixteen were in quick Succession blown to atoms." Cockburn managed to capture the seventeenth barge and several merchant schooners that were nesting with the Americans.

Commodore Barney and his men undoubtedly heard the violent explosions that shook the Patuxent Valley. After marching quickly through Upper Marlboro just ahead of the advancing British land troops, they joined forces

---

Preceding spread: **After routing the first and second American lines, the British faced fierce fire from the Chesapeake Flotillamen, Marines, and cannons under the command of Commodore Joshua Barney on the Bladensburg Road. With the town of Bladensburg off to the east, British troops attack the third and final desperate line of defense at the Maryland boundary line with the District of Columbia as rockets streak through the sky. Having chased off the militia on both flanks, the British will soon force their way through the third line and find an open road to the U.S. Capital.**

with Captain Samuel Miller and his U.S. Marine reinforcements promised by the Secretary of the Navy. Barney's command, all battle-tested veterans, joined the thousands of untried militia gathering at Woodyard Plantation (Prince George's County) anticipating battle with the British invaders. Barney's landlocked sailors and marines would soon be tested again at the hands of their approaching foes.

On August 22, 1814, the British rounded Pig Point and spotted the elusive and long-sought Chesapeake Flotilla. Upon approaching, they soon discovered that the gun barges had been abandoned and trains of gunpowder ignited. One by one the boats, under orders of the Secretary of the Navy, were "blown to atoms."

Days One and Two

August 19 and 20, 1814
Benedict, Maryland

"as long as his [the British] point of attack is unknown, so long must our force remain divided; that these considerations suggest the preference he will probably give the Patuxent."

—Secretary of War John Armstrong, July 1, 1814

Over four thousand British troops landed and encamped at Benedict, Maryland, on August 19 and 20, 1814. Here British pickets guard the heights west of the encampment.

The British had chosen the Patuxent River for their invasion in part because of its relatively deep waters and access to good roads to Washington. The destruction of the flotilla had the added benefit of concealing the real intent of the British presence in the river.

The British landing overwhelmed Benedict, called "a small, straggling place," with their ships and troops. No one in tidewater Maryland had ever seen such a frightening forest of enemy masts and sails. From 3 p.m. on August 19 until the morning of August 20, more than fifty warships, transports, and boats disgorged 4,370 men from four veteran regiments, all burdened with ammunition and rations issued for the campaign. The force included fifty local escaped slaves, trained and ready to fight as Colonial Marines. Troops, small-caliber field cannons, and piles of stores were laboriously rowed ashore in boats often fighting tidal currents.

Secretary of State James Monroe was eagerly embracing his new role as the U.S. government's unofficial scout. Monroe had assembled some Washington dragoons as an escort. Gathering a flurry of garbled reports indicating that a large British force had entered the Bay, he galloped around Southern Maryland trying to find out where the force was headed. Watching from a height near Aquasco Mills, Monroe found his answer. The British were landing at Benedict.

Eighteen-year-old Lieutenant George Robert Gleig (1796–1888) was one of the elite riflemen of the 85th Light Infantry, Bucks Volunteers, who landed at Benedict. Gleig, a Scot fresh from studies for holy orders at Oxford, would later become the Chaplain General of the British Forces. In 1814, the teenage Gleig was keeping a lively diary that recorded his military adventures in America. He and his comrades were enjoying terra firma after the long sail from Bermuda, "lying at full length upon the grass, basking in the beams of a sultry sun, and apparently made happy by the feeling of the green sod under them."

The invading troops, who now outnumbered the entire white adult male population of Charles County, Maryland, camped overnight in and around the deserted town. They were waiting for marching orders and were prepared for trouble. Warships in the river had broadsides ready for any attackers. The field cannons, placed on the heights to the west overlooking the landing, were loaded with gunpowder and shot with slow-burning matches at the ready. Pickets were spread out around the perimeter of the camp. There had been no hint of opposition to the vulnerable landing. In fact, Lieutenant Gleig was astonished that "apparently, [there was] no enemy within many miles of the place."

Finally, late in the afternoon of August 20, the British army commander Major General Robert Ross (1766–1814) rode briskly through the camp to the sounds of bugles and the cheers of his waiting men. Lacking cavalry but with flanking parties flaring out in all directions to guard against surprises, the troops were soon on the march. They did have the benefit of sympathetic local spies and guides. One volunteer from Benedict was a victim of leprosy described as "a most awful spectacle of a man named Calder . . . a very shrewd, intelligent fellow, and of the utmost use to us." Local horses were scarce and only the commanding general and his staff would be mounted for the ride over land. Sailors were assigned the thankless task of pulling three light field guns and their accoutrements by hand. The new-fangled Congreve rockets were carried on the backs of the soldiers.

After weeks of confinement onboard ship, the troops were in no shape for the march in the stifling heat. Carrying heavy packs laden with extra provisions, about a third of the men succumbed to exhaustion and heat stroke in just six miles. To add to the misery, that night's tightly guarded camp was hit by thunder and lightning accompanied by buckets of rain. Lieutenant Gleig was fascinated by the scene. "The effect of the lightning, as it glanced for a moment upon the bivouac, and displayed the firelocks piled in regular order, and the men stretched like so many corpses beside them, was extremely fine."

Where were the defenders? American commander Brigadier General William Winder (1775–1824), a model of misdirected energy and indecision, was peppering the capital city with messages, orders, and questions. His task, gathering troops and supplies to defend the capital or other nearby potential British targets, was all but impossible. The region was in a panic, his civilian superiors were meddling with his preparations, and the secretary of war gave him little or no assistance. Militiamen were being summoned from all directions, but Winder, despite the efforts of cavalry squadrons sent out to find the enemy, still had no idea where the British were aiming their assault.

Two Generals

"Nine-tenths of tactics are certain and taught in books; but the irrational tenth is like the kingfisher flashing across the pond, and that is the test of generals."

—Lieutenant Colonel T. E. Lawrence (Lawrence of Arabia) (1888–1935)

Two very different generals faced off during the 1814 British invasion. British Major General Robert Ross was a seasoned and professional veteran while American Brigadier General William Winder was a controversial officer in the U.S. Army called up for a military emergency.

General Ross was the quintessential Napoleonic-era soldier. Born in County Down, Northern Ireland, Ross joined the 25th Regiment of Foot as an ensign after attending Trinity College in Dublin. He had found his calling, steadily advancing in rank as he fought in the Netherlands, Egypt, Italy, and Spain. Noted as a tough but fair and popular leader, Ross became a right-hand man to the Duke of Wellington during the bloody 1813 Spanish Peninsular War. Just months before coming to the Chesapeake as a general in command of land forces, Ross was seriously wounded in the neck.

General Winder, of Somerset County, Maryland, was a lawyer by trade. He practiced successfully in Baltimore before the War of 1812. Winder was sent to the Niagara frontier as an army colonel then promoted to brigadier general. In his first combat in 1813, he was captured during the night battle at Stoney Creek and spent most of a year as a prisoner of war. When exchanged in 1814, Winder was placed in charge of the 10th U.S. Military District defenses, which included Maryland and Washington. The promotion by President Madison undoubtedly was designed to curry favor with the general's uncle, Maryland's Federalist Governor Levin Winder who was against the war, and the Republican leadership in the U.S. capital.

Both of these generals faced the unpredictable fortunes of war as that irrational kingfisher flashed across the pond in 1814.

British Major General Robert Ross was a decorated and wounded veteran of the Napoleonic Wars in Spain.

Brigadier General William Winder was a Baltimore lawyer who had limited military experience.

A Neighborhood Hero

> "We believe that Baron Steuben has made us soldiers and that he is capable of forming the whole world into a solid column . . ."
>
> —The 1782 Creed of the 1st U.S. Army

In 1814, the British invaders marched through Aquasco, unaware that the sleepy village was the hometown of a military hero. Leonard Covington (1768–1813) was a part of the small U.S. Army that inherited the traditions and tactics codified by the Baron von Steuben during the American Revolution.

As a 24-year-old coronet of cavalry, Covington served valiantly with General "Mad" Anthony Wayne's army during his campaign against Indians on the western Ohio frontier. When his cavalry commander was killed at the 1794 Battle of Fallen Timbers, the young officer led a squadron into the center of the fighting, personally killing two Indian warriors.

By 1795, Covington was a farmer back in Maryland, but he was soon voted into the state House of Delegates, then the U.S. Congress. Upset by the *Chesapeake-Leopard* affair, he again joined the army as a lieutenant colonel of dragoons, heading a force that occupied Mobile, Alabama. By 1813, Covington was a brigadier general commanding a brigade of regular infantry in Canada.

An ill-conceived campaign against Montreal, designed to sever supply lines to the west, got off to a late start and was all but stopped by unrelenting rain. A veteran and disciplined British force caught up with the invaders during a snowstorm at Crysler's Farm, Ontario, on November 11, 1813. The disorganized Americans were soundly defeated. Covington, mounted on a conspicuous white charger, bravely led his infantry against fierce British musketry and was shot. He died three days later and was eventually buried at Sackets Harbor, New York.

TO THE MEMORY

OF

LEONARD COVINGTON,

Brigadier-General;

WHO "FELL WHERE HE FOUGHT AT THE HEAD OF HIS MEN"

AT WILLIAMSBURG, IN CANADA;

AND

WILLIAM BURROWS,

Lieutenant in the Navy:

The conqueror of the Boxer; who, mortally wounded, entreated, "that the Flag should wave while he lived"—

THE FIFTH VOLUME OF THE WEEKLY REGISTER

IS MOURNFULLY,

BUT RESPECTFULLY, DEDICATED

BY THE EDITOR.

"PEACE TO THE SOULS OF THE HEROES; FOR THEIR DEEDS WERE GREAT IN THE FIGHT."

Dedication page to Brigadier General Leonard Covington in Baltimore *Niles' Weekly Register*, 1814

U.S. Army veteran and war hero Brigadier General Leonard Covington was mortally wounded at Crysler's Farm, Ontario, Canada, on November 11, 1813. Covington is nearly unknown in his home state of Maryland, but at least twenty-one cities, towns, and counties in Alabama, Kentucky, Mississippi, Oklahoma, Texas, and Virginia are named in his honor.

Day Three

AUGUST 21, 1814

NOTTINGHAM, MARYLAND

"...detached bodies of [American] riflemen lay in ambush among the thickets; and the very expectation of having something to do, created a degree of excitement which, till now, we had not experienced."

—Lieutenant George Robert Gleig on the march and in anticipation of an American attack, August 21, 1814

With no American defenders yet in evidence, Lieutenant Gleig and his platoon, flanking the British column, thought they saw the "glitter of arms" in the nearby woods.

I contrived to surround the spot . . . I beheld two men dressed in black coats, and armed with bright firelocks and bayonets . . . as soon as they observed me, they . . . took to their heels, but . . . they quickly perceived that to escape was impossible, and accordingly stood still . . . I heard one say to the other . . . "Stop, John till the gentlemen pass . . ." I could not help laughing aloud . . . by their attempts to persuade me that they were quiet country people, come out . . . to shoot squirrels. When I desired to know whether they carried bayonets to charge the squirrels . . . they were at a loss to a reply, but they grumbled exceedingly when they found themselves prisoners, and conducted as such to the column.

Cautiously marching ahead and chasing phantoms in the woods, the British were approaching the substantial little port of Nottingham. There General Ross planned to join up with Admiral Cockburn and his barge flotilla rowing up the Patuxent. Suddenly, late in the afternoon, some long-anticipated hostile fire halted the right front of the column. Following his brave but sometimes reckless routine, the general charged into a deserted Nottingham with a few of his staff.

At that moment, "Colonel" James Monroe was galloping out of town into the setting sun. He and his dragoons had trotted unwittingly into Nottingham just ahead of the British, trying to find Barney's flotilla. The Americans were gone but Monroe saw British barges coming up the river and knew the enemy was close. He paused just long enough to dash off a note to General Winder, requesting that five hundred American troops be sent to meet the threat. His dragoons fired some shots at the enemy barges before they dashed west.

As the British column marched toward Nottingham on their way to Washington, they detected a reflection in the nearby woods. Surrounding the area, the troops discovered two American militiamen who pleaded that they were out squirrel hunting. They had no answer when officers inquired why they were hunting squirrels with bayonets.

The British, with thirty to forty barges anchored close by, enjoyed the night unmolested in and around the village. Lieutenant Gleig admired the "abundant and luxuriant crop of tobacco" that dominated the neighborhood. His men were more interested in the bread left in the ovens by the fleeing townspeople. They also collected "a parcel of turkeys and geese on which [they] made a capital supper and slept under the shade of an old barn full of Tobacco." While his army enjoyed the evening at the expense of the departed Americans, General Ross met with Admiral Cockburn who continued to press for an attack on the capital city.

Winder and his small army reached the Woodyard Plantation, only nine miles west of the sleeping British, about midnight. He had decided that Woodyard was "a position from which they [the American army] can, at two hours notice, reach the banks of the Patuxent and Potomac, as either may be menaced." After a miserably hot march from Washington, the thousand-man D.C. Columbian Brigade had arrived a few hours earlier. An exhausted Secretary of State Monroe rode in, announced that he estimated about six thousand British were dangerously close, and went to bed.

Winder was still flummoxed about the intended target of the British. Were they headed for the Potomac River and Fort Washington guarding the southern access to the capital? Could they still be headed north toward Annapolis and Baltimore? Were they after Barney and the flotilla? Would there be a quick dash for Washington itself? A baffled general ordered his small army, now eighteen hundred strong, to be awakened and preparations to move out commenced. While the sleepy citizen-soldiers packed tents, reloaded wagons, and then waited at the ready, General Winder went to his tent. He spent the several hours until dawn writing out orders and puzzling over his next move.

Save the Documents!

When the British threatened the nation's capital on August 23, 1814, State Department clerk Stephen Pleasonton (shown here in a photograph taken later in his life) led a contingent of twenty-two carts loaded with the most important United States documents to safe temporary storage near Leesburg, Virginia.

Precious federal documents saved by a team led by Stephen Pleasonton were stored in this brick-arched chamber in the basement of the Rokeby Mansion until it was deemed safe to return them to Washington.

Secretary of State James Monroe had sent a terse note to President Madison on August 22: "you had better remove the records." The very next day, precious documents started moving out of Washington. The tiny government bureaucracy tapped junior officials to transfer those documents to safety in the surrounding countryside. Supply wagons assigned to the army were quickly reassigned to the new task.

Soon the vehicles, laden with all manner of boxes, bags, and stacks of paper, were lumbering on the dirt roads out of the city. A 24-year-old clerk named Lewis Machen piled up the Senate records and rolled twelve miles to Brookeville Academy. Clerks John Frost and Sam Burch spirited the House of Representative papers to a secret location. They moved some of the claims, pension, and committee records a few doors down from the U.S. Capitol, only to see them destroyed by the fires lit by the raiders. While the Library of Congress burned in the Capitol building, Supreme Court clerk Elias B. Caldwell saved the court's books by moving them to his own nearby house. Dr. William Thornton moved Patent Office papers to his farm in what became Bethesda and then talked the British into sparing the patent models by convincing them that they were works of art, not the property of the government. Post Office materials ended up in a farmhouse cellar guarded by a 19-year-old named Brown.

While other important records were floated up the Potomac River in canal boats, national treasures were in the hands of Stephen Pleasonton, a State Department

clerk. He and his companions stuffed the Declaration of Independence, probably the U.S. Constitution, the Articles of Confederation, the Bill of Rights, much of George Washington's correspondence, treaties, laws, and who knows what else into coarse linen bags. The new nation's priceless papers were loaded onto twenty-two carts.

The first stop was a grist mill on the Virginia side of Chain Bridge. Deciding this was too close to a cannon foundry, a likely British target, Pleasonton secured wagons from nearby farms, loaded the bags a second time, and rolled another thirty miles to a brick vault in deserted Rokeby Mansion near Leesburg, Virginia. As the humble State Department employee completed his assignment, the fire from burning buildings in the national capital glowed in the night sky.

The National Archives in Washington, D.C., is the present home of many of the documents saved from destruction when the British occupied Washington in 1814.

Day Four

*"The enemy are in full march for Washington.
Have the material prepared to destroy the bridges.
You had better remove the records."*

—Secretary of State James Monroe to President James Madison, August 22, 1814

The dawn of the fourth day of the British invasion revealed continued confusion on both sides. General Ross, now many miles from his fleet at Benedict and his naval barge support on the river, took his time launching the veteran army on Southern Maryland's hot and dusty roads. The general's officers, Lieutenant Gleig included, were accustomed to marching at dawn and wondered about the delay. "It seems indeed to be something like hesitation as to the course to be pursued." When the column got underway around 8 a.m., Gleig remembered, "The road was well wooded, so the rays of the sun did not oppress us as much as usual." Later, Charles Ball, a former slave who became a Chesapeake Flotillaman and wrote a memoir, claimed that if the Americans had attacked, "in these woods and cedar thickets, not a man of them [the British] would ever have reached Bladensburg."

The Americans were finally on the road as well and headed in the direction of their invaders. General Winder was struggling to organize this home-grown militia. Alongside some experienced regulars, there was a sizeable and growing mix of sipping and singing societies in band box uniforms—mostly poorly trained infantry, some riflemen without rifles, old cannons of various

This bucolic section of the sunken Fenno Road survives and illustrates the probable road conditions in 1814.

sizes mixed in with the new, and inexperienced cavalry, many riding sub-standard mounts. The units descending on the area from all directions were, for the most part, ill-supplied by an overwhelmed and disorganized system. The command structure was a minefield of civilian and military egos and inexperience.

At 8:30 a.m. on this muggy morning of August 22, the two combat forces first met at a simple fork in the road; one route headed west to Woodyard (now Duley Station Road) and another to Upper Marlboro (now Croom Road).

A vanguard of several hundred American infantry, cavalry, and artillery waited nervously west of the intersection. The rest of the American army, including the U.S. Marines who had marched out from Washington to join Commodore Barney, was strung out on the same road to the Woodyard. General Winder and Secretary Monroe, galloping ahead with a bold army surgeon named Hanson Catlett, found the vanguard of the advancing British first at Page's Chapel (now St. Thomas Church). Having quickly ridden a few miles northwest, they were again straining to see the glint of red uniforms from a second-floor window at Bellefields, the home of Benjamin Oden, who supported the war but had fled with his one hundred thirty-five slaves.

When the British, feeling their way without cavalry, reached the fork, they saw the backs of the American horsemen as they rode westward toward Woodyard. The British followed them and an anticipated collision seemed imminent as the invaders methodically maneuvered to do battle. At the same moment, breathtaking explosions roared and reverberated through the countryside. The Chesapeake Flotilla was meeting its demise.

General Winder immediately ordered a wholesale retreat. Confusion reigned as Yankee units withdrew and got tangled up on the road west. Instead of pursuing, the British, blind to the confusion ahead, turned around and headed north toward Upper Marlboro. Joshua Barney quizzed the commander about his motives. Winder replied that he intended to find a place to put his army between the attackers and the Federal City. After hovering near the enemy army all afternoon, still trying to divine its intentions, Winder returned to his now twenty-four-hundred–man force repositioned for the night at the Long Old Fields (now Forestville). Winder's prospects became even more complicated when he discovered that the president of the United States and members of his cabinet had arrived to review the troops.

By 2 p.m., the British had marched on to the Prince George's County seat of Upper Marlboro. No longer concerned about the Chesapeake Flotilla,

From this gable end window in the Bellefields Mansion, Secretary of State James Monroe and Brigadier General William Winder observed the British column advancing on the Woodyard (now Duley Station) Road.

Admiral Cockburn was bringing along four hundred Royal Marines and sailors from his barges to beef up the land forces.

Ross and his men were enchanted by the century-old town named for the celebrated Duke of Marlborough. Lieutenant Gleig admired the sheep-covered hills and the abundant fruit trees before enjoying a "hearty dinner undisturbed." General Ross spent the night with a prominent local physician and antiwar Federalist named William Beanes. The next morning, Admiral Cockburn—ignoring the concerns of his superior, Vice Admiral Alexander Cochrane, that the expedition was marching too far from its base of support in Benedict—convinced Ross to strike at Washington.

Frederick Hall Becomes William Williams

"A bright mulatto . . . so fair as to show freckles."

—Benjamin Oden's newspaper ad describing his runaway slave Frederick Hall, Spring 1814

Not all of the slaves who fled or were taken from Chesapeake plantations joined the British. Before Bellefields Plantation owner Benjamin Oden escaped from the British invasion with his slaves in August of 1814, he was seeking a runaway named Frederick Hall.

It appears that the light-skinned, 22-year-old Hall could and did pass as a white man. He soon appeared as Private William Williams on the muster rolls of the 38th Regular U.S. Infantry. He collected his $50 cash bonus for enlisting and private's wages of $8 a month.

On September 13–14, 1814, Private Williams was stationed with his company in Fort McHenry's dry moat, enduring the British bombs and rockets raining down on the Americans. An incoming bomb blew his leg off, and he died two months later in Baltimore Public Hospital, one of the few casualties of the day-long bombardment.

How do we know the story of this escaped slave turned American soldier? Determined not to lose his investment, Benjamin Oden later tried to claim the 160 acres of land due Private Williams's heirs for his military service. Congress denied Colonel Oden's request, claiming that he had not tried hard enough to find and recapture his escaped slave. The runaway was known to have sought refuge in the Baltimore home of a man named Williams, and that may be where Hall got the name that he enlisted under.

Frederick Hall, a runaway slave from Bellefields Plantation in Prince George's County, did not choose to fight for the British. On April 14, 1814, he enlisted in the 38th U.S. Infantry as William Williams. Serving in the dry moat at Fort McHenry during the September 13–14, 1814, bombardment, he lost a leg to a cannonball and died two months later.

Forty Dollars Reward

For apprehending and securing in jail so that I get him again, *NEGRO FREDERICK*; Somtimes cails himself FREDERICK HALL a bright mulatto; straight and well made; 21 years old; 5 feet 7 or 8 inches high, with a short chub nose and so fair as to show freckles, he has no scars or marks of any kind that is recollected; his clothing when he left home, two months since, was home made cotton shirts, jacket and Pantaloons of cotton and yarn twilled, all white. It is probable he may be in Baltimore, having a relation there, a house servant to a Mr. Williams, by the name of Frank who is also a mulatto, but not so fair as Frederick.
BENJAMIN ODEN.
Prince George's County, May 12th.
may 16   d

Major Benjamin Oden of Bellefields advertised a reward for the return of his escaped slave Frederick Hall.

Day Five

"I made up my mind that if [General] Ross . . . was a man of enterprise, he would be upon us in the course of the night, and, being determined to die like a trooper's horse, I slept with my shoes on."

—Brigadier General James Wilkinson, August 23, 1814

Tuesday, August 23, began with an early-morning pep rally. With the British only miles away, President Madison reviewed the troops camped at Long Old Fields. In a short note to the first lady, Dolley, the upbeat president noted that the mostly green militiamen, what we today might call weekend warriors, were "in high spirits & [made] a good appearance." But, after Madison mounted his horse and departed for Washington, the fortunes of the young United States rapidly went downhill.

The fate of Washington and possibly the republic as a whole rested largely on the shoulders of General William Winder. His assignment was admittedly Herculean. His unflagging energy was indisputable. His command decisions, however, were anything but inspired. Based on Winder's latest hunch, the president returned to the President's House thinking the British were headed for Annapolis.

An incident the night before painted a picture of an edgy and confused defense. Exhausted after a hot day of marching with no result, the troops were roused at about 2 a.m. by a false alarm. Some cattle driven through the camp kept the panicky soldiers on alert the rest of the night.

British General Ross, who was still hesitant about a strike on the American capital, was again taking his time. His army didn't get on the road until the early afternoon of August 23. Several miles after passing a hundred-year-old house called Melwood, the British ran into an advance line of six cannons and hundreds of defenders stretched across the road. The ever-cautious General Winder had already ordered them to fall back. Determined to show some pluck for a change, the Americans fired some parting cannon and musket balls at the British. As usual, General Ross was at the front of his column. One of his mounted officers jumped a fence and helped chase the Yankees into a hasty retreat. American Major George Peter, their commander, was convinced that had his men been carrying rifles rather than muskets, they could have picked off the British commander.

Peter and his men fell back to Long Old Fields. With General Winder headed north to meet reinforcements from Baltimore, D.C. militia General Walter Smith, now commanding over three thousand men, decided to stand his ground. But when Winder returned he envisioned nothing but a looming

About 2 a.m. on August 22, 1814, cattle were driven through the American camp at Long Old Fields. The thirty-two hundred troops were thrown into a panic, thinking the British were attacking. Later that morning, the sleep-deprived citizen-soldiers were reviewed by President Madison.

limped into one of the young country's darkest days with a sore right arm and ankle.

On the morning of August 24, Washington was in a total panic with rumors of an imminent British attack in full circulation. General Winder had fretted in the wee hours of the morning over whether to destroy the lower bridge near the Navy Yard. Barney's much-needed rest was disrupted when Winder woke him at 2 a.m. searching for combustibles with which to burn the bridge. The resultant fire failed to destroy the bridge completely, so barges with kegs of gunpowder were placed under the span ready to blow it up if necessary. Calling on Barney and some of his men to guard the bridge, Winder summoned the president and his cabinet to a morning war council at the Navy Yard.

The general now feared that the British might be veering south to attack Fort Washington. An ever-skeptical secretary of war, John Armstrong, maintained that the invaders were mounting a "mere Cossack Hurrah," a raid that would not amount to much if the militia withdrew to the city and ambushed the attackers. When definitive word arrived during the meeting that the enemy was headed for Bladensburg, all the activity immediately flowed in that direction. President Madison and his party quickly headed for the action. Still assigned to defending the south bridge, the combative Commodore Barney persuaded Madison to allow him to march with his Chesapeake Flotillamen and the marines to meet the advancing British.

After covering only five miles on August 23, the British had camped near Belle Chance Plantation, located on today's Andrews Air Force Base. They were on the road again at 2 a.m. and soon passed the former American encampment at Long Old Fields. Lieutenant Gleig commented that, "smoking ashes, bundles of straw, and remnants of broken victuals were scattered about." As the cool of the early morning turned into another hot and dusty summer day with temperatures approaching 100 degrees, Gleig could not remember a more punishing combination of heat and fatigue with "men [falling] behind from absolute inability to keep up."

fight after dark. Winder's experience of capture during a chaotic nighttime British raid at Stoney Creek on the Niagara frontier in 1813 led him to believe that his inexperienced troops would be subject to "certain infallible, and irremediable disorder, and probable destruction." He ordered yet another retreat and almost ushered in a night of "irremediable disorder" of his own making. Winder later defended his decision by claiming that the superiority of his artillery and cavalry would have been lost in a night attack.

Now with their backs at the very door to Washington, the Americans withdrew behind the Eastern Branch (today's Anacostia River). Barney and his men slept comfortably in bunks for the first time in months at the nearby Washington Navy Yard. General Winder was now faced with defending three bridge crossings. Which one would the British use? Winder was on his usual frenetic pace, galloping about with no sleep in sight. In the early morning darkness, his horse threw him into a ditch. Undaunted, the army commander

The Greatest Disgrace Ever to American Arms

AUGUST 24, 1814

BLADENSBURG, MARYLAND

"They ran like sheep chased by dogs."

—Flotillaman and former slave Charles Ball describing American militia fleeing the British at Bladensburg

This 1806 pencil and watercolor sketch depicts the Eastern Branch (Anacostia) wooden bridge, which was probably little changed when the British attacked across it in 1814. Looking southeast past the buildings on its western edge, the sails and masts in the distance mark the port of Bladensburg.

Everyone remembered August 24 as a day of boiling heat and choking dust. In that oppressive atmosphere, the gathering amateur American militiamen were struggling with their own private fears of a collision with a veteran enemy. Standing on the west side of the Eastern Branch opposite the town of Bladensburg, the green and frightened citizen-soldiers wondered how they would act when facing British bayonets.

Once General Ross aimed his invading army at Washington, Bladensburg became the obvious target. Its attraction for both armies was a humble narrow wooden bridge on the road to the U.S. capital. British informers told them that even if the bridge were destroyed, the invaders could ford the shallow Eastern Branch just above the town.

American reinforcements had begun pouring into Bladensburg from the north on August 23. General Tobias Stansbury led 1,350 hot and tired Baltimore troops and set up his position on Lowndes Hill east of town. The 5th Maryland Regiment, 800 strong, arrived at 11 p.m. after an arduous forced march. Dating back to the Revolution, the red-plumed 5th claimed Baltimore's best on its rolls.

The morning of August 24 brought more troops, more civilian and military leaders, and more confusion. Secretary of State James Monroe, without authorization, ordered the redeployment of some of the troops. Everyone warily watched an approaching cloud of dust that, to their relief, turned out to be Colonel William Beall with eight hundred Annapolis militiamen, raising the number of American defenders to six thousand. General Stansbury and his men had already abandoned Lowndes Hill and joined the other units west of Bladensburg and the Eastern Branch. The British were expected soon, yet no one seemed interested in destroying the bridge to slow the enemy advance. In fact, President Madison, in his haste to find General Winder, rode onto the bridge just as the British were entering town. A scout, scurrying back to the American lines, fortunately warned the president and his entourage. Stunned to learn the British were so near, they quickly turned tail and galloped to safer ground.

"Final Stand at Bladensburg" depicts U.S. Marine Captain Samuel Miller directing his marines firing a 12-pound cannon and muskets in the fierce fighting on the third American line.

Private John Pendleton Kennedy was bivouacked with American troops on Bladensburg's Lowndes Hill on August 24, 1814. At 1 a.m., shots roused the men and Kennedy mistakenly put on his dancing shoes, brought along for use at the expected victory celebration. He wore the pumps throughout the Battle of Bladensburg and as he carried a wounded friend from the battlefield. These shoes, unfortunately, never danced in victory.

As General Ross and his army streamed into Bladensburg after their grueling twelve-mile march, the Americans supported by eighteen cannon were arrayed to the west of the bridge. Lieutenant Gleig observed that the American defensive position was one of "great strength and commanding attitude. They were drawn up in three lines upon the brow of a hill, having their front and left flank covered by a branch of the Potomac [Eastern Branch], and their right resting upon a thick wood and a deep ravine." In truth, with all the shifting of troops and second guessing, the first line, except for some cannons and riflemen, was too far from the still-intact bridge to successfully contest the enemy crossing.

After observing the American lines from the upper floor of the Parthenon, a house since demolished that once sat on the slope of Lowndes Hill, General Ross realized that the American lines were too far apart to support one another. He launched his light infantry across the bridge at the double quick while the rest of his troops were still arriving. Lieutenant Gleig watched as two American cannons fired into the packed bridge and "an entire company was swept away." After a pause, Colonel William Thornton, Jr., led the light infantry who gained a foothold beyond the bridge, "trampling on many of their dead and dying comrades." American riflemen stood sniping for awhile, but the fierce discipline kept the British pushing ahead.

The red-coated regiments, 4th followed by 44th, arrived, streaming across the bridge. The 4th aimed at an orchard on General Stansbury's left flank. And now, the infamous British Congreve rockets were flying in all directions from launchers near the bridge. It did not take long for the flanked first American line to waver and then break. No one was willing to face British bayonets. John Pendleton Kennedy, who later became Secretary of the Navy, fought as a private in the battles of Bladensburg and North Point. He admitted that the elite 5th Maryland "made a fine scamper of it" as the first line collapsed despite the encouragement of their officers to stand and fight.

The attackers next confronted the now-panicking second line as Americans fled in all directions. General Winder bravely tried to stem the tide, but the second line soon evaporated. Rushing uphill on the Bladensburg Road to what appeared to be an easy victory, the British crossed a ravine on another narrow bridge only to see some large cannons in the road on the heights ahead. With the American army melting before him, Commodore Barney, arriving on the scene after the battle had begun, was sitting on his horse, determined to stop the enemy attack in its tracks. He had five big guns loaded with grapeshot, 500 flotillamen, 114 U.S. Marines, and hundreds of militiamen on each flank to make his point. The commodore eloquently described what happened next in his after-action report:

> In a few minutes the enemy again advanced, when I ordered an 18 lb. to be fired, which completely cleared the road, shortly after a second and a third attempt was made by the enemy to come forward but all were destroyed. The enemy then crossed over into an Open field and attempted to flank our right, he was there met by three 12 pounders, the Marines under Capt. [Samuel] Miller and my men acting as Infantry, and again was totally cut up, by this time not a Vestige of the American Army remained except a body of 5 or 600 posted on a height on my right from whom I expected much support, from their fine situation. The Enemy from this point never appeared in force in front of us, they pushed forward their sharp shooters, one of which shot my horse under me, who fell dead between two of my Guns. The enemy who had been kept in check by our fire for nearly

The mistress of Riversdale, Rosalie Stier Calvert, wrote that she heard and saw "cannonballs" (probably Congreve rockets) from her bedroom window during the Battle of Bladensburg. Mrs. Calvert's husband, George, helped bury the dead after the battle with the assistance of slaves from his plantation.

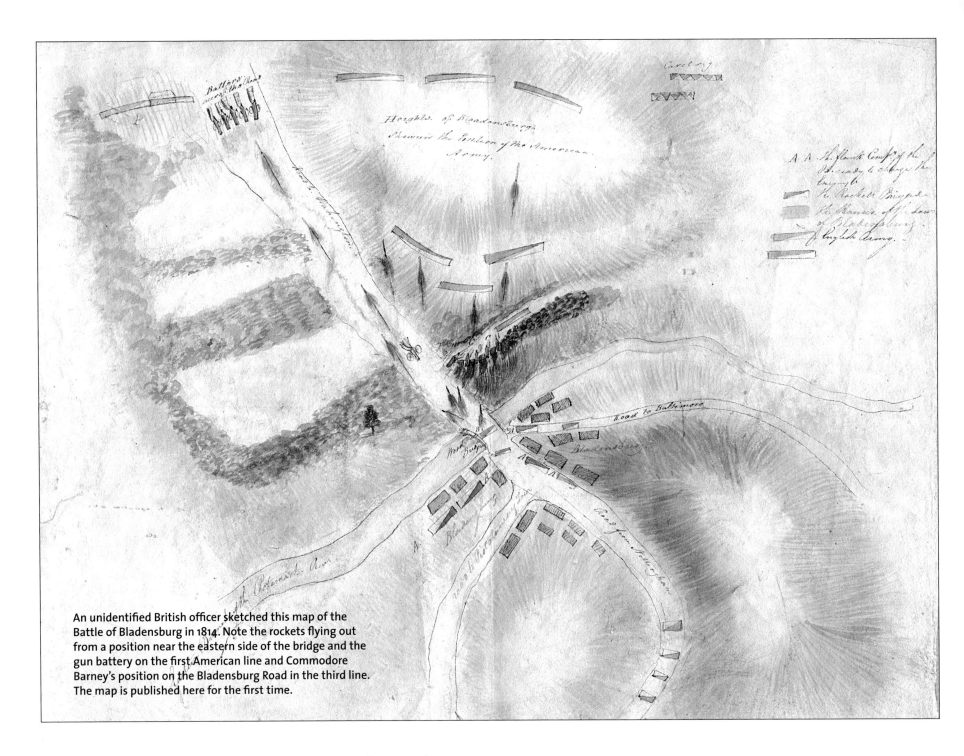

An unidentified British officer sketched this map of the Battle of Bladensburg in 1814. Note the rockets flying out from a position near the eastern side of the bridge and the gun battery on the first American line and Commodore Barney's position on the Bladensburg Road in the third line. The map is published here for the first time.

half an hour now began to out flank us on the right, our guns were turned that way, he pushed up the Hill, about 2 or 300 towards the Corps of Americans station'd as above described, who, to my great mortification made no resistance, giving a fire or two and retired, in this situation we had the whole army of the Enemy to contend with; Our Ammunition was expended, and unfortunately the drivers of my Ammunition Waggons had gone off in the General Panic, at this time I received a severe wound in my thigh . . . Finding the enemy now completely in our rear and no means of defense I gave orders to my officers and men to retire.

At one point, Barney ordered the marines to charge the advancing British. The seagoing infantry was heard to yell "Board 'em! Board 'em!" Captain Samuel Bacon, the marine quartermaster, galloped on the field on a borrowed horse and was swept up in the melee. "Barney now had the whole British army to fight; he mowed them down by hundreds; the marines are a dead shot. They killed more than each his man." In truth, the British reported only sixty-four British troops killed, not hundreds, and not all of them by the flotillamen or marines.

Joshua Barney, faint and bleeding profusely from a deep thigh wound, met Admiral Cockburn and General Ross for the first and only time. After they paroled Barney for his brave stand and summoned a British surgeon to attend him, the admiral was heard to say of Barney and his men, "They gave us the only fighting we have had."

The day's fight at Bladensburg had seen a combination of disgraceful disorder and some gallant defense. Militia captain and Maryland congressman Joseph Hopper Nicholson was outraged. "Good God! How have we been disgraced? Our cursed militia have been coming in one, two, and three at a time, and all speak highly of their gallantry." Marine Captain Bacon minced no words. "[General] Wi[nder] ought to be hung and would b[e in] any other country." An anonymous poet nicknamed the sad and largely forgotten American flight the "Bladensburg Races." "And, Winder, do not fire your guns, nor' let your trumpets play/Till we are out of sight—forsooth, My horse will run away."

Commodore Barney's fighting days were over. Although the British had suffered heavier casualties than the Americans, they had won a signal victory. The road to America's capital was wide open.

The First Family Flees

"Our kind friend [Mr. Charles Carroll] *. . . is in a very bad humour with me because I insist on waiting until the large picture of Gen.* [George] *Washington is secured."*

—Dolley Madison, writing to her sister, Lucy Todd, from the President's House, August 24, 1814 (an after-the-fact recreation of the original lost letter)

Imagine the U.S. president fleeing for his life. James Madison, in the company of Attorney General Richard Rush, U.S. Commissioner for Prisoners Brigadier General John T. Mason, and a handful of aides, galloped through Washington as the American defense collapsed behind them at Bladensburg. Madison had sent word ahead to the first lady to save what she could and flee.

With the president's hastily scribbled distress call in hand, Dolley Madison had a wagon loaded with clocks, silver, cabinet papers, even velvet curtains from the oval drawing room. George Washington's portrait was ordered taken away or destroyed. Crowding a carriage with her maid, Sukey, and an older sister, Anna, with her three children, Mrs. Madison picked up Secretary of Navy William Jones and his family then rode over to the home of the Carroll family, close friends, at Bellevue (later Dumbarton House) on Georgetown Heights. The caravan quickly crossed the Potomac River on Chain Bridge and spent a restless night at Rokeby Farm as distant fires in Washington lit up the sky.

When Madison arrived at the President's House, Dolley had already gone. Exhausted, he sat and poured himself a glass of wine and probably pondered the future. In the face of the day's disastrous reverses, the prospects looked bleak. Would the capital city be destroyed? Would the American army escape to fight another day? Would the British pursue the president, and what would happen if he were caught? How would the country respond to this

Saving George Washington's Portrait

"The precious portrait [was] placed in the hands of two gentlemen of New York for safekeeping."

—First Lady Dolley Madison recreating a note to her sister, Lucy Payne Todd, written on August 24, 1814

The first lady was a whirlwind of action. Writing hastily to her sister in a mixture of anxiety and resolve, Dolley Madison laid out the dilemma. "I must leave this [President's] house or the retreating [American] army will make me a prisoner in it by filling up the road I am directed to take. When I shall again write to you or where I shall be tomorrow, I cannot tell!!" Her husband, President Madison, had sent strict instructions to flee immediately. The British army would soon be at her door.

But what to save among the treasures of a young nation? Dolley frantically had Jean Pierre Sioussat, the doorkeeper, and Tom Magraw, the gardener, pile some silver, large urns, red curtains, papers, and other valuables into a wagon. She also remembered the large Gilbert Stuart portrait of President Washington in all his black suit authority. Washington was the iconic hero of the country. She could not allow the painting to be defaced and destroyed by the British.

Mrs. Madison gave orders to have "the frame broken and the canvas taken out of it." In the hurried confusion, two visiting New Yorkers, Jacob Barker and Robert G. L. De Peyster, saw to it that the painting, still on its stretcher, was safely removed. Barker was back with the painting three weeks later. The grateful and relieved Madisons reportedly gave him a three-piece silver tea set that is now in the White House collection. The great portrait still hangs majestically in the White House East Room.

First Lady Dolley Madison is credited with saving a White House portrait of President George Washington from certain destruction by the British. (In order to free the portrait from the wall, the frame was destroyed and the painting on its stretcher taken for safekeeping.)

embarrassment? Losing a war of its own making, could the United States survive as an independent country?

In the confusion of the day, Madison had sent word to Dolley suggesting they rendezvous at Wiley's Tavern, nearly twenty miles away. President Madison, with his small party and no bodyguard in attendance, crossed the Potomac on a ferry at Mason's (now Roosevelt) Island. It took a day and a half of hard traveling before the frantic couple were reunited.

Madison and his party rushed to Falls Church looking vainly for the first lady. After picking up two cavalry escorts and enduring a frightening storm, Madison finally found Dolley safe at Wiley's Tavern the next evening. Rumors of pursuing British sent the president and his small entourage back on the road at midnight. Most of August 26 was wasted trying to again ferry across the Potomac, swollen and impassable owing to the recent storm.

The party rode into Maryland to Montgomery Courthouse (now Rockville) looking for General Winder and what was left of his scattered army. Winder had already moved on, so the exhausted president and his party rode another eleven miles to Brookeville.

Caleb Bentley, a local Quaker, loaned his house to this illustrious but harried visitor. The tiny hamlet of Brookeville became the de facto capital of the United States for about fifteen hours. Mrs. Bentley, offering her room to the president, spent the night sleeping on the floor with her daughter. One consequence of her hospitality was trampled rose bushes and vegetables, victims of the boots of the twenty or so dragoons who arrived to protect the president. As villagers gathered at the Bentley windows to catch a glimpse of history unfolding, Madison busied himself with dispatches coming in from his scattered aides. It is not clear if Madison had any inkling that the U.S. Senate records had been temporarily moved to Brookeville Academy only a block away. Madison wrote to the first lady, who would soon return to Washington. "My dearest . . . I have just received a line from Col. [James] Monroe saying that the enemy is out of Washington & on retreat to their ships, and advising immediate return to Washington . . . I know not where we are in the first instance to hide our head but shall look for a place on our arrival."

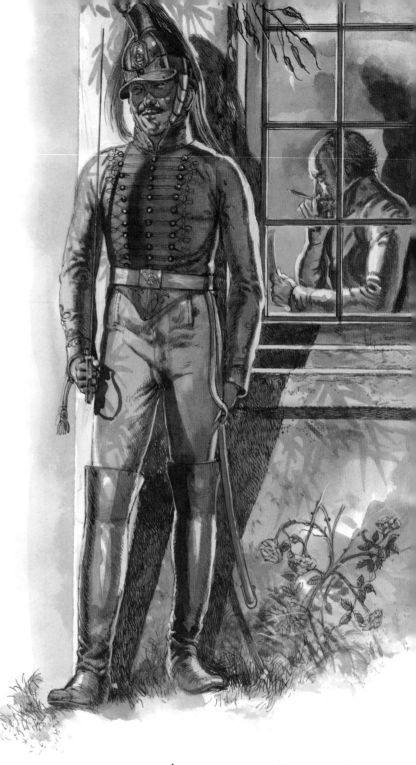

Faced with the prospect of a British occupation of Washington, President James Madison was forced to flee for his life. He spent most of the night of August 26, 1814, writing letters at the Bentley House in Brookeville, Maryland, while dragoons stood guard. The small town still claims that it was "The United States Capital for a Day."

5 *Washington Is Burning!*
AUGUST 1814

The British Ensign Flies Over Capitol Hill

"The spectators stood in awful silence, the city was light and the heavens redden'd with the blaze."

—Author and Washington chronicler Margaret Bayard Smith (1778–1844) describes the burning of the U.S. capital, August 24, 1814

Hundreds of terrified citizens of America's brand-new capital city followed the fleeing president and first lady. They packed up what they could and hastened out of town, many crossing the new Potomac River "Long Bridge" (now the 14th St. Bridge) stretching a mile to Virginia. Many who stayed behind feared death and destruction. The capital's defenders were nowhere to be seen, government officials were leaving the Federal City, and the entire British Army was only a few miles away

Washington had heard the distant thunder of battle at Bladensburg all afternoon. When legions of exhausted and retreating American soldiers appeared, concern turned to chaos. The British commander-in-chief of North America, Vice Admiral Alexander Cochrane, had received a letter from the governor-general in Canada calling for "severe retribution" for the American sacking of York (now Toronto) and Newark (now Niagara-on-the-Lake). What better retribution than reducing the U.S. capital to ashes?

Preceding spread: **Washingtonians couldn't believe their eyes. In one savage night, August 24, 1814, the British Army had laid to waste the new, unfinished U.S. Capitol. Depicted in this 1815 painting, the two houses of Congress were left as mere shells and the Library of Congress, housed inside the Senate Chamber, was burned to ashes.**

For their part, the invaders were exhausted. On the road at 3 a.m., the British Army had marched twelve miles in sweltering heat, fought a pitched battle for three hours, and now faced another five-mile trek to the American capital. Major General Robert Ross rested his men for two hours after the battle. Then, in the gathering dusk, led his three fifteen-hundred-man brigades to what became Washington's "Old Circus Grounds" (15th St. and Bladensburg Road, N.E.). Leaving two brigades there as backup, the general and Rear Admiral Sir George Cockburn rode into the city with the other brigade and a flag of truce. The British may have been looking for ransom money rather than revenge.

Any chance for negotiation evaporated as the invaders climbed Capitol Hill and approached the Capitol building. Heavy musketry suddenly rang out from nearby buildings. Several soldiers went down and General Ross's horse was shot out from under him. Commodore Joshua Barney's tough flotillamen, still stinging from their recent hasty retreat, may have been the culprits. A local slave, Michael Shiner, later vividly described what happened. "The British army . . . looked like flames of fier all red coats . . . in a twinkle of the eye the house [the Sewall-Belmont House, now rebuilt on 144 Constitution Ave., N.E.] wer sorounded by the British army and search all through upstairs an downstairs . . . but no man whar found . . . They put a globe match to the house and then stood oft a sertin distance . . . and those rockets burst until . . . they made the rafters fly East and West."

The British took on the U.S. Capitol next. After a long, grueling, dangerous day, the suddenly bushwhacked Englishmen were in no mood for compassion. Lieutenant Gleig thought the Capitol was the only building worth any notice in what he called the "infant town." "These modern republicans are led to flatter themselves, that the days are coming when it will rival in power and grandeur the senate-house of ancient Rome herself . . . This, however, is, or rather was, an edifice of great beauty."

Margaret Bayard Smith, married to the president of the Bank of Washington and founder of the Washington *Daily National Intelligencer,* saw the British approach the Capitol. "50 men, sailors and marines were marched by an officer, silently thro' the avenue . . . when arrived at the building. Each man was stationed at a window, with his pole and machine of wild-fire . . . the windows were broken and this wild fire was thrown in, so that an instantaneous conflagration took place and the whole building was wrapt in flames and smoke."

Washington in 1814

"Like other infant towns, it [Washington] is but little ornamented with fine buildings; for, except the Senate house [U.S. Capitol], I really know of none worthy to be noticed."

—Lieutenant George Robert Gleig, remembrance of 1814 published in 1821

At the time of the destructive British visit in 1814, Washington City was still an unfulfilled grand vision. That vision had begun with a congressional mandate in 1791. Federal officials, led by President Washington, would create a national capital. They selected ten square miles, some of it swampy farmland on the shores of the Potomac River, not far from Washington's Mount Vernon Plantation.

The chosen designer was a French architect who had fought with Washington's army during the Revolution. Pierre Charles L'Enfant (1754–1825), who preferred to be called Peter, had bold ideas. He conceived European-style grandeur with a "Congress House" and a "President's Palace," complete with public gardens and monuments, anchoring each end of a long ridge. An elaborate grid of avenues running in all directions would intersect at circular and rectangular plazas and a local creek called the Tiber would be tamed as a canal system. L'Enfant, difficult to work with, soon ran into economy-minded critics like Thomas Jefferson and was fired when he wouldn't share his plans with the D.C. surveyor Andrew Ellicott. It was Ellicott who made the final plans for the city, but he incorporated much of what L'Enfant had envisioned.

By 1814, the national capital was still a rude and crude place with about three thousand inhabitants sparsely settled in a motley assortment of wood and brick structures. Besides the Capitol and the President's House, still under construction as funds allowed, there were only a handful of fine homes like the brick Sewall-

The U.S. Capitol, as seen circa 1800, was a modest building far from completion. Approached by a dirt road, it was surrounded by open fields and trees.

Belmont House on Capitol Hill. Gentlemen hunted quail near the Capitol, and a wood picket fence kept grazing cattle out of the Capitol grounds. In spite of President Jefferson's efforts, the planned "Grand and Majestic Boulevard" between the Capitol and the President's House was often a muddy mess. Carriages lost wheels to stumps and pedestrians lost boots and shoes in the ooze.

Riding through the hustling and bustling nation's capital today, it is hard to imagine the planned city's rustic beginnings. As late as the 1820s, President John Quincy Adams often took an early morning skinny dip in the Potomac near the White House. But, in the end, an under-appreciated, ill-paid French architect helped to create a now much-celebrated plan that conceived the creation of one of the world's great capitals.

The conflagration soon turned into a smolder. With ceilings covered in sheet iron, the Capitol proved a challenge to burn down. The British fired Congreve rockets through the windows with little effect. They finally entered the large chambers, piled up tables, desks chairs, and curtains, heaped on rocket powder, then fired rockets into the pile. The subsequent blaze was so intense it was reported the glass lighting globes were melted. A giant plume of fiery embers flew up into the night and set a nearby boardinghouse, built for George Washington, aflame. Lieutenant Gleig was bedazzled by the scene and declared it sublime. This successful and unorthodox fire-starting technique was used on both houses of Congress then on other public buildings, including the President's House (White House).

Still, many important pieces of the Capitol survived the fire. Architect and artist Benjamin Henry Latrobe (1754–1820) later described the ruins of the Capitol as "a melancholy spectacle . . . However, many important parts are wholly uninjured . . . the picturesque entrance of the House of Representatives, the Corn Capitals of the Senate Vestibule, the Great staircase, and all the vaults of the Senate chamber, are entirely free from any injury which cannot easily be repaired."

The entire Library of Congress, then housed in the Capitol, was consumed by the flames. Thomas Jefferson later jumpstarted a new library by selling his personal collection to the government in 1815 for $23,950, one half of its assessed value. Meanwhile, Admiral Cockburn had busied himself inside the Capitol before the fire. He pilfered a book of 1810 government receipts bearing President Madison's stamp. The volume, with an inscription by Cockburn, "Taken in President's room in the Capitol of Washington 24th August 1814," was returned to the Library of Congress by a rare book dealer in 1940.

Left: As the British advanced down Maryland Avenue toward the U.S. Capitol, Major General Robert Ross's horse was shot out from under him, probably by Chesapeake Flotillamen firing from the nearby Sewall-Belmont House. Any chance for negotiation disappeared after this incident. In retaliation, the house was burned, one of the few private structures destroyed by the British.

Right: The corn capitals, designed and drawn by Capitol architect Benjamin Henry Latrobe and carved by Giuseppe Franzoni in 1809, survived the 1814 fire and still stand today in the east entry of the Old Senate Vestibule.

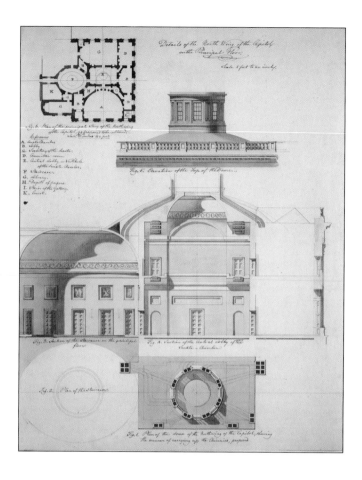

Drawing of the North Wing of the U.S. Capitol by Henry Latrobe between 1803 and 1814. Obviously Latrobe's plan was never fully completed before it was burned by the British in August 1814. "Fig. 1 Plan of the dome of the North Wing of the Capitol, showing the manner of carrying up the Chimnies, [sic] proposed." "Fig. 2. Plan of the staircase." "Fig. 3. Section of the Staircase on the principal floor." "Fig. 4. Section of the Central Lobby of the Senate - Chamber" "Fig. 5. Elevation of the Top of the Dome." "Fig. 6. Plan of the principal Story of the North wing of the Capitol, as proposed to be altered."

Right: Initially the British tried to fire Congreve rockets into the ceiling of the Capitol Senate Chamber, not realizing it was covered by sheet metal. When that failed to start a blaze, combustibles, such as furniture and curtains, were piled in the middle of the chamber and sprinkled with rocket fuel. A rocket fired into the heap provided ignition and resulted in a substantial fire.

Will Washington Be Destroyed?

"Greater respect was certainly paid to private property than has usually been exhibited by the enemy in his marauding parties."

—Washington Journalist Joseph Gales, Jr., August 31, 1814

British vengeance was aimed at Washington's major public buildings and military headquarters. The Capitol, President's House, and Treasury and Executive Buildings were the main targets, although some nearby buildings were damaged and destroyed in the confusion. General Ross and even Admiral Cockburn often heeded the pleas of locals trying to save their dwellings and businesses, but three private rope walks were burned because they produced supplies that could potentially be used by the navy.

Much of the damage occurred at the hands of the Americans themselves. Three bridges were burned, one on the Potomac and two on the Eastern Branch (Anacostia), and the Navy Yard was put to the torch to keep it out of enemy hands. A great glow in the sky, visible from as far away as Baltimore and Leesburg, Virginia, thirty-five miles away, was the result of these fires as well as the buildings burned by the British.

One of the embarrassments for Americans was the amount of damage caused by local looters. Joseph Gales, Jr. (1786–1860), editor of the Washington

This modern painting recreates the burning of the Navy Yard ordered by Captain Thomas Tingey in an effort to avoid the British capture of armaments. The Tripoli Monument, the oldest U.S. military monument and now located at the U.S. Naval Academy, is in the foreground. The British reputedly vandalized the monument when they further damaged the yard the following morning.

Daily National Intelligencer, was shocked that "[n]o houses were half as much plundered by the enemy as by the knavish wretches of the town who profited by the general distress." Paul Jennings (1799–1874), President Madison's body servant, reported that "a rabble, taking advantage of the confusion, ran all over the White House, and stole lots of silver and whatever they could lay their hands on." Captain Thomas Tingey (1750–1829), commander of the Navy Yard, was amazed at how the neighborhood moved in to plunder after the fire. "[It] is disgraceful to relate—not a movable article from the cellars to the garrets has been left us—and even some of the fixtures, and locks of the doors, have been shamefully pillaged." The British were not above joining in this behavior. British officers attempted to prevent looting by their troops and some British soldiers were flogged, or even shot, for theft.

Washington's two bookends, the Capitol and the President's House, were the pivots of the city's design. With the burning Capitol lighting up the sky behind them, General Ross and Admiral Cockburn rode down the wide expanse of Pennsylvania Avenue. They were leading one hundred fifty men through the heart of the city. The President's House was about a mile ahead.

The President's House, hurriedly deserted in late afternoon, was an easy target. Lieutenant Gleig was unimpressed with the place. "[It] was remarkable for nothing, except the want of taste exhibited in its structure . . . in no

respect likely to excite the jealousy of a people peculiarly averse to all pomp or parade, even in their chief magistrate." It was 11 p.m. when the invaders picked through the furnishings and food left in the empty building. It was soon set ablaze and, by morning, was a roofless shell.

Much has been written about the British partaking of a "victory dinner" set out in the President's House. There is no doubt that food and drink were available. Paul Jennings, Madison's 15-year-old slave, remembered that he had laid the table himself. There were always refreshments for messengers and the like. Whatever was on hand, British officers, even possibly Ross and Cockburn, took full advantage of the spread. British officer James Scott certainly enjoyed it. "Never was nectar more grateful to the palates of the gods than the crystal goblets of Madeira and water I quaffed off at [James] Madison's expense."

The British commanders chose to enjoy a midnight supper with nine other officers at the nearby Mrs. Suter's Boardinghouse, watching the burning President's House light up the night. While the British bivouacked on Capitol Hill they raised the Union Jack, the national ensign of Great Britain, at the heart of Washington City.

After some rest, the marauders were at it again on the morning of August 25. The Treasury Building was already burning when at about 8 a.m. enemy soldiers attacked the Southwest Executive Building, offices for the secretaries of state and war. Luckily, through heroic efforts, the records had been carted to safety along with the prized colors and standards seized from the British during the Revolutionary War.

Admiral Cockburn had a personal vendetta against the *Daily National Intelligencer,* located on 6th Street, N.W. Editor and English immigrant Joseph Gales, Jr., had been regularly attacking the admiral in the newspaper. Cockburn ordered the newspaper headquarters burned, but when neighbors pleaded that a fire would be disastrous for the whole block, he instead ordered Royal Marines to pull down the building with ropes. Some accounts claim the neighbors then pleaded that the structure was private property belonging not to Gales but to a judge opposed to war with Britain. Impressed,

---

Major General Robert Ross and Rear Admiral George Cockburn must have been in a celebratory mood when they occupied President "Jemmy" Madison's mansion; possibly even toasting their success before they ordered it torched.

After marching down Pennsylvania Avenue from the burning Capitol, British troops entered an empty White House, reputedly ate the food and drank the wine laid out, then set the building on fire. This modern painting depicts the fire that lit up the midnight sky.

This contemporary view from the northeast of the once-elegant and imposing White House shows the extent of the damage from the August 24, 1814, fire. The s-shaped curve above the near corner of the roof is part of the metallic conductor that encircled the roof, loosened from its mooring.

Benjamin Henry Latrobe designed some elegant, neoclassical White House chairs that were destroyed in the 1814 fire. A replica chair at the Maryland Historical Society was constructed based on his surviving drawings.

Cockburn instead ordered the contents of the office removed and destroyed; some burned in a bonfire in the street and some dumped in the nearby canal. But most of all, the admiral made certain that all the type was destroyed, especially the letter "C," so his name would not be found in future issues of the newspaper.

Meanwhile, Dr. William Thornton (1759–1828), the multi-talented designer of the U.S. Capitol and the superintendent of patents, was frantically trying to save the Patent Office, housed in Blodgett's Hotel (8th and E Streets, N.W.), as was the U.S. Post Office after 1810. The patent records had been spirited away but the patent models were too bulky to move. In a stroke of inventive thinking, Thornton convinced the British that "to burn what would be useful to all mankind [the patent models] would be as barbarous as formerly to burn the Alexandrian Library for which the Turks have been ever since condemned by all enlightened nations." Unfortunately, many of the models, saved by the good doctor for posterity, were later lost in an 1836 fire.

Rear Admiral George Cockburn claimed that Joseph Gales, editor of the *Daily National Intelligencer,* was printing lies about him in editorials. He ordered the publication's office burned, but when locals pleaded that neighboring houses would be affected as well, Cockburn relented and ordered that the structure be pulled down instead, as suggested in this illustration. When a bystander told him the building did not belong to Gales, the admiral relented and instead had all the furniture, presses, and type removed to the street where they were burned and smashed.

Reverses Then Retreat

"The capture of Washington was more owing to the blindness of the Americans themselves than to any other cause.

—Lieutenant George Robert Gleig, 85th Regiment of Foot

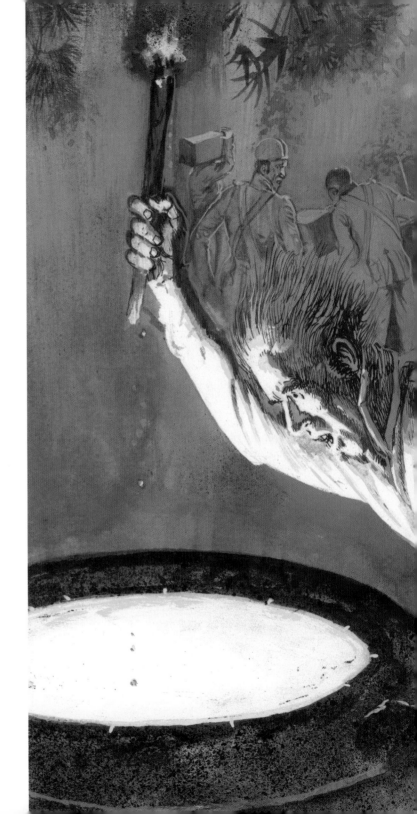

The law of unforeseen consequences plagued the British toward the end of their unwelcome visit to Washington City. Two enormous setbacks put a damper on their foray and hastened their departure.

The Greenleaf Point Federal Arsenal was tucked away on a peninsula between the Potomac and the mouth of the Anacostia. After surging through the smoking Navy Yard and further destroying what was left from the Americans' burning the previous night, seventy-five British soldiers swarmed over the arsenal. Cannons were spiked and fired muzzle to muzzle to put them out of action. Unmounted tubes were rolled into the river along with shot and shell. What happened next was later gravely reported in a London newspaper.

> One of the artillery-men most unfortunately dropped a lighted port-fire into the well, which, with a magazine about twenty yards distant . . . blew up with the most tremendous explosion. One house was unroofed and walls of two others [burned earlier] . . . were shook down. Large pieces of earth, stones, bricks, shot, shell, etc., burst into the air, and, falling among us . . . killed about twelve men and wounded above thirty more, most of them in a dreadful manner . . . The groans of the people almost buried in the earth, or with legs and arms broke, and the sight of pieces of bodies lying about, was a thousands times more distressing than the loss we met in the field that day before [Bladensburg].

One of the British targets was the Federal Arsenal at Greenleaf Point, now Fort McNair. Americans had dropped over one hundred barrels of gunpowder into a dry well. No one knows for sure how this gunpowder was ignited (one story claims that an Englishman dropped a burning port-fire into the well), but the resulting explosion killed at least twelve men and wounded another thirty.

Another version claims a spark from the fires landed in the arsenal well, setting off the explosion—not because of the proximity of the nearby magazine, but because the Americans had hidden about a hundred thirty barrels of gunpowder in the well itself. No matter what the source, the explosion left a crater nearly twenty feet deep and about forty feet in diameter.

After these devastating losses, the British army, in fact all the people left in the vicinity of the capital city, faced another frightening calamity, this time at the whim of Mother Nature. While British depredations spread through Washington, the weather remained hot, hazy, and humid. In the early afternoon of August 25, an ominous bank of black clouds came rolling in from the west. No one was prepared for the violence that followed. Sheets of lightning and deafening claps of thunder were suddenly accompanied by the "frightening roar" of wind that announced the arrival of a strong line of thunderstorms, possibly accompanied by one or more tornadoes.

Roofs blew off and buildings were flattened. Chain Bridge across the Potomac buckled in the wind. People darted for cover and cowered as the storm blew through the center of town. Trees were uprooted and reportedly small-caliber field cannons were picked up and turned on end. Lethal debris flew in all directions and those unlucky enough to be in the open when the storm came through lay face down and prayed for their survival.

The freight train of wind was soon gone, leaving destruction in its wake. The rain, however, drenched the area for two more hours. Most if not all the fires still burning were drowned in the downpour. A story survives that a soaked Admiral Cockburn ran into a local lady while picking his way through the downed trees and debris. He cried, "Great God, Madam! Is this the kind of storm to which you are accustomed in this infernal country?" "No Sir," the lady answered, "This is a special interposition of Providence to drive our enemies from our city."

The British wasted no time abandoning the ruins, quietly leaving the shattered Federal City as darkness again descended. To fool the Americans into thinking their enemies were still in town, the British stoked smoldering campfires with more fuel, and a few men were ordered to walk about in front of the fires, their shadows creating silhouettes that would convince the locals that their enemies were still there in force.

By midnight, the majority of the dog-tired troops were again marching through the Bladensburg battlefield, herding about sixty beef cattle ahead of the column. A motley assortment of horses, carts, wagons, and coaches collected in Washington carried the wounded, although about ninety badly injured soldiers were left behind.

Lieutenant Gleig had an eerie and humbling experience marching through a silent Bladensburg. "The dead were still unburied, and lay about in every direction completely naked . . . having been exposed to the violent rain . . . they appeared to be bleached to a most unnatural degree of whiteness . . . when you come to view the dead in an hour of calmness . . . you cannot help remembering how frail may have been the covering which saved yourself from being the loathsome thing on which you are gazing." In his personal analysis of the campaign, Gleig credited the inexperienced Americans for handing the British victory at Bladensburg. "The [American] troops were drawn up . . . like so many regiments on parade . . . In maintaining themselves, likewise, when attacked, they exhibited neither skill nor resolution . . . they have not the experience nor the habits of soldiers."

Along the way many of the men in the column filled their haversacks with raw flour scooped up from barrels captured as war booty. But over time the greedy but tired soldiers dumped the flour from their packs to lighten their loads, thereby leaving a ribbon of white along the line of march. One soldier commented, "If it had not been for the flour thus marking the track, the whole column would have lost its way."

By August 27, only three days after the Bladensburg battle, the British had picked their way through downed trees and other damage from the recent storm. Reaching Nottingham they loaded their wounded, equipment, and pilfered flour and tobacco onto their boats. The rest of the army marched on to Benedict. Proud of a sortie that had brought their enemy to its knees, the entire force was methodically rowed out to waiting ships in the Patuxent River by August 30.

For the men who had been left behind with the ships on the Patuxent the harsh rhythms of the British navy had continued with scheduled punishments aboard the flagship, H.M. ship-of-the-line *Albion*. In the ship's log dated August 21, 1814, it states, "Read the Articles of War and punished Henry Farley (S) [Seaman] with 40 and Peter Anderson (M) [Marine] with 14 lashes for drunkeness, Michl Sullivan (S) with 18 lashes for neglect of duty, Wm. Smith (M) with 48 lashes for drunkeness and sleeping on his post, Jno. Sheridan (Arts) [Artillery] with 48 lashes and Henry Halls (M) with 36 lashes for drunkeness and violence."

Captain Sir Peter Parker

"And gallant PARKER! Thus enshrin'd,
Thy life, thy fall, thy fame, shall be;
And early Valour, glowing find
a model in thy memory."

—Lord Byron eulogizes his cousin, Captain Sir Peter Parker, 1814

Second Baronet Captain Sir Peter Parker (1785–1814) inherited a family tradition that put him in harm's way. He was the fourth generation of a distinguished Irish family that was dedicated to naval service during the age of fighting sail. It was well known that the Parker "pride was to bleed for their country." A doting Admiral Peter Parker said about his grandson and namesake, "His heart is in the right place, he is made of fine stuff. These are the sure prognostics of future distinction, if he lives . . . "

In the British fleet by age thirteen, the handsome and capable Parker rose quickly in the service, both because of his grandfather's friendship with Admiral Lord Nelson and because he was perfectly suited to the rough-and-ready world of sea service. By age twenty, he commanded a brig and was the first to discover the French and Spanish fleet leaving Cadiz, setting in motion events that led to the 1805 Battle of Trafalgar. During fifteen years of active, dangerous, and challenging service, the young captain faced death many times. He briefly served in Parliament, married and sired three sons, and toyed with the idea of resigning his commission. But, as the Napoleonic Wars wound down, he was ordered to America in 1814 with his frigate, H.M. *Menelaus*.

Actively, heartlessly, almost recklessly, 29-year-old Captain Parker pursued his assigned raids on Chesapeake Bay targets. His appointment with fate did not occur on the bridge of a square-rigger, trading cannonballs with an enemy on the high seas. He died bleeding in the arms of his men during a self-styled "frolic" in a moonlit field, miles from the water. Far from much-celebrated glory, it was a tragic and needless death on a little-known battlefield.

Captain Peter Parker, commander of the British feint to the Upper Chesapeake

A Frolic Becomes a Nightmare

"It was the height of madness to advance into the interior of a country we knew nothing about . . ."

—British Midshipman Frederick Chamier in an 1850 reminiscence

Captain Sir Peter Parker was a rising star. The 29-year-old scion of a noble British naval family had sea water flowing in his veins. As young as he was, the bold and efficient veteran officer was in command of a frigate and leading a raiding party up the Chesapeake Bay in August of 1814.

The British strategy called for feints on the Bay and the Potomac River, keeping the Americans confused about enemy objectives while the main force attacked Washington. Captain Parker was assigned the northern Chesapeake, a region that had felt the sting of enemy raids in 1813. In fact, the raids, practically unopposed, had never completely stopped. In July, a squadron of barges had fanned out to attack targets on both the eastern and western shores.

Captain Parker sailed up the Chesapeake in August aboard his flagship, the 38-gun H.M. frigate *Menelaus*. He was accompanied by two schooners, *Mary* and *Jane*, as well as a sizeable contingent of Royal Marines. Beginning on August 18, the squadron of raiders picked off tidewater targets. An Easton newspaper reported that on August 23, two enemy row barges "captured a small boat and canoe, fired four guns, and after amusing themselves on the beach, returned to their vessels."

A tender to the schooner *Mary*, anchored off Rock Hall on the Eastern Shore, was hit by the same terrible storm that laid Washington low. The fierce winds capsized the tender and a cannon, ammunition, muskets, and swords were sent to the bottom of the Bay off Swan Point.

On August 27 the schooner *Jane* sailed into the Patapsco River within view of Fort McHenry to sound the river channel depth. Alarms went out to the city from the fort as the garrison pondered what might happen next. Baltimore had its own gunboats that mirrored Barney's Chesapeake Flotilla boats in size but not in numbers. These lightly armed gunboats were used more for scouting and communication than for combat and were relatively powerless in the face of the enemy raiders.

Tensions increased as Captain Parker began observing "the Enemy's Regular Troops and Militia in Motion along the whole coast." The British strategy seemed to be creating confusion among the American defenders. Where would the raiders strike next?

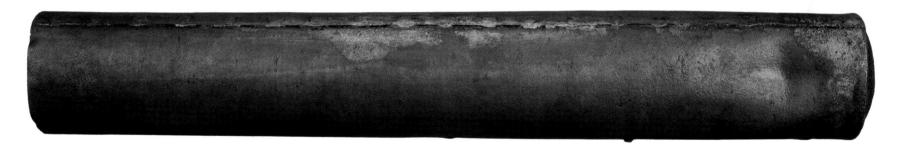

This Congreve rocket casing was recovered at the Henry Waller Farm in Kent County, Maryland, after the British spotted American cavalry there. In retaliation for this show of defiance, rockets were fired. Troops then landed and burned the farm. This casing is on display at Fort McHenry National Monument and Historic Shrine.

Early on a moonlit morning, Captain Peter Parker, a popular young British naval officer, was mortally wounded during the Battle of Caulks Field. His dedicated troops refused to leave him, taking turns carrying his body back to their boats. The next morning, Americans visiting the battlefield discovered a bloody shoe with the name Parker inscribed inside.

On August 28, Parker and his lieutenants decided to go after some militia in fancy uniforms near Fairlee Creek in Kent County. After a day of cat and mouse with local horsemen, the British began throwing rockets and 18-pound cannonballs at the Americans. One of the British lieutenants, Benjamin George Beynon, described the late afternoon action. "At five landed and set fire to the house [Big Fairlee] . . . I offered them [the American cavalry] Battle . . . and giving them sharp and galling fire for ten minutes which must have laid some of them low; they were extremely well mounted—smashingly dress'd in Blue and long white feathers in their hats. Our fire completely routed them . . . at dusk . . . we all embarked much pleased with our excursion." Henry Waller, owner of the devastated Big Fairlee Plantation, spent seventeen years seeking compensation and finally received $7,000 from the U.S. government. Francis Scott Key served as his attorney.

An episode on August 30 set the wheels in motion for another turn of events. While raiding and burning two Frisby family plantations, with "a great many [American] horsemen . . . close to us in the woods," the British quizzed some slaves about a nearby militia camp. Captain Parker decided on what he called a midsummer's night "frolic with the Yankees." Along with his bellicose confidence, Parker appears to have had some premonition that things would not go well. He sealed up a will and a farewell letter to his young wife before setting out.

That night, under the light of the moon, Captain Parker himself, leading 150 (some said as many as 260) sailors and marines, marched five miles to a place remembered as Caulks Field. At 1 a.m., the British raiders, several armed with pikes, ran into about 200 Yankee militiamen. Unfortunately for the intruders, the well-organized militia was led by a hard-bitten Revolutionary War veteran named Philip Reed.

From the start, the fight didn't go according to Parker's plan. The American encampment was not where Parker had first been told, but further inland from his boats. The Brits were stunned when at close range they were fired upon soon after turning at a junction in the road, with woods on both sides where trees had been felled to slow their progress. Parker advanced his men, who stood and traded flashing volleys with the militiamen in the night. These advanced Americans withdrew and reformed with the rest of the militiamen in a line supported by five cannon. As the British moved forward, they sustained many casualties. A flanking attack on the American right seemed to have gained the upper hand when a sudden bugle call announced an enemy retreat. Yet, according to later reports from Lieutenant Colonel Reed, the obstinate and hard-fighting militia had run out of ammunition. So why the British retreat?

In pressing the Americans, a cocky British force had sustained significant casualties: fourteen killed and twenty-seven wounded compared to three wounded militiamen. The real story, however, was the loss of Captain Parker. A musket ball had cut an artery in his thigh, and the young officer soon bled to death in the arms of his subordinates. His death stemmed the British attack. Carried off the field with his retreating force, Parker left behind an unusual calling card, a bloody shoe marked with his name. Parker's premonition had come true.

The frolic had turned into a disaster for the British. Withdrawing their squadron to the western shore, they mourned the loss of a rising young star in a trivial skirmish. For the Americans, however, the Battle of Caulks Field was no trifling matter. The local militia had shown some real spunk. Their small victory was much celebrated around the Chesapeake during that difficult summer of 1814, less than two weeks before the next big battle, this time at Baltimore.

Confusing the Americans

"A Tolerably good Diversion should ... be sent up the Potowmac with Bomb Ships &ca [etc.] which will tend to distract and divide the Enemy ..."

—Rear Admiral George Cockburn to Vice Admiral Alexander Cochrane, July 17, 1814

While Captain Sir Peter Parker was chasing fate in the Upper Chesapeake, another young fighting British fleet officer was looking for his own trouble on the Potomac River. Thirty-two-year-old Captain James Alexander Gordon had served nobly at sixteen with Admiral Nelson during his celebrated Nile victory in 1798. A tough customer, he was commanding a frigate in 1811 when he lost a leg, crushed by a cannonball. By 1814, he was back on the ship's bridge with a wooden leg, leading the Potomac Squadron.

Gordon's squadron was the largest flotilla yet to take on the hundred-mile sail upriver to Washington. Besides the 36-gun and 38-gun frigates *Euryalus* and *Seahorse,* the captain commanded an 18-gun rocket vessel, *Erebus,* three 8-gun bomb vessels, *Aetna, Devastation,* and *Meteor,* and a 2-gun schooner/dispatch ship, *Anna Maria.* The innovative and sturdy bomb vessels launched large exploding shells from a heavy mortar mounted amidships.

Largely powerless Americans, including Secretary James Monroe, had been watching closely. In July, an enemy squadron with a frigate, two schooners, and about ten barges had been sounding some shallows and placing buoys in the Potomac River. The Yankees were counting on two obstacles that would slow and even stop an invasion. One was a vexing series of shifting shallows near the Wicomico River known as the Kettle Bottom Shoals. Even experienced pilots couldn't determine the ever-changing river bottom. Larger

Captain James Alexander Gordon, commander of the British diversion up the Potomac River.

Sir James Alexander Gordon

"The Last of Nelson's Captains"

—Macmillan's magazine honors Gordon's long career in 1869

Captain James Gordon (1782–1869) had one of the toughest Chesapeake assignments of all. During the 1814 American invasion, the veteran 32-year-old, one-legged Scot led frigates, bomb vessels, and a rocket ship in a diversion up the Potomac to Washington. Gordon was the officer for the job, taking on arduous river shallows and enemy forts and fire ships in stride. He would soon command the same vessels during the bombardment of Fort McHenry in Baltimore.

The captain had been at sea since the age of eleven. Serving aboard at least nine different vessels in two decades, his amazing record throughout the high drama of the Napoleonic era, including losing a leg in battle, made him a model sailor from that time. Some claim that Gordon was the prototype for C. S. Forester's legendary fictional Captain Horatio Hornblower.

After his celebrated career at sea, James Gordon became the superintendent of naval hospitals and dockyards. His career on land went on for decades and, at age eighty-six, in the emerging age of steam, he was promoted to Admiral of the Fleet. Seventy-five years after he had stepped onto the deck of the 74-gun H.M. ship-of-the-line *Arrogant* as a midshipman, he was buried at Greenwich Hospital, the last of Lord Nelson's captains.

vessels had to warp through the sand bars, rowing a kedge anchor out ahead of the ship, dropping it overboard and then winching the vessel forward foot by tedious foot.

Captain Gordon, fighting contrary winds as well as the shallows, described the back-breaking process. "I believe each of the Ships was not less than twenty different times aground and each time we were obliged to haul off by main Strength—and we were employed warping for five whole successive days, with the exception of a few hours, a distance of fifty miles."

Finally clear of the infamous Kettle Bottom Shoals, the squadron was next hit by the same vicious August 25 storm that punished the whole region. The ships were tossed about, sails were ripped, and *Euryalus, Seahorse*, and *Meteor* had masts and spars damaged by the fierce winds. On a calmer August 27, a full two days after the British occupation of the Federal City, they passed Washington's Mount Vernon Plantation. Captain Charles Napier, skipper of the *Euryalus* and known as "Black Charlie" for his jet black hair, saw in "the retreat of the illustrious Washington for the first time since we entered the Potomac, a gentleman's residence."

The second major obstacle on the river was now just ahead. Fort Washington (or Warburton, named after the original plantation owner) consisted of a 5-gun water battery, 13-gun small star-shaped earthwork with a circular gun battery in front, a 6-gun blockhouse, and two supporting guns on a hill. Because the channel narrows and swings close to the Maryland shore here, ships other than mortar vessels could only bring guns to bear when directly opposite the fort. Still, Captain Gordon thought the fort was assailable, stating "the bomb vessels [with mortars] at once taking up their positions to cover the frigates in the projected attack at daylight next morning [August 28], and began throwing shells. The garrison to our great surprise, retreated from the fort and a short time afterward Fort Washington was blown up . . ."

Fort commander Captain Samuel T. Dyson, with only forty-nine men at his disposal, claimed he was expecting the water attack to be reinforced by land troops supposedly marching from Benedict. Setting off 3,000 pounds of

In order to ascend and descend the Potomac River, the British naval squadron was forced to use kedge anchors to ease their warships over the shallow and ever-changing Kettle Bottom Shoals. This time-consuming and exhausting work, called "warping," continued uninterrupted for five successive days. Each ship reported going aground at least twenty times.

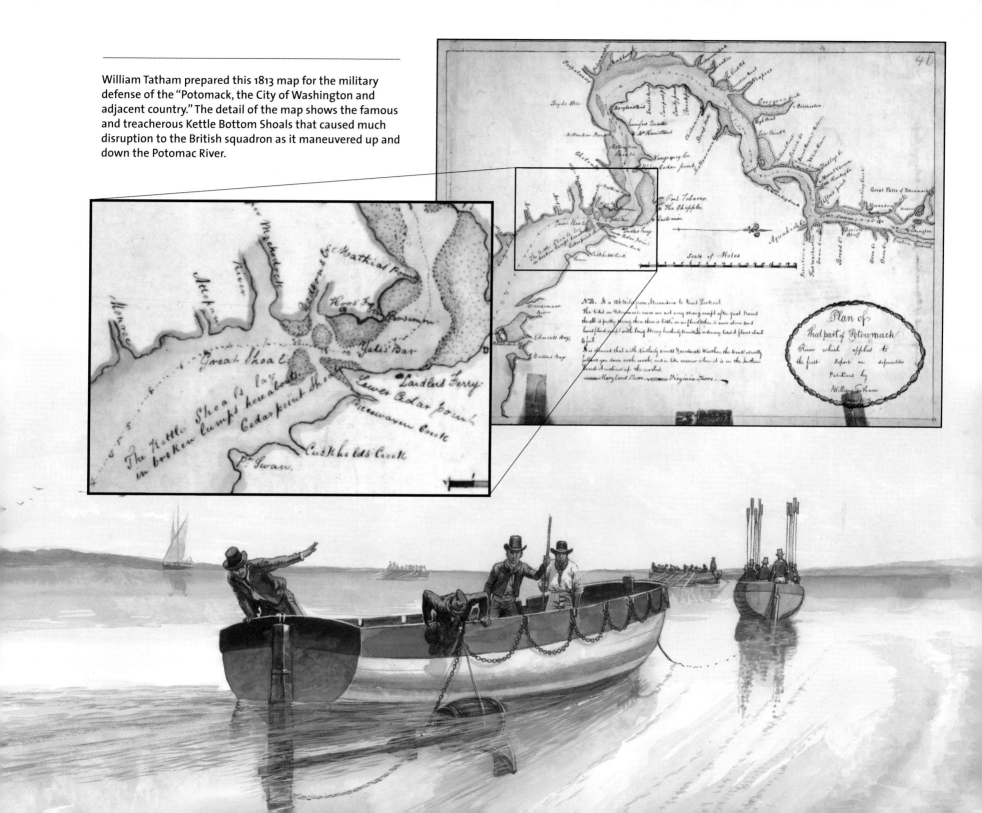

William Tatham prepared this 1813 map for the military defense of the "Potomack, the City of Washington and adjacent country." The detail of the map shows the famous and treacherous Kettle Bottom Shoals that caused much disruption to the British squadron as it maneuvered up and down the Potomac River.

Captain Porter Causes Trouble

"The town was providentially preserved from destruction, by the accidental circumstance of the . . . neck handkerchief giving way . . . "

—Alexandria Mayor Charles Simms describes an August 28, 1814, incident

U.S. Navy Captain David Porter, Jr., brought in to help defend Washington, was upset. Hard on the heels of the destruction of the capital's public buildings, Alexandria was disgracefully surrendering without firing a shot. Dashing on horseback into George Washington's hometown with two companions, Porter may have been the one who decided to take his frustration out on the nearest enemy officer he could find.

A young British lieutenant, John West Fraser, was busy supervising the "requisition" of flour barrels stored in a warehouse in the now-occupied Alexandria waterfront. Suddenly, one of the officers swooped down and grabbed the lieutenant by his neck handkerchief. He rushed away with his enemy dangling behind his horse by the scarf.

An alarmed Alexandria Mayor Charles Simms fumed that Lieutenant Fraser might have been killed had not the neck scarf separated, leaving the would-be hostage, "kicking and squalling quite lustily," in the dust behind the galloping American. Simms complained that "this rash act excited the greatest alarm among the Inhabitants of the Town. Women and children running and screaming through the Streets and hundreds of them layed out that night without Shelter."

The incident also "created a considerable alarm [among the British]; the men retreated to the boats, and prepared their carronades, and were with difficulty prevented from firing." The mayor did some fast talking to prevent real trouble. Two representatives rowed out to the British commander, Captain Gordon. The brouhaha was explained and "the Signal of Battle was annull'd." The British "recommended that proper precautions should be taken as a repetition . . . might lead to the destruction of the town."

Captains David Porter, Jr., and John O. Creighton and Lieutenant Charles T. Platt rode into Alexandria to reconnoiter the British occupying the town. At a warehouse, they spotted a young British lieutenant, John West Fraser, and a squad of men rolling out barrels of flour. Suddenly one of the daring American officers grabbed Fraser by his neck scarf and would have abducted him had not the scarf given way, thus avoiding a potential British reprisal.

gunpowder without firing a shot and then fleeing upriver with his men, the disgraced Dyson was later arrested, tried, found guilty of destruction of government property, and dismissed from the service. President Madison, just back from his own flight, heard the enormous explosion along with everyone else in Washington. Were the British attacking a second time?

After all their frustrations ascending the river, Captain Gordon and his squadron were suddenly on a roll. A boat with a flag of truce appeared at 8 a.m. on August 28. In order to save defenseless Alexandria from destruction, the town fathers negotiated a surrender. Although Mayor Charles Simms pointed out that "[i]t is impossible that men could behave better than the British while the town was in their power," the occupiers had a field day confiscating ships, flour, tobacco, and cotton. Criticism instantly came from all quarters. Newspapers claimed that "surrender without resistance . . . [has] everywhere excited astonishment and indignation." Even first lady Dolley Madison weighed in, telling friends that Alexandria should have burned rather than accept such humiliating terms.

After a five-day uncontested occupation, the British withdrew down the river. Even then, newly arrived American naval Captain John Rodgers had to threaten to burn Alexandria himself before the thoroughly demoralized town leaders would let him raise a U.S. flag. Rodgers had been brought in along with Lake Erie naval hero Oliver Hazard Perry and Captain David Porter, Jr., to punish the British as they sailed downriver. The ever-vigilant Secretary of State James Monroe, having replaced John Armstrong as Secretary of War, was now wearing two hats. Everyone agreed that they would launch fire ships and torpedoes against the British and establish gun batteries at White House (modern Fort Belvoir) and Indian Head to harass the withdrawing enemy squadron.

Between September 3 and 8 the Americans threw everything they could at the enemy ships moving through the gauntlet. At first they attacked with fire ships and heavily armed barges. The Americans used cannon, muskets, and rifles to take pot shots at the passing ships. Flying a conspicuous white

President James Madison, Secretary of the Navy William Jones, Brigadier General John Hungerford, and U.S. Navy Captain David Porter, Jr., met atop Shuter's Hill in Alexandria (now the site of the Masonic Temple) to plan countermeasures for attacking the British as they withdrew down the Potomac River.

A Hero and a Villain
Captain Oliver Hazard Perry and Major General James Wilkinson

"The most consummate artist in treason that the nation ever possessed."

—Historian Frederick Jackson Turner about James Wilkinson

Several American senior military and naval officers were present in the Federal City during the 1814 crisis. Two deserve special attention; one the renowned "Hero of Lake Erie," the other "a villain, from the bark to the very core."

Oliver Hazard Perry (1785–1819) was thirteen when he joined the United States Navy, serving on his father's ship, the 30-gun U.S. frigate *General Greene*. By 1813, he was commanding the naval forces on Lake Erie and facing a substantial British squadron. The September 10 Battle of Lake Erie began badly for the Americans and Perry was forced to row from his crippled flagship to another vessel. He and his small fleet soon won a great victory against all odds and Perry understated the first-ever capture of a whole British naval squadron with the simple, immortal words, "We have met the enemy and he is ours." Much celebrated as the "Hero of Lake Erie," Captain Perry came to Baltimore in 1814 to command the 44-gun U.S. frigate *Java*, then under construction. He saw his last combat, however, commanding a gun battery on the banks of the Potomac River after the attack on Washington.

James Wilkinson (1757–1825) was born near Benedict, Maryland. Studying medicine in Philadelphia, he joined the Continental Army in 1775 and began a long military career with the American forces. Although twice an army commander (1796–1798, 1800–1812) and governor of the Louisiana Territory (1805–1807), General Wilkinson was regularly in trouble throughout his career for incompetence,

Captain Oliver Hazard Perry, the hero of Lake Erie, aided in the defense of Maryland.

conspiracy, corruption, self-aggrandizing, and intrigue. Wilkinson was in Washington during the 1814 invasion, criticizing the American defense, while a military inquiry was investigating his own failures leading two disastrous invasions of Canada. After his death it was determined he had been a paid agent of the Spanish Crown. A modern historian called the villainous General Wilkinson, "a general who never won a battle or lost a court martial."

This flag, recalling the last words of Captain James Lawrence aboard the U.S. frigate *Chesapeake*, was flown during the American victory on Lake Erie in 1813. The flag is now on display at the U. S. Naval Academy Museum.

Major General James Wilkinson, a soldier and statesman, was associated with several scandals and controversies.

flag declaring "Free Trade and Sailors' Rights," the overmatched White House gun battery took on British bomb vessels, resulting in casualties on both sides. More fire ships and torpedoes followed. But these efforts only delayed and lightly damaged the enemy. The last defense, another gun battery erected at Indian Head on the Maryland side of the river, was said by commander Captain Perry to be "too small a caliber to be much impression on the enemy," and didn't even slow the passing ships down.

By September 8, Captain Gordon's squadron had made contact with H.M. frigate *Havannah* sailing from the main British fleet to meet them. The frigate *Euryalus* was grounded for a day on the notorious Kettle Bottom Shoals, but the eventful twenty-three-day "feint" up the Potomac was finally all but over.

Admiral Cochrane thought of leaving the Chesapeake and sailing to the Gulf of Mexico. But the potential for violent annual storms that accompanied the arrival of the equinox (when the sun was on the same plane as the Earth's equator) called for a delay. Cochrane wrote, "Major General Ross and myself resolved to occupy the intermediate time to advantage, by making a demonstration upon the City of Baltimore, which might be converted into a real attack should circumstances appear to justify it."

To harass the withdrawing British, the Americans made at least three attempts to send fire ships against the naval squadron. All of the efforts failed because the wind either died or changed direction or the British were able to pull away or fend off the burning vessels.

6 *The Battle for Baltimore*
September 1814

Going Toe to Toe

"When little more than a hundred paces divided the one line from the other, both parties made ready to bring matters more decidedly to a personal struggle."

—Lieutenant George Robert Gleig describing the Battle of North Point, September 12, 1814

It was another dog day in that hot summer of 1814, and now the British invaders were on the doorstep of Baltimore. The nervous American militiamen were attempting to stand tall at the edge of a field as they confronted long lines of red-clad British troops brandishing muskets with shining bayonets accompanied by the sounds of bugles blaring and drums beating. There would be no repeat of the Bladensburg Races. These three thousand or so Yankees were defending hearth and home and there were thousands of citizen-soldiers dug in further west prepared to back them up.

This was toe-to-toe battle with the enemy in the age of the musket. The American infantry, sporting plumed hats and high-collared wool coats, had their long, muzzle-loading muskets at the ready. Their double line stretched across the narrow Patapsco Neck peninsula, anchored on Bear Creek to the south and the marshes of Bread and Cheese Creek flowing into Back River to the north. They were blocking the way, daring the British to attack. Cannons were sitting in the road from Baltimore to North Point, barking canister and grapeshot at red targets massed for the assault. The British responded with cannon blasts and their signature, noisy Congreve rockets. Local militiamen knew the veteran enemy would soon close with their feared bayonets. It was a personal battle of nerves, shoulder to shoulder with comrades, lost in the smoke, listening for commands above the roar of battle, making every shot count, shouting oaths of defiance, holding the line.

British Lieutenant Gleig, marching with his 85th Regiment, later described the face of this fight with professional detachment: "...the enemy, now raising a shout, fired a volley from right to left, and then kept up a rapid and ceaseless discharge of musketry. Nor were our people backward in replying to these salutes; for giving them back both their shout and their volley, we pushed on at double-quick, with the intention of bringing them to the charge."

Young militiaman John Pendleton Kennedy lined up sweating with his gunpowder-stained friends and neighbors in the elite, smartly dressed, gentlemanly company of United Volunteers, the disgrace of Bladensburg flashing in his memory. Again in ranks and facing down his fears, he had his mother's

---

Preceding spread: The Battle of North Point (more correctly the Battle of Patapsco Neck or Godly Wood) was fought in the afternoon of September 12, 1814. In this painting, the North Point Road, running left and right (south to north), is joined by Trappe Road near the far center. Back River is in the foreground, Bear Creek is to the far left center, and Bread and Cheese Creek is to the right. The white Methodist Meeting House is to the left of the bridge. The American reserves are posted near Cook's Tavern to the right. A rocket launcher is in action on the Bouldin Farm to the left. The burning log house is near today's Battle Acre Park. While British troops attack the main American line, others are maneuvering through the woods and marsh to flank the American left.

A modern National Guard Heritage painting depicts the elite 5th Maryland Regiment, with red-plumed hats and blue wool coats, fiercely defending the American right-center flank during the Battle of North Point. They are firing at will after unleashing a devastating volley at the approaching British line.

Baltimore in 1814

"In the varied scenes which have put to the test the constancy of the nation Baltimore ranks among the portion most distinguished for devotion to the public cause."

—President James Madison, April 22, 1815

Baltimore was the kind of city that could challenge the mighty British Empire. It was a scrappy, tough-minded, melting pot sort of place with a seafaring population that reached out to the world. President Madison honored America's third largest city for displaying the public fighting spirit that the new nation's capital was unable to muster.

Dating back to 1729, when Maryland's settlers were moving up the Chesapeake Bay, Baltimore "took off" during the American Revolution. Spared most of the fighting, the town and the state became the breadbasket of the new nation, supplying food and supplies to the Continental armies. The mercantile success story grew as ports as far away as China were regularly visited by Baltimore-built and -based merchant ships.

Blessed with a large natural harbor and miles of waterfront, the inland port of Baltimore, almost two hundred miles from the Atlantic, both dominated trade in the Chesapeake and looked west into the American heartland for new markets. Three communities growing along the inner harbor, Baltimore, Jonestown, and Fells Point, soon merged into a vibrant seaport. Bustling shipyards were building distinctive, fast ships. A nearby hill, christened "Federal" in 1789 after a boisterous dinner party celebrating the new United States Constitution, flew flags announcing waterborne traffic coming and going. The Jones Falls, cutting through the heart of the city, powered new industry.

By 1814, wealthy and influential families—the Pattersons, Carrolls, Howards, and Smiths—occupied large townhouses in Baltimore but fled to new

"villas," neoclassical country houses, during the heat and disease-prone months of summer. Their money spawned a homegrown golden age of decorative arts and the new city became a cultural center. Beautiful public buildings, like the Roman Catholic Cathedral, the first great metropolitan cathedral in the United States, under construction for a decade, announced prestigious achievements for the young United States.

The majority of Baltimore's fifty thousand inhabitants were immigrants, and its waterfront, where most found work, was a rough-and-tumble place. The community's toxic politics and virulent anti-British opinions earned it the nickname "Mobtown." That same toughness, however, helped defeat the British invasion force.

This 1804 painting shows Federal Hill looming over Baltimore's inner harbor. The heart of the city's maritime pursuits was at Fells Point, further down the harbor.

Spartan warning to spur him on. "Do not let me hear, my son, of your turning your back disgracefully upon the enemy."

Baltimore had been bracing for battle for almost two years. Since the spring of 1813, British warships had been roaming the Chesapeake, having their own way at nearly every turn, raiding towns and plantations with little or no opposition. Menacing enemy ships had appeared at the mouth of the Patapsco River on several occasions—once even sounding the channel to Baltimore. Local defenses, anchored at Fort McHenry, hoisted alarm flags, but each time the threat had evaporated.

Every Baltimorean knew that a serious attack could be coming. The notorious port, with its fleet of vexing privateers, had earned heaps of British scorn. Among the influential city fathers, Baltimore found a potential savior in 61-year-old local merchant and politician Samuel Smith. With the mature looks of a matinee idol and a nationally recognized political reputation to match, the decorated Revolutionary War hero hit the ground running.

Smith was given carte blanche to prepare a daunting defense. He was closely connected to rich and influential citizens. Fast-growing Baltimore, as the nation's third largest city (only New York and Philadelphia were larger), had many maritime-based fortunes already on its account books. A city council–appointed Committee of Public Safety evolved into the Committee of Vigilance and Safety, facing the life-and-death emergency at hand.

Newly minted Major General Samuel Smith used all his energy, leadership, and prestige to get the entire community working together in a united cause. Nothing escaped Smith's attention: raising funds; laying rings of defense on land and water; recruiting, equipping, and supplying thousands of militiamen from all over the region; seeking scarce federal help, if available; and, most important of all, keeping Baltimore's spirit in fighting trim.

Preparing for the Worst

"My friends I have but one life to lose, and that I have at all times been willing to hazard in defense of my beloved country . . ."

—Major General Samuel Smith to the Committee of Vigilance and Safety, August 25, 1814

In mid-1813, Baltimore had a skimpy defense. During the Revolution, an earthen fort had been built at strategic Whetstone Point, the intersection of Patapsco River's Ferry and Northwest Branches, and it had deteriorated in the years since. During the early 1790s, the Washington administration, Secretary of War James McHenry, and Congress had authorized permanent coastal fortifications. As a result, Fort McHenry was established in 1798. Other than a small battery on Federal Hill overlooking the inner harbor, the now-familiar brick walls added to the star fort in 1803 were the only barriers faced by potential attackers.

By the summer of 1814—just a year later—Baltimore harbor was bristling with guns, forts, and sunken harbor obstacles. How did this happen in such a short time? While Captain Joshua Barney was building his Chesapeake Flotilla, which included some gun barges built in local shipyards, the city was busy beefing up its own defenses. Gun batteries at the water's edge and a larger garrison strengthened Fort McHenry. A battery was added on the other side of the channel at Lazaretto Point to provide a cross fire with the fort. A floating boom of ship masts chained end to end was stretched across 600 yards blocking the entrance to the inner harbor. Brick and earthen Forts Covington and Babcock, named for a fallen Maryland hero and a U.S. Army engineer, protected the Ferry Branch west flank of Fort McHenry. An elaborate flag-and-lantern signal system kept a network of lookout stations on land and schooners and gunboats on the water in touch with Federal Hill. A

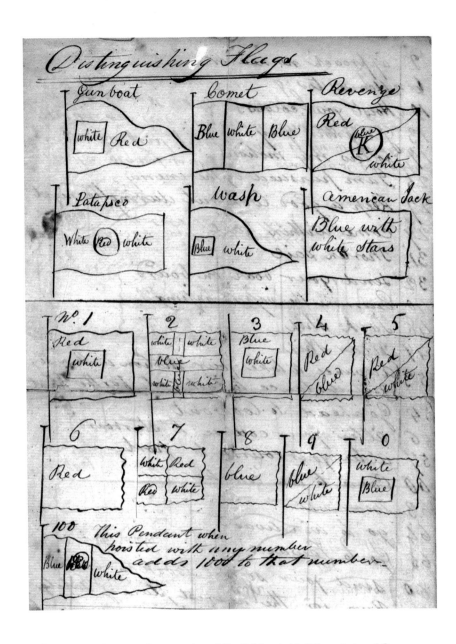

This manuscript records examples of the thirty-eight different signal flags used to communicate between shore lookout stations along the Patapsco River, gunboats, and Federal Hill in Baltimore's inner harbor. At night, lanterns were used in place of the flags.

line of old scows provided a rickety bridge for troops and supplies to cross the inner harbor between Hampstead Hill and Fort McHenry.

Organization of this backbreaking work fell to a trusted ally of General Smith. Veteran merchant and ship's captain George Stiles (1760–1819) put together an amphibious artillery unit of two hundred mariners dubbed "The First Marine Artillery of the Union." Smith and the city paid the bills and this "Seamen's Corps" raised the earthworks with pick and shovel. Stiles ran regular recruiting ads appealing to the patriotism of his neighbors on the docks. "We have a right to expect every master and mate in port. The cloud gathers fast and heavy in the East, and all hands are called." Working with steamboat inventor Robert Fulton (1765–1815), Stiles began building a "Steam Battery," a floating, catamaran-hulled gun battery powered by a steam engine. Baltimore raised $150,000 for the venture, but the 1814 emergency passed before it became seaworthy.

General Smith was certain that the British attack would come from both land and water. He ordered earthworks across the road from North Point up the Patapsco Neck to the east. Baltimore's main defensive line was a mile-long series of trenches and bastions stretched across three hills (Hampstead, Loudenslager, and Potter) rising as high as 100 feet on the eastern edge of town (Johns Hopkins Hospital on Broadway is now on a portion of the heights). Robert Cary Long, Sr., Maryland's first native-born architect (1770–1833), and William Stuart (1780–1839), a local stone cutter and lieutenant colonel of the 36th U.S. Regiment, were brought in to lay out the defensive lines. If this formidable defense was breached by the British, plans called for another stand on the high ground where the Roman Catholic Cathedral (now the Basilica of the Assumption) was under construction.

By August 25, 1814, all the news arriving from the nation's capital was sobering. Baltimore had sent its best militia to the defense of Washington, but the American troops had been no match for the British. The disgraced army commander, Brigadier General William Winder, was headed for Baltimore, leaving a burning Capitol and President's House in the Federal City behind him.

Arriving at Montgomery Courthouse (now Rockville), Winder delivered an unambiguous message to Baltimore: "There remains no doubt but the enemy are on the advance to Baltimore. Are the people animated there?" Rumors were flying that the British were marching to attack the city from the south.

The Indispensable Defender

"A Hero of Both Wars for Independence."

—The inscription under the Federal Hill statue for Samuel Smith, General, Senator, and Mayor

The portraits of Samuel Smith (1752–1839) depict a man very much in charge. His string of important successes during a long, event-filled career proves that he was among the country's most influential founding fathers.

Born into the sturdy families that settled frontier Pennsylvania, Smith was raised in Baltimore. At twenty-five he was already commanding a fort defending Philadelphia during the Revolution and winning praise from the Continental Congress for his bravery. After the war, the hero took full advantage of Baltimore's growth and became a power broker in the shipping business.

Beginning his political career as a Federalist, the party of George Washington, Smith joined the Jeffersonian revolt in 1800 but always remained a maverick who opposed many of the Jefferson and Madison policies. As a born leader, he moved easily into politics and was a powerful and influential force in the U.S. Congress, serving both as a congressman and a senator almost continuously from 1793 until 1833.

Through the tempestuous days of the Quasi-War with France and the Whiskey Rebellion, Samuel Smith also found time to serve the nation as an officer in the Maryland militia. In 1813, the sixty-one-year-old elder statesman took over Baltimore's defenses and he became the highly popular and effective choice to command the forces that repelled the British in 1814.

After spending almost his entire career in public service, the venerable eighty-one-year-old veteran of two wars against Great Britain still had enough drive and energy to lead a troubled Baltimore as mayor (1833–1835). Only a handful of founding fathers can claim so much influence and success during the first fifty years of the United States.

Major General Samuel Smith, the commander of American forces in Baltimore, was among the most important leaders in early America. After Baltimore's victory in 1814, Smith was painted for posterity in his general's uniform. He was still active well into his eighties, leading the city as mayor during some turbulent years.

That same day, Baltimore's Committee of Vigilance and Safety was called to an emergency meeting in the city council chambers. Revolutionary War hero and former governor John Eager Howard (1752–1827) emotionally captured the tension in the room. "My wife, my children, my friends and all that is nearest to me on Earth are here, but I had sooner see them all buried in Ruins and myself along with them, then see Baltimore make a last and disgraceful surrender to the Enemies of our beloved Country."

Rejecting the leadership of the absent General Winder, the committee recommended that Major General Samuel Smith "take command of the Forces which may be called into federal service." Recalling the group's revered General George Washington taking command of the Continental Army in 1775, Smith responded with humility; "Tell the members of your convention that I willingly obey their call, and confidently expect their hearty cooperation in every necessary means of defense."

Manning the Earthworks

"All hearts and hands have cordially united in the common cause. Every day, almost every hour, bodies of troops are marching in to our assistance."

—Private George Douglas, Baltimore Fencibles, writing to a friend, August 30, 1814

It was as if an electric spark had ignited Baltimore. Now that everyone was certain trouble was coming, few could imagine ignoring the call. African-Americans, slave and free, were called out to work side by side with white volunteers, creating a long ribbon of freshly dug earthworks on the city's east end. Some fifteen thousand militiamen hailing from Maryland, Virginia, Pennsylvania, the District of Columbia, and Delaware were marching in to man those defenses and save the city.

Naval hero and Marylander John Rodgers, credited with firing the war's first shot in anger, brought a new burst of energy to the defense on September 6. Working closely with General Smith and Fort McHenry commander Major

Army food rations have long had the reputation of being inedible. When one militia unit received some spoiled meat, they held a mock funeral on Hampstead Hill. Pall bearers placed straw bands on their hats and marched solemnly to a grave as a drummer beat the Death March. The bad meat was buried with the traditional "three taps and three cheers."

The lore associated with Reverend Joshua Thomas, the parson who brought Methodism to Maryland's Eastern Shore islands, is an important part of the area's culture. This illustration of Thomas preaching peace to the British troops on Tangier Island in 1814 accompanied a retelling of that event in a popular biography published in 1861.

The Parson of the Islands Chides the British

"...a natural roughness, a polished diamond of the first order, to whom lawyers, judges, doctors and preachers gave more heed than they would to the most cultured man in the community."

—The Reverend Adam Wallace, 1861

Joshua Thomas (1776–1853) was always a pious man. Raised in the hard-scrabble world of Eastern Shore watermen, he found his religious calling early. During a long and dedicated life, Thomas singlehandedly sailed his log canoe *Methodist* through the chain of Chesapeake islands and spread the gospel to the water communities.

The parson's reputation for powerful sermonizing grew. The British high command, headquartered on Tangier Island during the troubles between 1813 and 1815, thought "Brother" Thomas might be an inspiration

for its sailors and soldiers. As the fleet prepared for the 1814 expedition against Baltimore, the admirals reportedly summoned Thomas to a prayer meeting.

Standing up in front of thousands of enemy troops, gathered dutifully in ranks in a pine-covered bible campground near Fort Albion, Brother Thomas shouted out the Lord's message as he saw it. "Thou shalt not kill," he implored the men before him. Anyone who resorted to the sword and war was doomed to "perish by the sword." He went on to claim that the Almighty had told him that the British could not take Baltimore. In fact, he counseled the soldiers, marines, and sailors to prepare for death.

The British seem to have taken the parson's stern prophetic message in stride. As the fleet went on to its appointment with destiny, Joshua Thomas returned to his lifelong calling as the "Parson of the Islands." The results of his memorable fifty-year career remain a vital part of today's Lower Eastern Shore culture.

The cupola of Ridgely House, once located at North Point, was used as a lookout and signal station during the War of 1812.

George Armistead (1780–1818), the veteran leader mobilized the sailors and marines into an effective work force, finishing entrenchments and sinking hulks to block the waterways. Rodgers also drilled his men into a potent fighting force. An important fortification at a strategic intersection entering the city was christened the "Rodgers's Bastion" and manned with one hundred seventy U.S. Marines. Lieutenant John Harris wrote his brother that the arrival of Rodgers and his mariners made a real difference to a struggling, fearful city that may have succumbed without them. Rodgers himself noted that "people now begin to show something like a patriotic spirit."

The long-anticipated alarms reverberated around the community on Sunday, September 11. A hostile fleet of thirty ships was sighted from North Point, about fifteen miles east of Baltimore. A succession of flag messages led to the firing of three cannon shots on Federal Hill, the dreaded signal of imminent attack. The Baltimore *American* newspaper reported that "all the [American] corps of every description turned out with alacrity." Parishioners were released early from church services and citizen-soldiers rushed through the city to their units. Dismissing his congregation, the Reverend John Gruber of the Light Street Methodist Church was reported to have said in parting,

The Hero of North Point

Brigadier General John Stricker was honored with Major General Samuel Smith, Major George Armistead, and Commodore Joshua Barney as a "Baltimore Defender." A Revolutionary War veteran from Frederick, Maryland, Stricker commanded the American forces at the Battle of North Point. The circa 1817–18 painting above shows Stricker in full uniform; to the right Stricker is shown in a circa 1814 painting issuing orders from a white horse.

"I give you joy, my dear friend, after a tremendous conflict we have got rid of the enemy for the present. Baltimore has maintained its honor. It has not only saved itself, but it must tend to save the country . . ."

—Private George Douglas, Baltimore Fencibles, to a Boston friend, September 30, 1814

Baltimore delivered a triple-barreled punch to the British in September of 1814. Three men quickly became national heroes. Major George Armistead, commander at Fort McHenry, and Major General Samuel Smith are the better known of the trio, but Maryland Militia Brigadier General John Stricker, the commander at the Battle of North Point, deserves just as much credit.

Stricker was born in Frederick, Maryland, the son of a militia general who also fought with George Washington. When only seventeen years old, John marched to the fighting at Princeton with the 1st Maryland Regiment. Along with other veterans, he proudly wore his blue Society of Cincinnati Medal, identifying him as one of the small fraternity of officers who had risked everything serving under General Washington.

John Stricker's career during the War of 1812 swung between two extremes. Within days of the declaration of war against the British, there was a riot in Baltimore that highlighted the dangerous division among Americans on the issue of going to war. General Stricker was then in command of the local militia charged with intervening and preventing bloodshed. Sympathizing with the rioters, the general dragged his feet before calling out the militia. The result was a night of mayhem and death that tarnished the whole town's reputation.

Just two years later, General Stricker was serving under General Smith. Sent out with a brigade to slow down the British land attack and buy time to strengthen the city defenses, Stricker handled the assignment with enviable patience and skill. He created one of the memorable moments for the Baltimore defenders at the Battle of North Point. In spite of his early war lapses, General Stricker won an honored place among the memorial portraits of the leading 1814 defenders.

"The Lord Bless King George, convert him, and take him to heaven as we want no more of him."

When General Smith heard the news he immediately ordered three thousand of his best militiamen, Baltimore's Third Brigade under the command of fifty-five-year-old Brigadier General John Stricker (1759–1825), to meet the threat brewing out on Patapsco Neck. At about 3 p.m., the brigade marched down Baltimore Street with flags flying, bands playing, and crowds cheering. The troops headed east on the Philadelphia Road to North Point Road. Arriving at a narrow part of the peninsula at about 8 p.m., they bedded down for the night in and around the Methodist Meeting House. A unit of riflemen advanced another two miles east and set up a skirmish line near a blacksmith shop. About one hundred forty mounted dragoons trotted a mile farther east to Gorsuch's Farm and set up vedettes, peering nervously into the darkness for any British activity.

As the Americans spent a restless night waiting for their invaders, British tars in the fleet faced a difficult task. Beginning at 3 a.m., they had to row almost five thousand soldiers and sailors with equipment and supplies to shore in small craft of all sorts. The invaders swarmed up the low bluffs at North Point, all the while facing possible ambush in unfamiliar enemy territory.

British Army commander Major General Robert Ross, confidently cautious as always, was leading his light infantry up the North Point Road by 7 a.m. The main column of soldiers, sailors, and black Corps of Colonial Marines were supported by four pieces of light artillery. These troops carried three days' rations, eighty rounds of ammunition, one blanket, an extra shirt, and pair of shoes. The plan was to quickly march the fifteen miles to Baltimore, brushing aside the Yankee militia in the process, punish the renegade city, and return to the ships before the issued rations ran out. Shallow draft support barges would shadow the soldiers along the shore of the peninsula.

The advanced British troops soon encountered the Todd House. Three mounted sentries who had been stationed there had hurriedly ridden north to warn their comrades as soon as they saw the British troops had landed. The now-empty house and some outbuildings were summarily burned and

A courier stationed at the Todd House gallops north to warn Baltimore that the British fleet had anchored at Old Road Bay off North Point early on September 11, 1814.

the Todds were forced to live in a granary for two years thereafter, until another house, still standing today on the same foundation, was built.

About three miles from North Point, the light infantry passed a "precipitately abandoned" and unfinished earthwork. Lieutenant Gleig, marching with the light infantry, was impressed that the trenches "showed a considerable degree of science" and "if completed, might have been maintained by a determined force against very superior numbers." General Ross surmised that the defenders might have been close at hand. Stopping briefly at the nearby Shaw House (the foundation of which still survives), he marched his light infantry slowly up the road prepared for a fight as the rest of his column caught up.

Ross, again accompanied by the notorious Rear Admiral George Cockburn, stopped for a late breakfast at the Gorsuch House, another American outpost. The meal was interrupted when three recently captured American dragoons were brought in for questioning. Lieutenant Gleig remembered that these "young gentlemen volunteers . . . being little accustomed to such service . . . had suffered themselves to be surprised . . ." They boasted to Ross that twenty thousand men were waiting to fight the invaders, and the general was reported to have said, "I don't care if it rains militia." Within the hour, British fortunes would take a dramatic turn in a thicket known as Godly Wood.

As the British marched north toward Baltimore, Major General Robert Ross and some advanced troops stopped at the Shaw House to wait for the main column to catch up. Local tradition holds that a British lieutenant tried to kiss Eleanor Shaw, a daughter of Mr. Thomas Shaw. She broke free and jumped out of a second-story window to escape her pursuer. General Ross allegedly ordered the officer back to the ships.

The Fight in Godly Wood

"The temple of God—of peace and goodwill towards men—vibrated with the groans of the wounded and dying."

—British Captain James Scott describes the suffering at the Methodist Meeting House, September 12, 1814

Anxious horsemen had galloped into the meeting house encampment with news that a large British force was landing. Calm and deliberate, the veteran American General Stricker was preparing his militia for a stand. Any fight would be a holding action, but Stricker wanted the enemy to know his defenders meant business. With rumors of possible British flank attacks coming from the water, the general's advance units, the eyes of his force, were falling back to the main defensive line. Stricker formed his regiments in a battle line along a zigzag rail fence at the edge of the Bouldin Farm clearing. He sent out Major Richard K. Heath with one hundred fifty Marylanders armed with rifles and muskets and a single cannon to re-form the skirmish line. Then, Stricker and his brigade waited patiently for the enemy.

Stretching all the way across the narrows of Patapsco Neck with another reinforcing line behind them, the two ranks of Sunday soldiers were receiving a crash course in military reality. These hours of watching, waiting, and lolling with comrades would soon be punctuated by confused and deadly bursts of combat.

British General Ross had no idea that a major American force was so close. As he rejoined his advance force of light infantry, firing suddenly broke

In this romanticized depiction, Major General Ross is shown falling into the arms of another officer while a Congreve rocket passes overhead.

Opposite: This 1820 hand-colored aquatint depicts an American officer pausing at the spot where Major General Robert Ross was mortally wounded during a skirmish before the Battle of North Point, on the North Point Road in Godly Wood.

133

out ahead. Ross and Cockburn galloped through the deep Godly Wood to investigate the fracas. Heath's small band of skirmishers was soon pushed aside, but there were casualties on both sides. One of them changed the course of the entire campaign.

Admiral Cockburn later reported to his commander, Vice Admiral Alexander Cochrane, what happened next: "[o]ur advanced Guard . . . soon obliged the Enemy to run off with the utmost precipitation . . . but it is with the most heartfelt sorrow I have to add in this Short and desultory Skirmish my gallant and valued Friend the Major General received a Musquet Ball through his arm into his Breast which proved fatal. . . Our Country Sire has lost in him one of its best and bravest Soldiers."

Lieutenant Gleig, rushing to the front with the riflemen, reflected the shock that quickly embraced the entire army: "[t]he General's horse, without its rider, and with saddle and housings stained in blood, came plunging onwards . . . In a few moments we . . . beheld General Ross laid by the side of the road, under a canopy of blankets and apparently in the agonies of death . . . It is impossible to conceive the effect which this melancholy spectacle produced throughout the army. All eyes were turned upon him as we passed, and a sort of involuntary groan ran from rank to rank, from the front to the rear of the column."

No one will ever be certain who shot General Ross. Later some gave the credit to two teenage leatherworking apprentices, volunteer riflemen attached to Aisquith's Rifle Company in the 5th Maryland Regiment. Daniel Wells and Henry McComas were killed in the skirmish and both of the young martyrs, epitomizing the sacrifice of the Baltimore defenders, were honored by and reburied under a 20-foot obelisk completed in the east side of the city during the 1870s. Others claim Aquila Randall shot Ross. A monument to him marks the spot where Randall died. With Ross's death, Colonel Arthur Brooke (1772–1843), a 42-year-old Anglo-Irish veteran of the 44th Regiment of Foot, suddenly found himself in command. Buried in the main column two miles behind the action, he rushed to the front and discovered a solid line of enemy troops standing firm just ahead. Ordering up his cannons and rockets and pausing to let his tired troops rest and eat, Brooke gazed across the 500-yard Bouldin Farm clearing at the American position. He decided that the Yankee left, anchored on Bread and Cheese Creek, was vulnerable. At about 2:30 p.m., the colonel sent the 4th Regiment of Foot into the woods to stay under cover as it went after that left flank. The British started an artillery and rocket duel

Thomas Ruckle, an Irish immigrant house painter who fought at the Battle of North Point with the 5th Maryland Regiment, painted this panorama of the September 12 clash not long after the event. Brigadier General John Stricker and his staff are on the North Point Road in the foreground as American cannons and infantry in the background fire at the long line of British attackers at the far side of the open field.

when a passing breeze swept away the cloud for a moment that either force became visible to the other . . . The flashes of the enemy's muskets alone served as an object to aim at."

With the two lines blasting away at each other, the 4th Foot managed to get some traction on the American left flank. The 51st Maryland Regiment, sent over to protect the position, soon broke and ran, taking a portion of the 39th Regiment on the fence line with it. Now flanked, General Stricker was forced to withdraw from the field, but the 5th and 27th Regiments on the right of the fence line left the contest only begrudgingly. They retreated, marching in ranks and turning to fire more volleys at their advancing enemy. The Americans lost a cannon and about fifty men were captured, but the much-criticized militia had shown considerable spirit and bravery. As long as they lived, these Baltimore defenders would proudly commemorate their courage at what became known as the Battle of North Point.

As General Stricker's Brigade slowly retreated to their main defenses, Colonel Brooke decided his fatigued troops, up since at least 3 a.m., would stay put for the night. They had chased the Yankees off the field of battle but had suffered more casualties than their opponents; almost 350 dead, wounded, and missing compared to 213 Americans. One British casualty, General Ross, was irreplaceable. Colonel Brooke, described as a good regimental commander, was still feeling his way as an army commander on the night of September 12, 1814.

The rain came after the battle, a driving, persistent downpour that soaked everyone to the skin. Even more disheartening for the British was being bivouacked near the Methodist Meeting House, which became a makeshift field hospital. British Captain James Scott was particularly touched by the suffering all around him: "The accents of human woe floated upon the ear, and told a melancholy tale of the ebbing tide of human life." One young American, James Haines McCulloh, Jr., a July 1814 graduate of medical school, risked a trip through the enemy lines that night looking for his militiaman father. He entered the Meeting House and described the scene he encountered: "on not finding my father—I instantly requested permission to go over the field of battle . . . In the course of a few hours I had the wounded brought in . . . which were 28 in number—2 of these died in the course of the night after I dressed them and extracted the balls one of which was a grape [shot]." Dr. McCulloh eventually did find his father, the Collector for the Port of Baltimore, recovering with a leg shattered by a British ball.

with the six American guns and set a nearby cabin ablaze. Thousands of soldiers, sailors, and marines methodically lined up in the open field amidst the Bouldin Farm's haystacks. They then launched a frontal attack on the American militia who were waiting and watching behind the rail fence.

Lieutenant Gleig described the 3 p.m. assault: "The British soldiers moved forward with their accustomed fearlessness, and the Americans, with much apparent coolness, stood to receive them . . . Volley upon volley having been given, we were now advanced within less than twenty yards of the American line; yet such was the denseness of the smoke, that it was only

Insurmountable Defenses

"If I took the place, I should have been the greatest man in England. If I lost, my military character was gone forever."

—Colonel Arthur Brooke, writing in his diary, September 1814

Colonel Brooke was stunned. After a miserable, rainy night for both sides, Brooke had roused his men at 5:30 a.m. As they marched toward Baltimore stripped of their packs, blankets, and extra gear, the army hacked a path through trees felled to slow their advance. They could hear the bombardment in the harbor as they approached the Yankee earthworks on Hampstead Hill during the morning of September 13. And now they were gazing at an amazing sight.

Colonel Brooke commandeered a good view out of a second-story window. He was staring at thousands of soldiers and scores of cannon behind stout earthworks nearly as far as the eye could see. The hills ahead were teeming with American militia in a display of colorful uniforms, and all were determined to stand and fight for the city behind them. Brooke thought there might be fifteen thousand men with one hundred twenty cannons on the heights, more than triple his own force. His heart undoubtedly sank when he saw the bloody task ahead for his troops, even with the support of a harbor assault that he expected from the Royal Navy.

Probing for a weakness, the colonel found the enemy "left was not so secure, and that by making a night attack, I might gain his flank, and get into his rear, so came to a resolution of attacking him in two columns, whilst a

---

The Methodist Meeting House served as an American encampment the night before and a British camp the night after the Battle of North Point. It was also a haven for the suffering wounded of both sides after the fighting.

third was to make a feint to the right." A chess game ensued with General Smith countering Brooke's every move. Smith, watching the whole scene unfold from high on Hampstead Hill, later reported to the new Secretary of War James Monroe: "He [the enemy] manoeuvred during the morning towards our left, as if with the intention of making a circuitous march . . . Gens. [William H.] Winder [having joined the defense as a subordinate commander] and [John] Stricker were ordered to adapt their movements to those of the enemy, so as to baffle this supposed intention."

After 1 p.m., Smith observed Colonel Brooke concentrating his soldiers directly in front of the strong American defenses: "[p]ushing his advance to within a mile of us, driving in our videttes and showing an intention of attacking us that evening. I immediately drew Gens. Winder and Stricker . . . to the right of the enemy, with the intention of their falling on his right or rear should he attack me."

As night fell and the drenching rain continued, Colonel Brooke knew he had been checkmated. Smith was brief and to the point: "To this movement [of Winder's and Stricker's brigade] and to the strength of my defenses . . . I am induced to attribute his retreat." Brooke held a war council and the always bellicose Admiral Cockburn pleaded to storm the defenses. But then a message arrived from Admiral Cochrane. The Royal Navy was stymied out in the harbor and couldn't assist in the attack. Cochrane was gloomy, stating "it is for Colonel Brooke to consider . . . whether he has force sufficient to defeat so large a number . . . and to take the town."

North Point defender Thomas Ruckle captured a rich variety of uniforms in this painting of American militia gathering by the thousands on Hampstead Hill, digging entrenchments and awaiting the British attack that never came. British warships are in the distance and Fort McHenry is on the far right. The Philadelphia Road on the left points toward the North Point Battlefield several miles to the east.

The difficult decision to attack or withdraw was now squarely on the colonel's shoulders. Sitting alone in the gloom of a stormy night, Brooke had no stomach for high casualties with low odds of success. As the tense night wore on, the Americans watched the British fires. First Lieutenant Jacob Crumbaker stated he "could hear the hogs squeal as [the British] killed them in their camp." Crumbaker wrote that at 3 a.m. he saw some rockets "down the bay as a signal for the [British] land forces to retreat which they did in great haste." A young sanguine Lieutenant Gleig was sorely disappointed: "when the order was given to fall in, and we were all in high hopes of obtaining death or immortal honor, to our mortification we found the troops on the main road for a retreat." Writing later to the British secretary of state for war and the colonies, Colonel Brooke had a straightforward defense of his decision; "the capture of the town would not have been sufficient to the loss which might probably be sustained in storming the heights."

Defending the eastern approaches to Baltimore, thousands of American troops, private citizens, and slaves prepared a mile-long line of earthworks on high ground with Hampstead Hill at the center. Fort McHenry is on the right in the distance and British forces are to the left about a mile away. The attackers wisely chose not to test the formidable, well-defended earthworks.

Sarah Trotten was living in this house in 1814 when, according to local legend, the British invaders demanded a horse, cart, and some blankets. The Trottens later learned that the cart was used to transport the body of Major General Robert Ross to a small boat, which then carried his corpse out to the fleet.

Stories abounded, good and bad, after the brief British visit to the Patapsco Neck. The English left a note of thanks after "a crowd of stragglers" broke into 5th Maryland Regiment commander Colonel Joseph Sterret's house and destroyed his extensive wine cellar. Other enemy soldiers purportedly took a horse, cart, and blankets to carry General Ross's body to a boat for conveyance back to the fleet, then dutifully returned the confiscated items.

As the British retreated past the bodies of American riflemen still hanging in trees where they had been killed while waiting to ambush their enemies, they had fifty-three prisoners in tow, the only tangible result of their costly invasion. Some American cavalrymen harassed the retreating army and captured a few Englishmen, but the victors were more interested in retrieving their dead. Two wagonloads of recovered bodies from the North Point battle were solemnly laid out on Hampstead Hill for identification by grieving families. About a dozen were never identified. Local Quakers interred them in a nearby potter's field.

A Fort Defended

"We were like pigeons tied by the legs to be shot at."

—Captain Joseph Hopper Nicholson, commander of the Baltimore Fencibles Militia stationed at Fort McHenry, September 1814

As he stood on the bridge of the 74-gun H.M. ship-of-the-line *Albion*, studying Baltimore's harbor defenses through his spyglass, Vice Admiral Sir Alexander Forrester Inglis Cochrane, the 56-year-old commander of His Majesty's North American Squadron, was confident of a quick victory. The September 13 dawn sky revealed sunken obstacles, hastily erected earthen gun batteries, and, in the center of it all, the low profile of a brick fort masked with tall trees. The admiral had a score of warships at his command. Blowing a hole through these defenses should take only a few hours.

Besides the terror of his rocket-launching ship *Erebus*, Cochrane counted on his bomb vessels. The five heavy, mortar-bearing ships had names worthy of horsemen from the apocalypse: *Terror, Volcano, Meteor, Devastation,* and *Aetna.* They were state-of-the-art weapon platforms, launching ten- to thirteen-inch exploding shells weighing as much as 200 pounds. The distinctive low "carrumph" of the initial mortar blast would be followed by the high arching flight of up to two miles of the sparking, sputtering shell and, finally, another low-pitched explosion as the shell spread shrapnel over its target. The bombs were inaccurate and unpredictable—often exploding prematurely or not at all, but one lucky shot could create havoc.

Anyone at the receiving end of this shower of death and destruction would be sorely tested. Fort McHenry's small garrison was reinforced by hundreds of local militia who endured the bombardment in the moats and water batteries in and around the star fort. Major General James Wilkinson pointed out that, "[t]he defense of Fort McHenry was of no ordinary character, for the passive resistance of danger is the test of valor."

This detailed pen, ink, and watercolor sketch shows defenses on Lazaretto Point *(near left)* with a string of gun barges, the steamboat *Chesapeake,* and scuttled merchant vessels blocking the Baltimore harbor entrance. Fort McHenry is on the right. Note the fort flag with an anchor and circle of stars. British warships are firing with support ships in the background. A sloop flying an American flag on the left of the British fleet is the truce boat. This circa October 1814 watercolor by Lieutenant Henry Fisher of the 27th Maryland Regiment is one of the most important renderings of the British bombardment known.

Alfred Jacob Miller (1810–74), famous for his frontier paintings, is credited with producing this image of the Fort McHenry bombardment as viewed from Camp Lookout (now Leone-Riverside Park) in 1828–29. He correctly shows the locations of Forts Babcock and Covington. His father, George Miller, a private in Captain John Berry's Washington Artillery, was at Fort McHenry during the fighting.

Opposite page: This painting, attributed to Francis Guy, is believed to be contemporary to the bombardment of Fort McHenry, which is depicted to the left. In the center is Fort Babcock and to the right is Fort Covington, both were built to defend Fort McHenry from naval flanking attacks. In the distance can be seen the British fleet. The view is to the southeast looking down Ferry Branch toward the Patapsco River. Painting from the collection of Stiles T. Colwill.

Fort commandant Major George Armistead had to hunker down with his garrison. None of his cannons could reach the bulk of the British squadron, which was anchored out of range. One lucky shot ripped through the mainsail of the H.M. schooner *Cockchafer* and another hulled a bomb vessel wounding a sailor. Armistead had requested two 10-inch mortars from Washington. The mortars were sent, but without carriages, fuses, or shells, so they sat useless in the fort. Even worse, after the capital was occupied and burned, government officials wanted some of Fort McHenry's armament back. General Smith told Washington that it could have the cannons but Baltimore owned the carriages. The request was quietly dropped.

With few offensive options, a pressed Major Armistead had to keep the British ships out of the inner harbor at all costs. If the British broke through, Baltimore defenses would be vulnerable and the city could be bombarded into submission. Damaging losses might include the new U.S. frigate *Java*, launched but not yet fitted with rigging and sails. Her chosen skipper, Lake Erie hero Captain Oliver Hazard Perry, was in town and promising to set her ablaze rather than give her up. But clearly there was little he could do as the British ships were anchored out of range of the fort's guns.

The bombardment began at 6 a.m. on the rainy morning of September 13 and continued for an entire day and night. Lieutenant Gleig watched the first shot, "…a solitary report, accompanied by the ascension of a small bright spark into the sky." It took about eight minutes for a bomb vessel to load and fire a mortar, so an estimated 1,500–1,800 shells were thrown at the city defenses.

It was an unrelenting sound-and-light show that both terrified and fascinated Baltimore. A local newspaper reported that "[t]he attack on Fort McHenry . . . was distinctly seen from Federal Hill and from the tops of Houses which were covered with men, women and children." A civilian watched from Federal Hill. "The night of Tuesday [September 13] and [early] morning of Wednesday presented the whole awful spectacle of shot and shells, and rockets, shooting and bursting through the air." The Reverend James Stevens described the dramatic scene to his sister. "I do not feel able to paint out the distress and confution half as it was with us to see the wagons, carts and drays all in hast moving the people, and the poorer sort with what they could cary

Sailing Master John Adams Webster, commanding seventy-five men from the U.S. Chesapeake Flotilla at Fort Babcock, saved Fort McHenry from a flank attack during the early morning of September 14, 1814.

Commodore Barney's Sailing Master

"During the firing of the enemy, I could distinctly see their barges by the explosion of their cannon which was a great guide to me to fire by."

—Sailing Master John Adams Webster describing his repulse of the enemy attack on Fort McHenry's west flank, September 14, 1814

John Adams Webster (1789–1877) was the type of capable, experienced, and loyal able-bodied seaman that every skipper needs to keep his ship in tip-top condition. Joshua Barney, a demanding captain with decades of experience, depended on Webster and was handsomely rewarded.

During the War of 1812, Webster served with Barney on the privateer *Rossie*, which early in the contest had brought back many prizes. His next assignment was the U.S. Chesapeake Flotilla. Webster commanded a gun barge throughout the Patuxent River campaign then marched overland with the flotillamen to Bladensburg. Protecting Barney's right flank during the last desperate stages of the battle, Webster lost his horse and had his hat shot off during the retreat.

Back in action without his wounded skipper a few weeks later at Fort Babcock, John Adams Webster again distinguished himself by protecting Fort McHenry's flank. As an unexpected complication, in the midst of a British attack, he had to defend himself against one of his own sailors, "an obstinate Englishman" determined to blow up the American powder magazine.

Webster's shoulder was permanently injured in the fracas, but he continued to serve as a captain in the revenue service for decades more, on one occasion losing his left thumb fighting pirates near the mouth of the Chesapeake Bay.

A Defiant Rooster

"A propitious omen"

—Sailors responding to a rooster in the rigging of the U.S. corvette *Saratoga* during the Battle of Plattsburgh, New York, September 11, 1814

The legends of chickens in battle go back a long way. Superstitious Romans reportedly kept sacred chickens on board ships to predict the outcome of battles. When they ate grain thrown to them the omen for a victory was favorable. One Roman consul, Pulcher, watched his sacred chickens lose their appetites and threw their cage overboard reportedly exclaiming, "If they won't eat, let them drink!" His fate, of course, was sealed, and he lost the battle.

Fort McHenry had its own resident rooster belonging to a defender named Henry Barnhart.

During the height of the bombardment, the rooster was struck in the foot by some shrapnel and flew up onto the parapet, even perhaps to the flagstaff itself, all the time cockadoodledooing his defiance.

One amused observer vowed that if he survived the shot and shell he would order pound cake for the brave rooster. When the danger had passed, the gentleman was good to his word. He had the cake delivered and fed it to the rooster with great ceremony.

and there children on there backs flying for there lives . . . the Bumbs lite and burst on the Shore at which explosion the hole town and several miles would shake." Lieutenant John Harris thought the bombardment was "the handsomest sight I ever saw . . . to see the bums and rockets flying and the firing from our three forts . . . it was much handsomer at night than in the day."

About four hundred shells fell in and around Fort McHenry. Considering the number of defenders present (about a thousand with sixty cannon), casualties were relatively modest: four killed and twenty-four wounded. An unfortunate woman carrying supplies to the troops was cut in half by a rocket. A runaway slave, Frederick Hall (also known as Private William Williams [see chapter 4]), who had joined the 38th U.S. Infantry, was mortally wounded by a piece of shrapnel. One bomb crashed through the roof of the powder maga-

zine but failed to explode. Having narrowly dodged a disaster, a chastened Armistead had the barrels of gunpowder scattered around the fort walls.

After eighteen hours of rocket, shot, and shell, Admiral Cochrane ordered some warships to move closer to the fortifications, but they were driven back by intense Yankee fire. Cochrane then tried to flank Fort McHenry and break the impasse. He ordered Captain Charles Napier to lead two hundred men on twenty-two barges with an armed schooner up the Ferry Branch of the Patapsco. Some Americans thought they saw ladders, designed to scale the fortifications, onboard the British vessels. What they probably saw were rocket launchers, an unfamiliar weapon of war. As the force quietly rowed up the branch in the rainy darkness, the attackers had no idea they would soon face about fifty of Commodore Joshua Barney's Chesapeake flotillamen led by Sailing Master John Adams Webster. They were manning Fort Babcock, the "Sailor's Battery," a 4-foot high, wood plank–faced earthwork with six 18-pound cannons that was protecting Fort McHenry's west flank.

Sailing Master Webster later described the British flank attack during the night: "I could hear a splashing in the water . . . we were convinced it was the noise of the muffled oars of the British barges . . . it was raining fast . . . I trained the guns and opened on them . . . a rapid firing followed from the barges . . . I could distinctly hear the balls from our guns strike the barges. My men stated to me that they could hear the shrieks of the wounded." The Fort McHenry gun crews, looking for a target after enduring an entire day of bombs and rockets, joined in for about two hours. The attackers were not only discovered but forced to quickly return to their ships.

With Colonel Brooke and his army retreating to their troop ships anchored near North Point, Admiral Cochrane called off the bombardment at 7 a.m. on September 14. A Virginia volunteer, Private John Leadley Dagg, spoke for the thousands watching from Hampstead Hill: "At the first dawn, every eye was directed towards the Fort, to see whether the American banner still waved there, and when the morning mists had sufficiently dispersed, we were filled with exultation at beholding the stars and stripes still floating in the breeze." As the British prepared to weigh anchor, the fort's storm flag was lowered and the large garrison flag raised. In the fort, Private Isaac Munroe of the Baltimore Fencibles described the scene with some irony: "At dawn . . . our morning gun was fired, the flag hoisted, Yankee Doodle played, and we all appeared in full view of the formidable and mortified enemy, who calculated upon our surrender in 20 minutes after the commencement of the action."

British Midshipman Robert J. Barrett saw the morning quite differently: "In truth, it was a galling spectacle to behold. And, as the last vessel spread her canvas to the wind, the Americans hoisted a splendid and superb ensign on their battery, and fired at the same time a gun of defiance."

There was also a contingent of three Americans who had watched the bombardment and the departure of the British warships from an unusual position—aboard a Royal Navy frigate anchored with the British fleet. Among them was Francis Scott Key. His reaction to the dramatic events left an indelible mark on American history (see chapter 7).

Victory . . . but the Raids Continue

"Rejoice, ye People of America! Baltimore has nobly fought your Battles! Thank God and thank the People of Baltimore!"

—Baltimore *Niles' Weekly Register,* October 1, 1814

Baltimore was ecstatic over its hard-earned victory. Church bells chimed, cannon and musket blasts echoed through the city, crowds assembled to cheer the defenders, and taverns rolled out kegs of spirits. But the town fathers, led by General Smith, weren't quite ready to take their bows. The British had a habit of returning to the scene of their attacks for another round, and the ramshackle, pieced-together city defenses needed attention. The handsome, debonair French immigrant architect Maximilian Godefroy was hired to beef up the entrenchments anchored on Hampstead Hill. (Godefroy later designed America's first battle monument, which is located at the intersection of Calvert and Fayette Streets in Baltimore.)

After sailing out of the Patapsco River, Admiral Cochrane's fleet anchored at Drum Point at the mouth of the Patuxent on September 18. Lieutenant Gleig saw preparations for a long voyage all around him: " . . . boats resorted in great number for water. Cattle and sheep were likewise purchased . . . flour which had been captured was converted into biscuit." At dawn the next day, several sailors were flogged for drunkenness, two were hung for desertion, and then most of the fleet weighed anchor. Some ships, with the remains of General Ross, headed for Nova Scotia; others, with Captain Parker's body, for Bermuda.

Amid the rejoicing in Baltimore, the Chesapeake region stayed on alert for more damaging raids. The reason was clear. British soldiers and sailors who remained in the Chesapeake still needed supplies. Enemy vessels sailed

The Saga of the Sacred Vestments

"The Sacred Vestments thrown and dragged here and there, the vessels consecrated to the service of God profaned . . ."

—Jesuit Brother Joseph P. Mobberly describing a British raid on St. Inigoes Manor, St. Mary's County, October 31, 1814

British depredations reached a new low when a Jesuit mission was attacked in the fall of 1814. St. Inigoes Manor, a Jesuit enclave on the St. Mary's River that dated to the origins of Maryland, was visited by a raiding party from H.M. sloop *Saracen* on Halloween. The Manor was an important food source for Georgetown College (now University) in Washington, so the raiders had many sheep and cattle to take back to their ship. What happened next, however, appalled local Brother Joseph Mobberly, who described their actions in the priests' chapel in horrifying detail: ". . . the Holy Altar stripped naked, the tabernacle carried off and the most adorable Sacrament of the altar borne away in the hands of the wicked." He calculated the cost at $1,033.70.

The Jesuits were prepared to chalk up their loss to the awfulness of war. But much to their surprise, the offending British Lieutenant William Hancock, in command of the raid, again appeared under a flag of truce on November 18. Hancock, under orders from his commander, Captain Alexander Dixie of the *Saracen*, delivered a letter of apology to the priests and the other St. Inigoes residents. He acknowledged the robbery, returned the pillaged holy articles, and handed Brother Mobberly a bill to the government of England for 22 pounds, 6 shillings, and 9 pence sterling along with a $9 gold piece. Apparently Lieutenant Hancock was then sent back to England for punishment.

The St. Inigoes Manor and farm on St. Mary's River was looted on October 31, 1814, by a British raiding party. Sheep and cattle were taken as well as sacramental objects from the chapel in the Jesuit priests' house. This 1856 painting of the manor house shows outbuildings and a windmill on Priests Point. To the right is a 1930s detail of what the manor house looked like before it was destroyed by fire in 1872.

to Tangier Island and local planters braced for the next shock. It came in the form of a raid up the St. Mary's River on September 27. Local militia attacked two unlucky British barges plundering at Porto Bello Plantation: "... we commenced a fire, they [British] held up their hands and begged for mercy ... Out of the first boat we got ten prisoners. Of the one [boat] that got off three were got, two fell overboard."

Punishing raids continued throughout October on the Virginia side of the Potomac. Plundering, burning, spiriting away of crops and slaves, and chasing militia was the usual routine. But now the Americans, angry and frustrated, were showing more and more spunk.

Amidst all the trouble, Joshua Barney, sufficiently recovered from his Bladensburg wounds, showed up at Hampton Roads commanding a schooner loaded with British prisoners. As part of his parole agreement after being captured at Bladensburg, Barney exchanged his prisoners for captured Americans, one for one. His parole obligations were now complete.

That fall, the British seemed to be everywhere. As most of the remaining fleet departed for New Orleans and a legendary and lopsided defeat at the hands of Andrew Jackson, barges and raiding parties appeared in the Choptank River. A whole regiment, one thousand men, started building barracks on Tilghman Island, collecting every cow for miles around. Protected by a small squadron, four ships, a brig, and two schooners, it looked like these unwanted squatters were settling into winter quarters. On October 27, British raiders crossed the Bay and attacked Tracys Landing and four days later Kirbys Wind Mill, both in Anne Arundel County. Militia skirmished with the enemy and were defeated at Tracys Landing, but successfully fought them off with casualties on both sides in what locals now call "The Battle of the Wind Mill."

December was ushered in with a foray up Virginia's Rappahannock River. Winter was coming on and British Captain Robert Barrie knew the Yankee militia wanted to go home. He wanted to keep his enemy "constantly on the alert, which in this Country at this advanced season of the year is most harassing Service." Barrie meant business when he started cannonading Tappahannock, sending in five hundred men including the now-veteran, home-grown Colonial Marines. Firing rockets to scare off the militia, the raiders torched many of the public buildings. Virginia Militia General John Hartwell Cocke was impressed with the Colonial Marines but condemned the results of their visit. "Three companies, of about 50 each, of negroes in uniform and apparently well trained ... They were said to be Virginia & Maryland negroes, trained at Tangier Islands ... There has been much wanton destruction of private property here ... and one deed of damnation has been performed which [out]does all their former atrocities—The family Vault of the Ritchies was broken open and the Coffins searched—I have seen the shocking spectacle."

Captain Barrie reported that the "Court House [in Tappahannock] was consumed without molestation from the Enemy though he frequently shewed himself with increased Force." The troubles peaked on December 6, when Barrie chased after six hundred militiamen and two cannons at North Farnham Church. "While the Main Body of the Troops were halted at the Church, I ... dispatched ... Marines ... with part of the new raised Colonial Corps [Marines] to release a number of slaves ... succeeding in releasing Twenty Negroes, several of whom ... [were] found in the Woods handcuffed round the Trees." The raid collected seventy slaves with no British casualties although twelve soldiers got "beastly Drunk [and] ... in consequence [were] lost in Wood and left behind." Desertion continued to be a problem for the British. As many as three hundred men had managed to disappear into the tidewater landscape since 1813.

After a daunting year, the Americans were not looking forward to 1815. They had no way of knowing that the treaty, signed by the British at the end of December, would be ratified by both sides in the coming year—putting an end to the devastating raids in the Chesapeake region.

During an early December 1814 raid on Tappahannock, Virginia, British looting reached new heights. One barge was stuffed with a large staircase clock clapped upon a few geese to keep them from escaping along with a bundle of books, some cabbages, a feather bed, and a small cask of peach brandy.

7 Peace, Jubilation, and Memory
1815

Baltimore's Pride

"As you look at her [Chasseur], you may easily figure . . . that she is about to rise out of the water and fly in the air, seeming to set so lightly upon it."

—Baltimore *Niles' Weekly Register*, April 15, 1815

A thrill spread through Baltimore as reports filtered in and signal flags went up on Federal Hill. Lookouts had spotted the sleek and stream-lined *Chasseur*, one of the city's famous privateers. As the clipper with her spreading sails came into sight, majestically entering the Baltimore harbor in the late afternoon of Saturday, March 18, 1815, clusters of townspeople gathered on shore to catch a glimpse. This was the brig-rigged schooner *Chasseur*, the Chesapeake's foremost high seas predator, soon to be rechristened *Pride of Baltimore*. Cannon salutes and a cheering crowd at her home port of Fells Point would punctuate the approaching nightfall.

This Baltimore haven for privateers could claim that during the amazing events of the previous year it had helped to stave off defeat. *Chasseur* and her resolute sister ships had boldly carried the war to faraway places throughout the seas. Along with other privateers up and down the Atlantic coast, the civilian fleet had done more damage to British shipping than the small U.S. Navy. Navy warships actually performed better based on a ship-to-ship ratio, but there were many more privateers than U.S. Navy warships.

Preceding spread: During a beautiful sunset on the Patapsco River on March 18, 1815, jubilant citizens line the shore to welcome one of Baltimore's most successful privateers home from her last cruise during the War of 1812. The brig-rigged *Chasseur*, commanded by the intrepid Captain Thomas Boyle and soon to be named the "Pride of Baltimore" for her exploits, is exchanging salutes as she passes Fort McHenry. Fells Point is just off the bow ahead and Federal Hill looms to the left of her stern.

Thomas Boyle: The Chesapeake's Greatest Privateer

"I do therefore, by virtue of the power and authority in me vested (possessing sufficient force), declare all the ports, harbors, bays, creeks, rivers, inlets, outlets, islands, and seacoast of the United Kingdom of Great Britain and Ireland in a state of strict and rigorous blockade."

—Captain Thomas Boyle declares his one-ship blockade of the British Isles, August 27, 1814

For a good privateer, success was all about speed. One unfortunate schooner, boldly named *Catch Me If You Can* and flying a pennant with the same challenging words, was caught and captured by the British in 1812. But most of the Baltimore privateers, better known as Baltimore clippers, manned by experienced captains and crews filled with bravado and braggadocio, easily overpowered unarmed opponents and outran warships.

Baltimore clippers were the height of cutting-edge sail technology. The daring, skilled, and resourceful Captain Thomas Boyle sailed the fastest vessels in the fleet—perhaps in the world. It seems that the Massachusetts-born Boyle had his sea legs firmly under him from the start. He was onboard by age ten and in command at sixteen. He was out quickly in 1812 and spent most of the war disrupting enemy shipping in the West Indies and off the Brazilian coast.

After a short career as a U.S. naval officer, Boyle snuck past blockaders in *Comet* and had twenty prizes in the West Indies by March of 1814. In July, he was at the helm of a new raider, *Chasseur*, heading for the enemy's homeland. Over the next few months, Boyle displayed his bravado by proclaiming a one-ship blockade of the entire British Isles. There is an earlier, similar proclamation signed "Paul Jones" dated May 17, 1814, but it is unclear if this was written by Boyle himself or by someone else that he copied from. Markets in London responded with some panic. Eighteen prizes were added to *Chasseur*'s impressive record right in His Majesty's own backyard.

"Wild Tom" Boyle turned for home with four enemy men-of-war in hot pursuit. Two brigs tried to trap him as he "edged down upon one of them . . . fired a shot to him, displayed the Yanky flag, hauled upon a wind, and outsailed them both with ease." *Chasseur* defeated the H.M. schooner *St. Lawrence* on yet another cruise near Cuba in early 1815. Boyle and his spirited crew returned to their home port in triumph, winning the title "Pride of Baltimore" for their plucky vessel. One of *Chasseur*'s integrated crew was a black seaman named George Roberts. The retired gunner lived long enough to be celebrated and photographed as an "Old Defender." When he died at age ninety, the amiable and humble Mr. Roberts was remembered as "a man whose patriotism, good sense and high moral character have won for him many friends for whom the news of his death will cause heartfelt sorrow."

George Roberts served as a gunner in the integrated crew on board the privateer *Chasseur* during the War of 1812. Roberts survived until the 1860s and had his photograph taken as a dignified and honored 1812 defender.

Baltimore privateer *Surprise* is shown in this undated watercolor capturing a prize. Note the tears in sails and rigging hanging in the water of the pursued vessel. *Surprise* reportedly captured twenty prizes in one month.

Chasseur and her skipper, Thomas Boyle (1775–1825), had been cruising in the Caribbean since December, searching for prey among the British merchant fleet. With Captain Boyle at the helm of one of the fastest vessels in the world, the privateer had seized seventeen prizes. Among her victims was *Chasseur*'s greatest war victory, the 14-gun H.M. schooner *St. Lawrence*. It was unusual for a privateer to capture a warship, but *Chasseur* was no ordinary privateer. The Americans had the same number of guns but a larger crew eager and ready for battle. In a bloody fifteen-minute collision not far from Havana, Cuba, the Yankees seized the British warship on February 26, 1815.

Precise dates did not matter much in that age of slower travel and communication. After a treaty was signed by both the American and British peace commissions in Ghent (today's Belgium) and then ratified by England in late December 1814, it was sent on its way to America for ratification as the fighting in the Chesapeake and elsewhere simmered on. In fact, on January 16, British Captain John Clavell assured his commander, Rear Admiral George Cockburn, that "every exertion shall be used by myself and the Ships under my Orders for the Annoyance and Destruction of the Enemy's Trade in the Rivers within the Capes of the Chesapeake."

The Odyssey of the *Atlas/St. Lawrence*

"People who handle dangerous weapons must expect wounds and Death."

—Commodore Edward Preble, 1804

Engagement between the American brig-rigged schooner *Chasseur* and H.M. schooner *St. Lawrence*, off Havana on February 26, 1815.

Men-of-war in the age of sail, no matter the size, were dangerous naval weapons. Battles on the water were particularly deadly. Cannons fired at close range created shrapnel-like splinters; sniping from ships masts and vicious hand-to-hand fighting resulted in high casualties and ghastly wounds. It was not a world for the faint of heart.

It was important for a swashbuckling skipper to get a "smart" ship, a dependable vessel that maneuvered well and could get the best of an enemy. For that reason, a captured ship with a good reputation was often recycled under the flag of its captor. One of the best examples was the schooner *Atlas*, built in 1808 at St. Michaels, Maryland. Sent to Philadelphia in 1810, *Atlas* became a very successful 13-gun privateer in 1812. She sailed between two enemy vessels, *Pursuit*

and *Planter*, laden with coffee, cocoa, and sugar, firing broadsides from both sides. Although seriously damaged herself, *Atlas* brought both prizes back to Philadelphia.

In 1813, the American privateer met British Admiral Sir George Cockburn and his squadron near Ocracoke Island, North Carolina. Captured, she was renamed as the 14-gun H.M. schooner *St. Lawrence*. In June of 1814, now operating back in the Chesapeake, she helped chase Joshua Barney's Chesapeake Flotilla into the Patuxent River. During the subsequent sharp fights in St. Leonard Creek, *St. Lawrence* was hit, run aground, and temporarily abandoned by her crew. Quickly

repaired, she was soon out with other warships in the Chesapeake capturing five American schooners.

The following year, as the war ended, *St. Lawrence* was back in the news. On February 26, near Havana, she was one of the many victims of the legendary privateer *Chasseur*. The short but destructive encounter left many casualties on both sides. *St. Lawrence*, again severely damaged, was carried back to Havana as an American prize. The much-traveled ship's wartime adventures were not over. Recaptured by the British after the war, she sailed to Bermuda where a British court, following the terms of the peace treaty, returned her to the Americans.

On January 12, a British raid on the Honga River in Dorchester County picked off six American vessels, one carrying 80,000 feet of wooden planking. A local militia lieutenant tried to negotiate a ransom but, when the British officer told him to bring thirty cattle in five minutes, the Yankee lieutenant quickly returned with about twenty armed companions instead. They drove the British off with musket fire and reclaimed the boats, smothering fires that had been set on two of them. By the end of that month, enemy raiders had captured and burned several vessels near the mouth of the Chesapeake Bay.

A February 6 cold snap brought ice to the Chesapeake while a raiding party from the British sloop *Dauntless* pillaged the little Eastern Shore town of Tobacco Stick (now Madison). After burning a few workboats and stealing some sheep, the raiders headed west for the open Bay and the western shore. Drifting ice forced them to the shelter of James Island, where they anchored for the night. The frosty morning found the vessel icebound, and American militia, led by Private Joseph Fookes Stewart, took full advantage. Climbing out on a mound of ice forced up by the wind and tide, they kept up relentless musket fire for two hours and forced the overwhelmed intruders to surrender. Thus the Battle of the Ice Mound was added to War of 1812 lore. Two officers, thirteen seamen, three Royal Marines, and two black servants were led off into captivity; the tender *Dauntless* and its contents were sold at public auction. Her carronade, commemorating the one-sided scuffle, is now part of a monument on Taylors Island.

A week later, hostile barges capped off the two years of British torment by running the privateer *Matchless* aground at Cape Henry. The last enemy warship, H.M. frigate *Orlando*, left the Chesapeake on March 10, but engagements continued on the high seas where news of the war's end was slow to reach the ships. "Old Ironsides," U.S. frigate *Constitution*, had bested H.M. frigate *Cyane* and H.M. sloop-of-war *Levant* off the coast of North Africa on February 20. U.S. sloop *Peacock* finally ended the fighting with a victory over East India Company Cruiser *Nautilus* in the Indian Ocean on June 30, 1815, over four months after the ratification of the Treaty of Ghent.

The last engagement of the war in Maryland took place on February 7, 1815. Known as the Battle of the Ice Mound, it was named for chunks of ice pressed by the tide and wind into a heap used as cover by Dorchester County militiamen as they shot at a British tender stuck in the frozen water. After two hours of relentless musket fire the British crew of twenty surrendered.

Peace and Jubilation

"The star-spangled banner of America and the red-cross flag of Britain displayed together at City Hall."

—The Baltimore *American & Commercial Daily Advertiser* reported on a Baltimore celebration, February 11, 1815

A circle, two rectangles, and a triangle were architecturally married into a fine mansion on an irregular Washington, D.C., lot. Together they became Colonel John Tayloe's stylish and innovative three-story brick home. Only blocks from the White House, its peculiar shape determined its name, the "Octagon." Built just as the U.S. capital was born, it served as a posh winter residence for Colonel Tayloe and his many children. Tayloe was a friend of George Washington's and an extremely wealthy planter who spent his summers at Mt. Airy Plantation on Virginia's Northern Neck. The Octagon House survived the destructive 1814 British visit because the Tayloes talked the French minister, who was their friend, into moving in. The minister flew the French flag over the house, thus making it official French territory with diplomatic immunity. After the President's House was burned, the Octagon served as a temporary residence for the first family while the damaged shell was restored.

Now, on the winter night of February 17, 1815, the house was aglow with light and crowded with noisy revelers. Punch flowed for guest and servant alike. Jean Pierre Sioussat (also known as "French John"), the White House doorkeeper who also looked after the presidential macaw, was reportedly hung over for two days after the party. There was patriotic music and dancing. Paul Jennings, President Madison's teenaged slave, treated everyone to a version of the "President's March" on his violin. Joseph Gales, Jr., the *National Intelligencer* editor, wrote that "among the members present were gentlemen of opposite politics, but lately arrayed against one another in continual conflict and fierce debate, now with elated spirits thanking God, and with softened hearts cordially felicitating with one another upon the joyful intelligence."

War had officially ended on the previous day. Peace negotiations had begun in August 1814, as the British were preparing to do their worst to the American Republic. The initial terms of peace were laid out in just ten days, but it took until Christmas before both sides agreed and the British ratified what came to be called the Treaty of Ghent. A fast British packet ship, *Favorite*, delivered the treaty with its American messenger to New York on February 11. The document reached Annapolis on February 13, and a post rider had it on Secretary of State James Monroe's desk the next day.

President Madison may have had misgivings about the treaty. After thousands of casualties, millions of dollars in property damage, several abortive invasions of Canada, unchecked ravages all over the Chesapeake and on the Niagara, most of the government buildings of the U.S. capital laid to waste, fierce Indian battles on the frontier, and threats of secession from New England states, the terms of the treaty called for a *status quo ante bellum*. Ratification meant returning to the same conditions as before the war. All of the blood and destruction had, on paper, accomplished nothing.

Depressed and confronting his personal failure, the president may have considered continuing the negotiations. Madison knew, however, that it would be next to impossible to get a better deal. Studying the document, he also realized that the terms of the treaty could have been much worse for the

United States. Besides, the support for "Mr. Madison's War" had dwindled to new lows. So, surrounded by the plush paneling of the Octagon's Round Room and buoyed by First Lady Dolley's always effervescent support, President Madison signed the treaty on Thursday, February 16, 1815. Surviving today as the museum home of the American Institute of Architects, the Octagon House had found its niche in American history.

As the news of the treaty spread, the entire country celebrated with a sense of jubilation and relief. The four-decade-old United States had emerged from the contest intact. In Washington, buildings were decked out in patriotic colors and the Stars and Stripes and the Union Jack flew together at city hall. Mayor James Blacke called for a "national demonstration of joy" and, as cannon salutes echoed through town, buildings, bedecked with candles and oil lamps, lit up the night.

Other towns celebrated in similar fashion. Baltimore rejoiced with its own version of Congreve rockets that pierced the sky. Alexandria called for a day of thanksgiving, then "brilliantly illuminated" its downtown. Norfolk chose a festive public dinner before lighting its lamps. Annapolitans used their prominent, illuminated State House as the centerpiece for cannon blasts, ringing bells, and grand bonfires. The Maryland *Gazette* reported, "In the midst of this scene of light stood the State House, conspicuous for its elevation and splendor. The Spacious Hall of this splendid building was decorated and honoured by a full length portrait of Washington as large as life, suspended in the centre of the inner dome."

Portsmouth and Richmond featured new crowd favorites, colored transparencies of patriotic scenes projected against buildings with the aid of gas lamps. Boston filled its streets with the choreographed peals of church bells. As the festivities spread through the nation, a special committee in Baltimore sent congratulations to their beleaguered president. Mr. Madison responded by thanking Baltimore for its "devotion to the public cause."

Everyone celebrated as the news of peace spread throughout the United States. Baltimore shot off fireworks that represented the dreaded Congreve rockets. In Annapolis, cannons saluted, bells rang, and great bonfires lit up public buildings. Maryland's capital may have also had fireworks, but the highlight was a great, full-length portrait of George Washington suspended from the center of the State House's inner dome.

Memory

BATTLE MONUMENT.

The Corner Stone of which was laid in Baltimore at the Solemnity of the 12.ʳ of Sepᵗ. 1815, in commemoration of the Defenders of Baltimore, who fell on the XII of Sepᵗ. 1814, at the Battle of North Point & the XIII during the Bombardment of Fort Mc Henry.

Published by S. C. Atkinson, for the Casket.

"It is a feast for the nation that we have an honourable Peace . . . We are all elated, and are to illuminate and proclaim aloud our grateful thanks."

—Lydia Hollingsworth, February 14, 1815

While most of the country put the war behind it, Baltimore set out to celebrate its battle victories and honor its 1814 heroes. Within a year of the Battle for Baltimore, a cornerstone was laid for a Battle Monument, the first substantial war memorial and the oldest commemorating the War of 1812 in the United States. The solemn ceremony accompanying the laying of that monument's cornerstone, on the first anniversary of the Battle of North Point, set a high bar for subsequent observances. The defenders, from top to bottom and fresh with memories of the fight, were there in force.

Six prancing white horses pulled a funeral car that was escorted by the spit-and-polish Baltimore Independent Blues, a company of the fighting 5th Maryland Regiment. The car bore a large rendering of the proposed monument. Rembrandt Peale (1778–1860), a renowned portrait painter who had

An impressive battle monument, the first erected in the United States commemorating the War of 1812, was begun with great pomp and ceremony only a year after the Battle for Baltimore. By the 1840s, Monument Square on Calvert Street became a favorite promenade in a fashionable neighborhood.

French immigrant J. Maximilian M. Godefroy, a prominent architect, designed the Battle Monument. After years in jail during and after the French Revolution, Godefroy sailed to the United States and had a successful career, designing several prominent Baltimore buildings.

militia, he had served as a civilian aide at the Battle of Bladensburg.

Key met with President Madison, who then met with Brigadier General John Mason, the commissary general of prisoners. They approved a mission to seek the release of Beanes and requested that Key accompany American Prisoner Exchange Agent John Stuart Skinner. Skinner had conducted many dealings with the British and was familiar with the commanding officers. After obtaining letters from British wounded attesting to the good treatment they had received at Bladensburg, Key and Skinner left Baltimore on a truce ship and sailed south to the British fleet near the mouth of the Potomac River. Boarding Vice Admiral Alexander Cochrane's flagship H.M. ship-of-the-line *Tonnant*, the party was greeted coldly by the senior British officers when the purpose of their mission was revealed.

At first General Ross was unwilling to release the doctor, but when shown the letters from wounded Englishmen lauding their medical treatment, the general and his naval colleagues agreed to let Beanes go. However, the doctor and the truce party were detained to prevent them from reporting the British plans to attack Baltimore, which they had been privy to. As the enemy fleet traveled north up the Bay, the three Americans were placed on H. M. frigate *Surprise* with their truce boat and crew towed behind. Before the battle commenced, Key, Skinner, and Dr. Beanes were transferred to the truce boat but kept under guard. There they unwittingly found themselves at the very center of the Battle for Baltimore. They and the truce boat were finally released on September 16, when they happily sailed for Baltimore over two days after the bombardment had stopped.

If not during the actual bombardment of Fort McHenry, then certainly when the garrison flag was

---

Mary Pickersgill, along with her teenaged daughter, mother, nieces, and servants, painstakingly hand sewed a new garrison flag for Fort McHenry in 1813. The giant flag (30 by 42 feet) would become the Star-Spangled Banner. Because of its great size, the flag needed to be spread on the empty malt house floor of a nearby brewery for assembly by Pickersgill and her helpers.

raised at 9 a.m., all three gentlemen undoubtedly saw the flag flying over the fort. The garrison flag (30 feet by 42 feet) had been ordered by the fort's commander, Major George Armistead, the year before along with a smaller storm flag (17 feet by 25 feet). The job went out to a 37-year-old widow, Mary Pickersgill, an experienced ship and signal flag maker. She labored for seven weeks with her 13-year-old daughter, Caroline, two nieces, 13-year-old Eliza Young and 15-year-old Margaret Young, a 13-year-old African-American indentured servant, Grace Wisher, and possibly her mother, Rebecca Young, who had taught her the trade. They pieced together strips of loosely woven English wool bunting then laid the whole flag out on the expansive floor of a brewery near Mrs. Pickersgill's Pratt Street house, now the Star-Spangled Banner Flag House Museum.

Key and his colleagues had perhaps the most unique location from which to observe the bombardment. The Americans occupied front-row seats amongst the enemy as the drama unfolded. First, on September 12, they heard the guns of the Battle of North Point a few miles away. On a gloomy, rainy September 13, they watched the bombardment of Fort McHenry many miles away. All day and into the dank, stormy evening, the noisy light show of rockets and bombs continued. During the night and early morning hours of September 14, there was more intense gunfire near the fort. At dawn, the men were all straining to see the fort and the flag. The British stopped their bombardment and an eerie quiet settled over the harbor. The three Americans slowly realized the British were retiring. The attack was over.

Released two days later as the British fleet sailed away, Key spent the evening at the Indian Queen Hotel in downtown Baltimore. It is there that he wrote the four stanzas to a tune that he probably had dancing in his brain while ship-bound. That original manuscript, entitled "The Defence of Fort M'Henry" and written with only a few revisions, is on display today at the Maryland Historical Society. From the beginning, Key intended for the stanzas to be sung to "The Anacreontic Song" or "To Anacreon in Heaven," an

eighteenth-century English club song that was already popular in America. An amateur poet and avid member of the gentlemen's clubs of the era, he had been toying with both patriotic ideas and various tunes, but his witnessing of the bombardment inspired him to write new lyrics to an old tune.

By September 17 printed versions of the piece were being handed out to the men in the fort and among the citizens of Baltimore. Within weeks it was published with its new name, "The Star Spangled Banner," in seventeen newspapers all over the east. A Mr. Harding is credited as the first to formally sing the new lyrics to the song on stage before a seated audience at the Holliday Street Theatre in Baltimore on October 19, 1814.

Bands played the song regularly during the Civil War and the U.S. Navy made it an official part of its flag ceremonies in 1889. President Woodrow Wilson ordered it be played for military ceremonies during World War I. The popular "Ripley's Believe or Not" cartoon series then pointed out that the United States had no national anthem. When famous composer John Philip Sousa published his opinion that Francis Scott Key's "soul-stirring" lyrics should become the national anthem, it helped begin a campaign to make it so. President Herbert Hoover finally signed a law on March 3, 1931, making "The Star-Spangled Banner" the official anthem of the United States. Since then, hardly a national sporting event has been played or an official ceremony opened without a rendition of the anthem.

The original Star-Spangled Banner flag remained in Major Armistead's family for ninety years. It was displayed in Baltimore on occasion and, as was the custom of the day, pieces were snipped off as gifts for friends and dignitaries. It was loaned, and later given, to the Smithsonian Institution after 1907 by Colonel Armistead's grandson, Eben Appleton. On public display for much of the last century, the remains of the giant flag became dangerously fragile. It recently underwent a decade-long, multimillion-dollar restoration and is again on permanent display at the Smithsonian Institution's National Museum of American History in the nation's capital. It is said to be among the most sought-after artifacts by visitors to the Smithsonian Institution.

This is the first published version of the "Star-Spangled Banner" that identifies the author. It incorrectly refers to Francis Scott Key as "B. Key, Esqr." and puts the dates of the bombardment as 12 and 13 September, 1814, rather than 13 and 14. A note at the beginning of the song states "With spirit." Set to the tune of a familiar club song of the day, "To Anacreon in Heaven," it proved very popular from the beginning and spread throughout the country in just a few weeks.

Opposite: After years of careful restoration, the giant flag that flew over Fort McHenry in 1814, better known as the Star-Spangled Banner, is preserved and displayed once again at the National Museum of American History in Washington, D.C. Several feet of the flag's fly end and one star are missing. During the nineteenth century, souvenir pieces were cut from the banner and given to distinguished visitors and well-wishers.

Postscript

WHAT DID A SECOND WAR WITH THE BRITISH ACCOMPLISH?

"The war has renewed and reinstated the national feeling and character which the Revolution had given . . . The people . . . are more American; they feel and act more as a nation; and I hope that the permanency of the Union is thereby better secured."

—Former Secretary of the Treasury Albert Gallatin (1761–1849), 1815

History taught in school tends to emphasize events as separate and distinct. In reality, history runs on a continuum that is better viewed in decades rather than years. Conflicts and issues are not so neatly packaged as the history books would have us believe. From our position today, it is not hard to see how the French and Indian War soon became the American Revolution and the Revolution foreshadowed the War of 1812.

The War of 1812 remains a largely forgotten footnote in the history of the United States. Although most of the fighting occurred between 1813 and 1815, the "War of 1812" label stuck. Attempts to call it something else, like "the second war for independence" have met with some success, but the emphasis on "independence" overstates the threat posed by the British in the early 1800s.

Mr. Madison's War grew out of unresolved issues, mostly an outgrowth of the Napoleonic War, over which Madison and the United States had no control. Would America's rights on the high seas as a new world trading rival and sovereign nation be respected by the European powers? Would Great Britain withdraw its troops and stop supplying guns to Indians on the American frontier? Would Canada, like the United States, throw off the yoke of the British Empire? Add a bitter, devastating, two decade–long European war and a brash young nation dependent on international trade, and one could hardly avoid trouble.

Yet, it is not difficult to find some important, even critical benefits that changed America during its self-created misadventure known as the War of 1812. After suffering about 6,765 battle casualties over nearly four years and an estimated cost to the country of $158,000,000, including property damage and lost economic opportunities it could ill afford, the United States was a different nation in 1815. The Treaty of Ghent, whose terms suggested that the war had accomplished little or nothing, nonetheless unleashed forces that significantly changed the United States in the years that followed. Having survived the war with no permanent losses, the country had new heroes, new symbols, new stories of patriotism, and a new sense of unity. Two of those heroes, Andrew Jackson and William Henry Harrison, later became presidents. Symbols from the war include Old Ironsides, Uncle Sam, and the Star-Spangled Banner. Most important, citizens had a new sense of confidence in their country and began to refer to themselves as Americans rather than as Virginians or Marylanders or residents of whatever state they lived in. While issues of slavery and states' rights continued to vex U.S. politics, an "Era of Good Feelings" after 1815 propelled the nation forward as the generation of the Revolution passed the baton to dynamic younger leaders.

Manufacturing, innovation, and central banking all fed a powerful national energy. A new emphasis on professionalism in the military led to the creation of scores of coastal forts to better defend the nation as well as forts along the western frontier that helped open a vast continent for settlement. By 1815, the American Indian nations had lost their British allies and Tecumseh, one of their greatest leaders. Their long fight for the Old Northwest and the frontier beyond was tragically doomed to fail.

Great Britain, a world power facing challenges more important than those proffered by the upstart United States, had 5,000 battle casualties of its own. During the war, it again came to the conclusion that victory over an underdeveloped country on the edge of a vast continent was not worth the necessary money and blood. In spite of some diplomatic scuffles and later tensions over the Canadian border, the British eventually became a close ally of the United States. For its part, Canada chose a different political path for its future after the 1812 struggles, but has also remained a friendly partner and neighbor ever since.

This painting by John Gast called *American Progress*, circa 1872, is an allegorical representation of the expansion of the American West. Columbia, a personification of the United States, leads civilization westward with American settlers, stringing telegraph wire in her wake. American Indians and animals flee while the many stages of economic development and modern forms of transportation envelop the west.

The War of 1812 remains a paradox for Americans. An ill-conceived conflict with a world power could have spelled doom for a struggling young republic. Instead, it launched the United States into a dynamic new era. In 1830, a young French visitor named Alexis de Tocqueville discovered greatness in America. "[It] lies not in being more enlightened than any other Nation, but rather in her ability to repair her faults."

Following spread: On September 12, 1839, over a thousand dignitaries, Old Defenders, and military units assembled at Battle Monument Square in downtown Baltimore. They had come to celebrate the twenty-fifth anniversary of the Battle of North Point. The throng marched to the inner harbor where they boarded steamboats bound for the battlefield. Here the distinguished guests joined with thousands of onlookers surrounding a platform on which the Star-Spangled Banner was laid. Upon the completion of speeches, and a gun salute, a granite block was laid as a cornerstone for an appropriate monument honoring those who risked their lives for Baltimore, Maryland, and the nation.

PART II
VISITING HISTORIC SITES AND OTHER ATTRACTIONS

1 Discovering the War of 1812

Picture a park that overlooks gently flowing waters where British and American troops once clashed . . . The distinctive wooden dome of an eighteenth-century building from which enemy warships could be observed . . . A star-shaped fort with a huge American flag fluttering high above its ramparts . . .

These historic sites are linked to important events that occurred two centuries ago during the War of 1812. But they also have something else in common: they, along with hundreds of other destinations throughout the Chesapeake region, exist today to be explored, admired, and enjoyed.

There has never been a better time for visitors to get out and retrace travel routes where history was made, to feel the drama that unfolded, to experience reenactments and demonstrations, and to view artifacts from two hundred years ago. In Maryland, Virginia, and Washington, D.C., there are museums and monuments, forts and battlefields, scenic byways and welcoming waterfronts just waiting to be explored.

The Chesapeake region has a wealth of fascinating places within a short drive (or boat ride!) of each other. Some, such as Fort McHenry, are known the world over. Others, like Benedict and Tappahannock, are less recognized. Yet, they all are intertwined with the story of the War of 1812.

And in this region, history often goes hand-in-hand with the beauty of charming small towns and inviting natural environments. Consider Havre de Grace, a "harbor of grace" situated at the confluence of the Chesapeake Bay and Susquehanna River. In the spring of 1813, it was savagely raided by the British. Or think about picturesque St. Michaels, one of the Eastern Shore's most popular locations. Twice, it was threatened by British forces—both times, the attacks were repelled.

In Southern Maryland, Jefferson Patterson Park and Museum is situated where St. Leonard Creek and the Patuxent River meet. Once the site of the largest naval battle to take place in Maryland waters, it is now a perfect spot for hiking, biking, or picnicking. And just an hour or so away, millions of visitors come to Washington, D.C., each year to snap photos of the White House and U.S. Capitol. During the War of 1812, both buildings were burned by the British until they were merely shells.

More than eight hundred historical sites in the Chesapeake region have connections to the War of 1812. Obviously, Part II of this book is not intended as a comprehensive list of war-related destinations, but as more of a launching point. While touring one of the destinations we've described, visitors just might learn about another place nearby that hasn't been mentioned here— so be on the lookout for other opportunities just down the road, around the next bend, and all along the clearly marked Star-Spangled Banner National Historic Trail.

For more comprehensive coverage of War of 1812 historical sites in the Chesapeake region, check in with the offices and information centers listed under "For More Info" in this section. Also refer to other valuable sources, such as *The War of 1812 in the Chesapeake: A Reference Guide to Historic Sites in Maryland, Virginia, and the District of Columbia*, and *A Travel Guide to the War of 1812 in the Chesapeake: Eighteen Tours in Maryland, Virginia, and the District of Columbia*, both published by the Johns Hopkins University Press.

Lace up those walking shoes, gas up the car or boat, grab a camera and smart phone, pack a picnic lunch, and maybe even take along a bike or kayak. Throughout the Chesapeake region, history comes alive. Now's the time to visit . . . and to live it!

Preceding spread: **Fort McHenry National Monument and Historic Shrine**

How Part II Is Organized

Part II is divided into this introduction and eight chapters that describe War of 1812–related sites in Maryland, Virginia, and the District of Columbia by region. They have been placed in roughly chronological order—beginning in the Norfolk area, where the Royal Navy established an important anchorage in February 1813, and ending in the Baltimore region, site of the Americans' triumphant stand at Fort McHenry in September 1814.

However, readers can tell from the history recounted elsewhere in this book that the progress of the war through the Chesapeake region had little regard for geographical tidiness. As an example, the Battle of the Ice Mound actually occurred on Maryland's Eastern Shore in the months following the Battle for Baltimore. Yet, based on the course of other events, it seems appropriate to place the Eastern Shore region chronologically ahead of Baltimore. The decision ultimately rests with the visitor as to where a War of 1812 tour should start. Some travelers prefer to set up home base at quiet, small-town accommodations and take a series of day trips in various directions. Others begin at the Fort McHenry National Monument and Historic Shrine, where their imaginations are sparked, resulting in the desire to see other places. And, of course, there are those hardy few who actually wish to tour war-related sites in a roughly chronological order. To them, we say, "Go for it!"

Each regional section not only includes a sampling of War of 1812 destinations and a little reminder of the history surrounding them, but also offers information about what else can be found in the area. Is a region popular for paddling sports? Should time be allotted for touring other museums and monuments? Considering the number of waterfront restaurants nearby, would a crab mallet and seafood bib be considered essential gear? So look to "What Else You'll Find" for some guidance.

Lastly, within the regional sections there are a handful of additional trails and byways we have assembled under the heading "By the Way." Look for theme-based auto tours as well as recreational opportunities such as hiking along a trail that ends at George Washington's Mount Vernon estate, spying wildlife around the scenic Patuxent River in Southern Maryland, or taking a bike ride through the Eastern Shore. Along the way, visitors will get a sense of the landscapes that served as staging areas for events that unfolded during the war in the Chesapeake.

Here are just a few of the trails, other byways, and heritage areas found within the regions described in Part II:

 The Star-Spangled Banner National Historic Trail—one of nineteen national historic trails recognized by Congress and administered by the U.S. National Park Service—is a 560-mile land and water route connecting the sites that tell the story of the War of 1812 in the Chesapeake and the events that led to the writing of the Star-Spangled Banner. The trail and the hundreds of individual sites along its length are linked by rich interpretive signage and a wayfinding system coordinated with the Star-Spangled Banner Byway in Maryland. Look for this trail logo marking places to explore the War of 1812 in the Chesapeake. Explore the trail online at www.starspangledtrail.net.

◆ Tied into the National Historic Trail, treasures are found all the time along the **Star-Spangled Banner Geotrail.** Using a handheld Global Positioning System (GPS), participants can enjoy hunting for hidden "caches" while exploring a series of more than thirty sites with War of 1812 stories. Start out by accessing the official geocache website at www.geocaching.com. More information can be found at www.starspangledtrail.net.

◆ Convenient access to the recreational bounty of America's largest estuary is provided through the **Chesapeake Bay Gateways and Watertrails Network,** a collection of more than 170 "Gateways" officially designated by the National Park Service. Visitors will want to park their cars and explore such destinations as wildlife areas, waterfront parks, historic ports, museums, nature trails, and ships with sails. Many Bay Gateways help tell the stories of the War of 1812, such as the Fort McHenry National Monument and Historic Shrine and the Fells Point Historic District in Baltimore. Others, like First Landing State Park in Virginia and Blackwater National Wildlife Refuge on Maryland's Eastern Shore, are great places to experience the diverse environment of the Chesapeake Bay. Find out additional information at www.baygateways.net.

Reenactment event at Fort McHenry

◆ Boaters and paddlers can enjoy the **Captain John Smith Chesapeake National Historic Trail,** a 3,000-mile-long water route that explores the Chesapeake Bay and its tributaries in Virginia, Maryland, Delaware, and the District of Columbia. Named in honor of the early-seventeenth-century explorer who said of the area, "heaven and earth never agreed better to frame a place for man's habitation," the trail utilizes state-of-the-art technology to make the experience of today's explorers a truly unforgettable one. Bobbing between Norfolk, Virginia, and Havre de Grace, Maryland, are ten "smart buoys" that can be contacted by cell phone (toll-free 1-877-buoy-bay) or any Internet-accessible device (www.buoybay.noaa.gov) in order to retrieve historical information and near-real-time climate and environmental data. There are plenty of ways to enjoy the Smith trail on land, too, while learning about American Indians, English colonists, and the abundance of the Bay from four hundred years ago. Discover more at www.smithtrail.net.

◆ Historic preservation blends beautifully with the scenery throughout twelve certified **Maryland Heritage Areas,** each of which is defined by a theme that fits with the area's historical, cultural, or natural significance. Learn more by going to www.mht.maryland.gov and selecting "Heritage Areas."

◆ Two of the National Park Service's forty-nine national heritage areas are found in the Chesapeake region, contributing to a better appreciation of the natural, cultural, and historic resources found here. Within the **Baltimore National Heritage Area,** visitors experience history dating back to the Revolutionary War, with additional emphasis on the War of 1812 and African-American heritage. The **Journey Through Hallowed Ground National Heritage Area and Byway** reaches from Gettysburg, Pennsylvania, south to Thomas Jefferson's Monticello in Charlottesville, Virginia, incorporating nine presidential homes, thirteen national parks, and hundreds of battlefields. Find out more at www.nps.gov/history/heritageareas.

Reenactment event, Bladensburg Region

◆ A 115-mile stretch of the lower Potomac River from Washington, D.C., to the Chesapeake Bay features some of the nation's premier sites for paddlers, boaters, anglers, and other outdoor enthusiasts. This **POTOMAC RIVER WATER TRAIL** features destinations such as Historic Alexandria, Mount Vernon, General Robert E. Lee's family home, and Point Lookout.

◆ **THE POTOMAC HERITAGE NATIONAL SCENIC TRAIL** is a network of locally managed trails, gathered under the auspices of the National Park Service that provides access to a host of outdoor activities between the mouth of the Potomac River and the Allegheny Highlands. Among the more than 800 miles of existing and planned trails within the network is the 238-mile Southern Maryland Tidewater Potomac Heritage Bicycle Route that starts and ends at Fort Washington Park and requires several days to complete. One of several trail options in Virginia's Northern Neck area is the 38-mile Leedstown Loop, which visits historic Colonial Beach and Leedstown as well as President James Monroe's birthplace (near Oak Grove). Information is available at the following websites: www.nps.gov/pohe and www.potomacheritage.net.

◆ In addition to the Star-Spangled Banner Trail, numerous **SCENIC BYWAYS** cover thousands of miles in Maryland and Virginia. Take these roads less traveled to find other exciting new discoveries throughout the Chesapeake region.

A pair of groups that actively support heritage initiatives in the District of Columbia and Alexandria, Virginia, areas have put programs in place to make visiting historical sites easier and more fulfilling. In Washington, **CULTURAL TOURISM DC** (www.culturaltourismdc.org) and its more than two hundred member organizations have established neighborhood heritage trails, walking tours, events, and other authentic experiences that involve art galleries, museums, parks, gardens, and entertainment venues. And the **OFFICE OF HISTORIC ALEXANDRIA** (www.alexandriava.gov/historic) has generated a long list of themed itineraries in addition to promoting seven premier destinations owned by the city, including the Alexandria Black History Museum, Gadsby's Tavern Museum, and The Lyceum: Alexandria's History Museum.

For More Info

Region-specific visitor information centers are identified elsewhere, but here are state and district offices that can provide general assistance with any traveling needs in the Chesapeake region. Welcome centers are located on major thoroughfares throughout Maryland and Virginia.

Destination DC
901 7th Street, N.W., 4th Floor
202-789-7000, 800-422-8644
www.washington.org

Maryland Office of Tourism
401 East Pratt Street, 14th Floor, Baltimore
410-767-3400, 877-333-4455
www.visitmaryland.org

Virginia Tourism Corporation
901 E. Byrd Street, Richmond
804-545-5500, 800-847-4882
www.virginia.org

Biking on the Eastern Shore

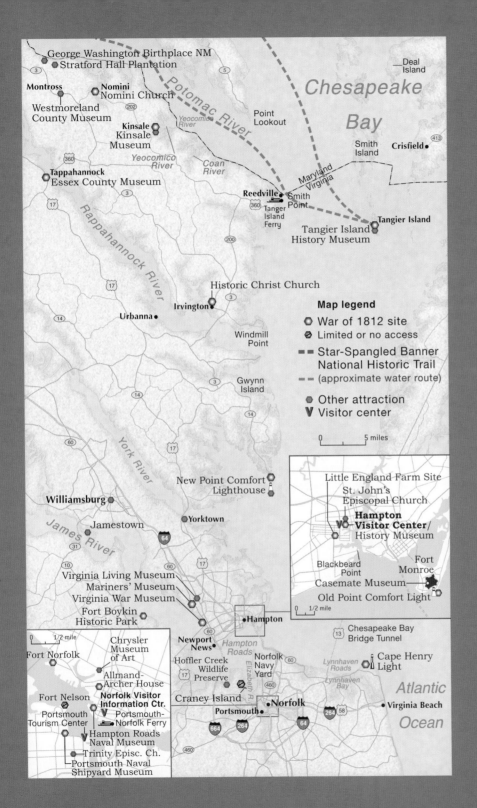

Map legend
- ◉ War of 1812 site
- ⊘ Limited or no access
- ▬ ▬ Star-Spangled Banner National Historic Trail
- ▬ ▬ (approximate water route)
- ⬡ Other attraction
- **V** Visitor center

0 _____ 5 miles

George Washington Birthplace NM
Stratford Hall Plantation
Montross
Nomini
Nomini Church
Westmoreland County Museum
Kinsale
Kinsale Museum
Tappahannock
Essex County Museum
Rappahannock River
Potomac River
Yeocomico River
Coan River
Point Lookout
Deal Island
Chesapeake Bay
Smith Island
Crisfield
Maryland Virginia
Reedville
Smith Point
Tanger Island Ferry
Tangier Island
Tangier Island History Museum
Historic Christ Church
Irvington
Urbanna
Windmill Point
Gwynn Island
York River
New Point Comfort Lighthouse
Williamsburg
Yorktown
Jamestown
James River
Virginia Living Museum
Mariners' Museum
Virginia War Museum
Fort Boykin Historic Park
Chrysler Museum of Art
Fort Norfolk
Newport News
Allmand-Archer House
Hoffler Creek Wildlife Preserve
Norfolk Visitor Information Ctr.
Fort Nelson
Portsmouth Tourism Center
Portsmouth-Norfolk Ferry
Hampton Roads Naval Museum
Trinity Episc. Ch.
Portsmouth Naval Shipyard Museum
Craney Island
Portsmouth
Hampton Roads
Norfolk Navy Yard
Hampton
Elizabeth R.
Norfolk
Chesapeake Bay Bridge Tunnel
Lynnhaven Roads
Lynnhaven Bay
Cape Henry Light
Virginia Beach
Atlantic Ocean

Little England Farm Site
St. John's Episcopal Church
Hampton Visitor Center / History Museum
Blackbeard Point
Fort Monroe
Casemate Museum
Old Point Comfort Light

0 ___ 1/2 mile

Maybe the War of 1812 didn't officially start in the Norfolk area of Virginia, but a harbinger of things to come occurred only a few miles offshore when, in 1807, the H.M. frigate *Leopard* fired on the U.S. frigate *Chesapeake*, fueling an American call for hostilities.

Protected by four forts, Norfolk was the best-defended city in Virginia. Yet, Hampton Roads, just a few miles across the mouth of the James River, served as an important anchorage for the Royal Navy throughout the war. And it was from this anchorage that the British fleet conducted its blockade at the mouth of the Bay.

One of several significant military targets quickly identified by British forces was a key American naval shipyard in Portsmouth; another was the U.S. frigate *Constellation*, which became bottled up in the Elizabeth River due to the British blockade. Last but not least, American forces scored a rare early victory in this area, at the Battle of Craney Island.

Today, an exploration of War of 1812 sites takes visitors along the waterfronts of both Norfolk and Portsmouth, which are connected by a scenic ferry ride. Other recommended sites include Hampton and Newport News, as well as Tidewater Virginia destinations that reach to the Northern Neck's 1,100 miles of shoreline. Along

2 The Tidewater Virginia Region

the way, visitors will discover an abundance of museums, beaches, restaurants, and recreational outlets.

For a quick and economical overview of the upper-river area, climb onboard the **Elizabeth River Paddlewheel Ferry.** Connecting Norfolk's Harbor Park to Portsmouth's North Landing, the ferry is a great way to travel among historical sites, restaurants, and retail centers. Near North Landing is the **Portsmouth Naval Shipyard Museum,** which is explained later in more detail.

Fort Norfolk, located on the narrows of the Elizabeth River, dates from the American Revolution but was upgraded after the *Chesapeake-Leopard* affair. Despite being used by both the Union and Confederacy during the Civil War, it remains today as one of the nation's best-preserved examples of pre-1812 fortifications to survive largely unchanged. Brick and masonry walls erected in 1810 are still standing, and visitors who step through the arched entryway may walk upon the ramparts to look downriver at the *Constellation*'s approximate anchoring position during the blockade. Please note that the U.S. Army Corps of Engineers Norfolk District headquarters is located on the grounds of the fort, and thus visitors must have photo identification in order to access the site.

Fort Norfolk

Exhibits about the U.S. Navy and the role it played in the Norfolk area for more than two centuries are found at the **Hampton Roads Naval Museum,** which sits in the shadow of the huge U.S. battleship *Wisconsin*. Among numerous artifacts displayed at the museum is a 1798 18-pound cannon from the *Constellation*. Narrated naval base cruises that are available from this area interpret Fort Norfolk and the site of Fort Nelson, which are now the grounds of the Portsmouth Naval Hospital.

The 1790s **Allmand-Archer House** is said to be the oldest standing house in Norfolk. Once owned by a merchant nicknamed "Old Gold Dust" because of his great wealth, the house served as headquarters for American forces during the war. Today, it remains a private residence, and thus only exterior views are permitted.

In Portsmouth, the eighteenth-century **Trinity Episcopal Church** is the burial site of many Revolutionary War patriots as well as U.S. Navy Commodore James Barron. Barron captained the *Chesapeake* during the *Chesapeake-Leopard* affair and gained infamy following the War of 1812 for fatally wounding fellow naval officer Stephen Decatur in a duel.

At the **Portsmouth Naval Shipyard Museum**, visitors can learn about Barron and the almost three-hundred-fifty-year history of

Historic Christ Church, Weems

America's oldest shipyard. Whether known as the Gosport Navy Yard or the Norfolk Naval Shipyard, this is one enterprise that has seen it all from the time of America's birth as a nation right on through to the twenty-first century. Along with ship models, uniforms, and a few War of 1812 artifacts, the museum also features exhibits on the Revolutionary War, Civil War, and World War II.

> **Did You Know?** Using an open boat named *Chesapeake's Revenge,* enterprising Americans hoping to cripple British warships set mines adrift in the mouth of the Chesapeake Bay. Though an actual target was never hit, one mine exploded so near a warship that it caused a cascade of water to fall on its deck. The British referred to these mines as "Powder Machines."

Defending the naval shipyard during the War of 1812 were American troops at Craney Island. Together with sailors from the *Constellation,* they repulsed a June 1813 attack by a superior British force and saved Norfolk and Portsmouth from probable destruction. None of the "battlefield" is visible because of landfill and the site now resides within a military installation.

East of Craney Island, the 142-acre **Hoffler Creek Wildlife Preserve** is located on the site where substantial British naval and marine forces assembled prior to the attack. Visitors to the preserve can get a sense of the landscape while exploring the diverse environment of the James River and Chesapeake Bay.

Seeking revenge for the embarrassing defeat at Craney Island, the enemy exacted bloody retribution on the town of Hampton. Visitors will learn the details at the **Hampton History Museum** and see artifacts such as a musket that had been taken back to England as a war prize following the attack.

Hoffler Creek Wildlife Preserve

Just across the road is **St. John's Episcopal Church,** which was completed in 1728 with handsome colonial brickwork. The British reportedly used the cemetery grounds for the butchering of cattle. Surrounding the church is a circa-1759 wall that is said to have "suffered the effects" of the Revolutionary War, War of 1812, and Civil War.

Several blocks away, a historic marker notes the location of **Little England Farm,** a 500-acre estate where Commodore James Barron lived. An American encampment and two gun batteries were located on his farm to defend the town.

Shedding some light on more war-related events in the region are three beacons built in the two decades prior to the start of hostilities. The **Old Point Comfort Lighthouse,** completed in 1802 at the entrance to Hampton Roads, was used as an observation station by the British. The beacon can be seen along the waterfront near **Fort Monroe.** The **New Point Comfort Lighthouse** is a sixty-mile trip to the north in the 105-acre, Mathews-based **New Point Comfort Natural Area Preserve.** This beacon was completed in 1805 and was said to have been utilized by British lookouts. The point was also used by the troops to replenish their fresh water supply. Bird watching is available from a boardwalk on the preserve and, for those with kayaks, beautiful marshes

> **Did You Know?** When the British attacked Hampton by water, they passed Blackbeard Point, named after the famous pirate whose severed head was displayed on a pole here a century earlier to warn other pirates to beware.

can be explored by water. Excellent views of the Atlantic Ocean and mouth of the Chesapeake Bay are revealed from atop the **Old Cape Henry Lighthouse,** completed in 1792 near Virginia Beach (the grounds of the nearby New Cape Henry Lighthouse, completed in 1881, are open to the public but there is no access to the tower). During the War of 1812, British troops removed meat from the keeper's smokehouse.

Geocaching activities on the Star-Spangled Banner National Historic Trail

Heading over to Newport News, one encounters the **Mariners' Museum,** one of the largest of its kind in the world. An anchor from the British troop ship *Dictator*, lost in the Patuxent River in 1814, is exhibited here amid 61,000 square feet of exhibition galleries and thirty-five thousand artifacts. The museum property also features a 167-acre lake and five-mile-long shoreline trail.

Visitors may also take the sixty-mile trip toward Irvington, located off the Rappahannock River. The town's National Register Historic District contains about one hundred fifty structures. For information about a British landing that was repulsed in 1813, as well as two more raids that were more successful in 1814, go to the **Historic Christ Church Museum** just north of Irvington.

Farther north is **Tappahannock**. In December 1814, the British seized this Rappahannock River port town, demolished the Essex County Courthouse, ransacked private homes, and pillaged a prominent local family's burial vaults. A

walking tour through the historic part of town reveals several properties that predate the War of 1812, including a couple located on the campus of the St. Margaret's School, established in 1921.

British forces were also present in the area of **Nomini Creek,** burning Nomini Church and taking the church's silver. A replacement church was constructed in the mid-1850s. In the town of Kinsale, walking tours incorporate a small museum on the village green that delves into the area's rich history. It was near Kinsale on July 14, 1813, that a vastly outgunned U.S. vessel was set upon by British forces. On the south bank of the Yeocomico River, a monument has been erected over the grave of a U.S. Navy lieutenant killed in that action.

In the Isle of Wight / Smithfield area, **Fort Boykin** stands high on a bluff overlooking the James River. Called "The Castle" when constructed in the seventeenth century, it was strengthened into a formidable star-shaped earthwork following the *Chesapeake-Leopard* affair. The present earthwork fort dates from the Civil War.

Fort Boykin is one of the southernmost points among more than thirty sites found along the **Star-Spangled Banner Geotrail,** a multistate initiative supported by the National Park Service featuring a series of caches tied to the War of 1812 and the birth of America's national anthem. At another location on the geotrail— the **Tangier Island History Museum and Interpretive Cultural Center,** accessible only by water—the story is told of the island's role as a base for British forces during the war. Visitors can use bikes or golf carts to further explore the island's deeply proud Chesapeake heritage.

1812 Destinations

Old Cape Henry Lighthouse
Fort Story, north off Shore Drive (U.S. Route 60),
Virginia Beach
757-898-2410
www.apva.org/CapeHenryLighthouse

Dating to 1792, the lighthouse has undergone numerous repairs, including some that were required after Confederate troops tried to render the beacon useless during the Civil War. One of the first British raids in the Chesapeake region took place here.

Historic Christ Church
Christ Church (Route 646) and Caskins Roads, Weems
804-438-6855
www.christchurch1735.org

This is one of the best preserved of colonial Virginia's Anglican parish churches. It has retained its original high-back boxed pews and triple-decker pulpit. A museum interprets a nearby British raid; War of 1812 veterans are buried here.

Fort Boykin Historic Park
7410 Fort Boykin Trail (Route 705), Mogarts Beach,
Isle of Wight
800-365-9339
www.historicisleofwight.com

Located along the Virginia Birding and Wildlife Trail, Fort Boykin is found on top of a bluff overlooking the James River. It is also part of the Star-Spangled Banner Geotrail.

Fort Norfolk
U.S. Army Corps of Engineers Norfolk District,
801 Front Street, Norfolk
757-640-1720
www.norfolkhistorical.org

Old Point Comfort Lighthouse, Hampton

> **Did You Know?** Near Lynnhaven in October 1813, a voluntary association of white men attacked a group of escaped slaves seeking to join the British, killing five or six and wounding others.

The best-preserved fort among nineteen that were authorized by President George Washington in 1794, Fort Norfolk features earthwork embankments, ramparts, officers' quarters, and other structures, many of which date to 1810.

Hampton Roads Naval Museum

Nauticus: The National Maritime Center,
One Waterside Drive, Norfolk
757-322-2987
www.hrnm.navy.mil

An official museum of the United States Navy, it is dedicated to celebrating two hundred thirty-five years of naval history in the region. Hundreds of paintings and photographs go along with ship models and artifacts.

Old Point Comfort Lighthouse

Fort Monroe, Fenwick Road, end of U.S. Route 258, Hampton
www.nps.gov/history/maritime/light/oldpt.htm

The lighthouse was used as a British observation post during the War of 1812. During the Civil War, it was one of the few beacons not to be damaged since it stood so near to the Union-held Fort Monroe. Within the fort is the Casemate Museum.

Portsmouth Naval Shipyard Museum

2 High Street, Portsmouth
757-393-8591
www.portsnavalmuseums.com

The museum traces the shipyard's history from colonial to Civil War times and on into World War II. Displays include ship models, uniforms, military artifacts, and exhibits.

Mariners' Museum, Newport News

For More Info

Hampton Convention and Visitor Bureau
1919 Commerce Drive, Suite 290, Hampton
757-315-1610, 1-866-484-HRCC
www.hamptoncvb.com/go/visitors

Hampton Visitor Center
Hampton History Museum, 120 Old Hampton Lane, Hampton
757-727-1102, 1-800-800-2202
www.hamptoncvb.com

Norfolk Visitor Information Center
9301 4th View Street, exit 273 off I-64 West, Norfolk
1-800-368-3097
www.norfolkcvb.com

The Northern Neck Tourism Commission
P.O. Box 1707, Warsaw
804-333-1919
www.northernneck.org

Portsmouth Tourism Center
6 Crawford Parkway, Portsmouth
757-393-5111, 1-800-PORTS-VA
www.visitportsva.com

Portsmouth Visitor Center*
6 Crawford Parkway, Olde Towne (at the North Ferry Landing), Portsmouth
757-393-5111, 1-800-PORTS-VA
www.visitportsva.com/maps.html#visitors

*There is also visitor information at the Starbucks Kiosk, 101 High Street (757-478-0056)

VisitNorfolk
232 East Main Street, Norfolk
757-664-6620, 1-800-368-3097
www.visitnorfolktoday.com

What Else You'll Find

History comes fast and furious in Tidewater Virginia. Fortunately, there are also plenty of places to just relax and unwind, so sightseeing can fill part of the schedule while additional time can be allocated for boat excursions, hitting the beach, or hiking along park trails.

From colonial settlements at Jamestown and Williamsburg to Revolutionary War success in Yorktown, and from War of 1812 sites to Civil War stories, the area brings more than four hundred years of history to life.

Hampton-based Fort Monroe, when completed in 1834, was the largest stone fort built in the United States. It was named for James Monroe, who served as secretary of state and secretary of war during the War of 1812 before becoming the fifth president of the United States. Construction of the fort was prompted in part by a lack of defenses that was exploited by the British. The Casemate Museum here places special emphasis on the Civil War period and offers a view of the prison cell once occupied by Confederate President Jefferson Davis.

Visitors wanting to devote some of their daylight hours to other pursuits have a number of options. Among several world-class museums just in the Norfolk area alone are the Chrysler Museum of Art, home to thirty thousand works from around the world, and the Hermitage Museum, which offers house tours and hosts live music events amid a breathtaking backdrop of wetlands, woodlands, and formal gardens.

Boat excursions are popular choices for travelers. And when evening arrives, there are still shopping adventures, eclectic eateries, theaters, and other entertainment venues to keep the good times going.

Downtown Norfolk's largest summertime event is Harborfest, which draws crowds in excess of two hundred thousand people each June. A spectacular Parade of Sail cruises down the Elizabeth River to kick off this three-day festival, and then the fun just keeps building from there. Live music, tasty food, children's activities, and fireworks displays are all highlights of this huge maritime celebration.

Portsmouth picks up right where Norfolk leaves off, with antiquing, restaurants, and the state's largest children's museum. Visit the Portsmouth Lightship, which operated from 1915 to 1963. Recreational boaters have easy access to the Atlantic Ocean and Chesapeake Bay from a deep natural harbor.

In Newport News—birthplace of performer Ella Fitzgerald—it's no wonder that fine cultural attractions take center stage. But the true star of this town just might be the Virginia Living Museum, where visitors can look in on wildlife amid living exhibits including a cypress swamp and mountain cove.

Virginia Beach promises leisurely strolls on the boardwalk, paddling trips around beautiful Back Bay, top-notch offshore fishing trips, boundless chances to sample coastal cuisine, and if you have a couple of hours left over, just sinking into a beach towel on warm, white sand.

Along the Northern Neck, the Westmoreland County Museum has plenty of local history together with a garden designed by noted landscape architect Charles Gillette. Known as the "Presidents' Garden," the layout incorporates marble busts of Presidents Washington, Madison, and Monroe, carved by Attillio Picciarilli, the same sculptor responsible for the Lincoln Memorial in Washington, D.C.

George Washington is also the subject of a National Park Service property dedicated to the first president's early life. Along with a seventeenth-century homestead, the George Washington Birthplace National Monument on Pope's Creek has a Living Colonial Farm (with livestock and tobacco) and a Washington family burial ground.

Spectacular views of the Potomac River are available from a high bluff in Stratford, where the Stratford Hall Plantation is located. This colonial property was the birthplace of Confederate General Robert E. Lee, and it is still managed as a 1,900-acre farm in addition to being a site on the Star-Spangled Banner Geotrail.

By the Way . . .

Extremely popular for kayaking, a Potomac River Water Trail dips down into the Northern Neck, the northernmost of three bayside peninsulas in Virginia, and runs south to the Rappahannock River. This area is teeming with American history, which is sprinkled amid several natural areas that seem virtually unchanged from centuries ago.

Scenic river views are available for walkers and bicyclists along an Elizabeth River Trail in Norfolk. Four interpretive markers along the trail tell the history of the area and environment.

A pedestrian-friendly heritage route called the Cannonball Trail connects historic sites woven among many popular attractions throughout downtown Norfolk. Pick up a map at the Freemason Street Reception Center.

For complete immersion in the state's War of 1812 experience, follow the Virginia War of 1812 Heritage Trail to more than a hundred sites, many of which provide tours, special events, and other attractions in addition to interpretive information. Look at Virginia welcome centers for brochures identifying the trail's major historic features, or go online to http://va1812bicentennial.dls.virginia.gov/places.html.

Did You Know? **A terrier dog accompanied one British barge during an attack on Craney Island.**

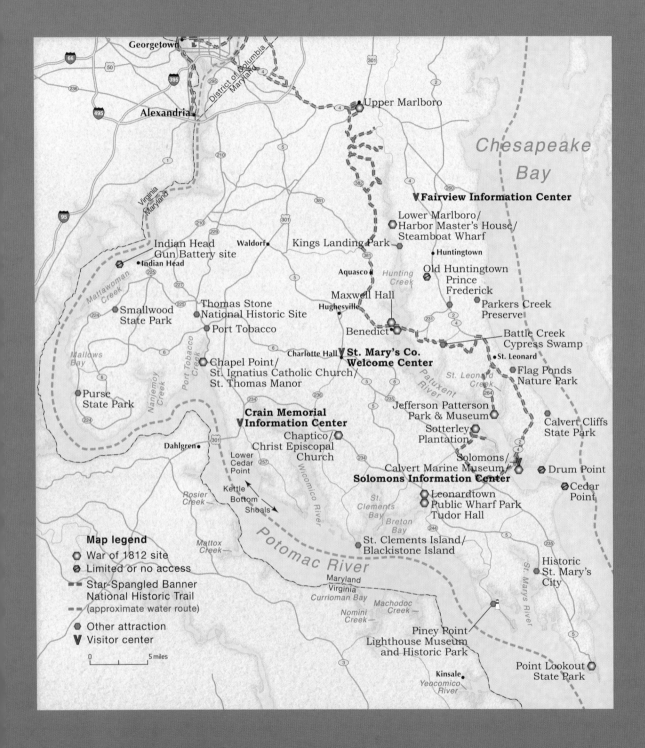

Map legend

- ⬡ War of 1812 site
- ⬗ Limited or no access
- – – – Star-Spangled Banner National Historic Trail
- – – – (approximate water route)
- ● Other attraction
- ▼ Visitor center

0   5 miles

Chesapeake Bay

Georgetown

Alexandria

District of Columbia
Maryland

Virginia
Maryland

Upper Marlboro

▼ **Fairview Information Center**

Lower Marlboro/
Harbor Master's House/
Steamboat Wharf

Indian Head
Gun Battery site
• Indian Head

Waldorf

Kings Landing Park

Huntingtown

Aquasco

Hunting Creek

Old Huntingtown
Prince Frederick

Maxwell Hall
Hughesville

Parkers Creek
Preserve

Thomas Stone
National Historic Site

Smallwood
State Park

Port Tobacco

Benedict

Battle Creek
Cypress Swamp

• St. Leonard

Charlotte Hall ▼ **St. Mary's Co.
Welcome Center**

Chapel Point/
St. Ignatius Catholic Church/
St. Thomas Manor

St. Leonard
Creek

Flag Ponds
Nature Park

Mallows
Bay

Purse
State Park

Nanjemoy Creek

Port Tobacco Creek

Patuxent River

**Crain Memorial
▼ Information Center**

Jefferson Patterson
Park & Museum

Calvert Cliffs
State Park

Dahlgren

Chaptico
Christ Episcopal
Church

Lower
Cedar
Point

Sotterley
Plantation

Solomons/
Calvert Marine Museum/
Solomons Information Center

Drum Point

Cedar
Point

Rosier
Creek

Kettle
Bottom
Shoals

Wicomico River

St.
Clements
Bay

Leonardtown
Public Wharf Park
Tudor Hall

Breton
Bay

Mattox
Creek

Maryland
Virginia

Currioman Bay

St. Clements Island/
Blackistone Island

Historic
St. Mary's
City

St. Marys River

Machodoc
Creek

Piney Point
Lighthouse Museum
and Historic Park

Point Lookout
State Park

Nomini
Creek

Kinsale

Yeocomico
River

Potomac River

Southern Maryland features a mostly rural landscape with natural beauty that flows from the Chesapeake Bay westward along both the Potomac and Patuxent Rivers. Reaching northward, it nearly touches Washington, D.C.

This last point, together with the region's deep natural waters and multitude of plantations and farms, helped make Southern Maryland an attractive target for British raiding parties during the War of 1812. No other region of the Chesapeake experienced more raids.

Places that are popular among anglers, boaters, and birdwatchers were once the sites of fighting that included the largest naval engagement

Sotterley Plantation

3 The Southern Maryland Region

Calvert Marine Museum, Solomons

on Maryland waters. Visiting the area offers the opportunity to explore majestic river views, quaint small towns, waterfront restaurants, and acres of open land dotted with the occasional tobacco barn.

Solomons is the perfect place to get this tour under way. In fact, it's the recommended starting point for the **Star-Spangled Banner National Historic Trail.** Some travelers prefer to arrive by car, others by boat, taking advantage of one of the Bay's best natural harbors. Within this former shipbuilding center and watermen's village— well known for its seafood dining and beautiful sunsets over the Patuxent River—the **Calvert Marine Museum** has an electronic map that

shows British troop movements up the Patuxent River during the War of 1812. Also on display are artifacts recovered from a U.S. Chesapeake Flotilla vessel scuttled thirty miles up the river.

In addition, the museum happens to be one of the finest facilities of its kind in the country. At least a couple of hours are required to scan the small-craft collection, search for fossils in the Discovery Room, see inside a lighthouse, stroll on a boardwalk over the salt marsh, and see Bubbles and Squeaks swimming in the River Otter Habitat.

On a side trip across the Thomas Johnson Bridge to the Patuxent River's western shore visitors can explore the three-hundred-year-old **Sotterley Plantation,** as well as **Point Lookout State Park**. On Sotterley's riverfront grounds,

> **Did You Know?** Roger Taney, a native of Calvert County and best known as chief justice of the Supreme Court, married Francis Scott Key's sister. He also penned an account of the writing of "The Star-Spangled Banner," which is a valuable historical contribution since Key himself never elaborated on the development of his lyrics.

near Hollywood, the British drove off three hundred militiamen, burned a warehouse full of tobacco, and allowed at least forty-eight slaves to flee on ships. Point Lookout, though more famous for its later role as a notorious Civil War prison camp, served as an observation post to monitor British activity on the Bay and was also the site of a British encampment.

Returning to Maryland Route 2/4, explore one of the most important War of 1812 sites in Maryland—the **Jefferson Patterson Park and Museum.** In this area during June 1814, a series of relatively large-scale naval battles took place pitting British forces against Commodore Joshua Barney's eighteen-vessel U.S. Chesapeake Flotilla. Informative panels in the park recount how Barney's cornered flotilla managed to thwart the superior British forces and then, in a surprise attack a few weeks later, slip past the British blockaders when they temporarily repositioned to repair their damaged vessels. The park's Exhibit Barn, which is open on weekends April through November, features a display called "Farmers, Patriots, and Traitors: Southern Maryland and the War of 1812." But this park offers much more. It is home to archaeology programs, hiking trails, a canoe launch, and a re-created American Indian village. The park's visitor center has exhibits, a

Flags at Charlotte Hall

museum shop, and a kid-oriented Discovery Room. Plan a trip to the park to coincide with the two-day Battle of St. Leonard Creek re-enactment, held each September.

Several charming small towns found along tributaries of the Potomac River offer visitors some Southern Maryland hospitality while providing background about lesser-known war-related sites.

In Leonardtown, the St. Mary's County seat, about fifteen hundred British troops attacked on July 19, 1814, and took the town without opposition. One force came from the west, then another approached from the east; a third landed at the **Leonardtown Wharf,** which is now part of a public park that is a favorite push-off point for canoeing and kayaking. Nearby is **Tudor Hall,** an eighteenth-century house that became the home of Philip Key, a relative of Francis Scott Key. Tudor Hall serves as the research library for the St. Mary's County Historical Society and houses the society's bookstore. The fertile countryside surrounding Leonardtown has sprouted a winery that hosts tours and special events.

During a British raid in Chaptico, the **Christ Episcopal Church** organ was smashed and grave vaults were reportedly desecrated. The church had been built in the 1730s under the supervision of Francis Scott Key's grandfather, and several members of the Key family are buried in a vault located immediately behind the church.

St. Ignatius Catholic Church–St. Thomas Manor is situated on a 90-foot hill at Chapel Point, overlooking the confluence of the Port Tobacco and Potomac Rivers. During the War of 1812, the U.S. Navy established an observation post at this strategic location to observe ship movements. Here, citizens watched the British squadron advance up the Potomac in August 1814 to threaten Alexandria, Virginia. Though the present church structure dates from 1798, the parish was founded in 1641, making it the oldest continuously active Catholic parish in America. Next door, **St. Thomas Manor** has been a Jesuit residence since its construction in 1741. While in Chapel Point, visitors may also stop at the 600-acre **Chapel Point State Park,** which has paddle-in campsites and fishing opportunities.

Not to be outdone, three small towns on the Patuxent River lay claim to their own intriguing tales. Prince Frederick, the Calvert County seat, was victimized by a night raid carried out by British troops that burned a jail and tobacco warehouse. They also set fire to the courthouse building, which is where some sick and wounded sailors from the U.S. Chesapeake Flotilla had been treated. Linden, a two-story frame house dating to the nineteenth century, is home to the Calvert County Historical Society.

Lower Marlboro is an early tobacco port town found along the river route taken by British troops heading toward the nation's capital.

Did You Know? There are two first ladies from Calvert County with connections to the war. Margaret Mackall Smith, born on St. Leonard Creek, married Zachary Taylor, who served as a U.S. Army captain during the War of 1812. Louisa Catherine Johnson, wife of John Quincy Adams, lived on a farm near the entrance of St. Leonard Creek and held a tenth anniversary ball in honor of General Andrew Jackson after his victory at the Battle of New Orleans.

During an enemy raid, warehouses were burned, a small schooner captured, and a civilian taken prisoner. But several buildings, such as the **Harbor Master's House,** survived, and the old steamboat wharf provides interpretation about the war as well as splendid river views.

> **Did You Know?** During the British occupation of Benedict in June 1814, legend holds that at least one barrel of poisoned whiskey was intentionally left for the British troops to drink, but an American with concern for humanity warned the unsuspecting troops.

On the same British-invasion route as Lower Marlboro is the town of Benedict. During the Civil War, it was the site of a camp where U.S. Colored Troops were trained, but back in mid-August 1814, Benedict encountered more than four thousand British troops that camped on nearby fields before marching on to Washington. The landing point was on the shore near the half-mile-long Benedict Bridge, which crosses the Patuxent River between Charles and Calvert Counties. North of town, local tradition claims British soldiers camped around what is now Maxwell Hall. The surrounding **Maxwell Hall Park** is a popular place for hiking.

Jefferson Patterson Park and Museum

1812 Destinations

Calvert Marine Museum
14200 Solomons Island Road, Solomons
410-326-2042
www.calvertmarinemuseum.com

A Maritime History Gallery at the museum helps orient visitors to troop movements on the Patuxent River during the War of 1812, while other exhibits delve into the Chesapeake region's ecology and prehistoric past.

Christ Episcopal Church
Intersection of Maddox and Budds Creek-Deep Falls Roads, Chaptico
www.christepiscopalchaptico.org

Founded by colonists, the Christ Church, King and Queen Parish, is located in Chaptico, which reportedly means "deep water." Established as a port of entry in 1683, Chaptico was visited by uninvited guests in the form of British troops during the War of 1812.

Jefferson Patterson Park and Museum
10515 Mackall Road, St. Leonard
410-586-8501
www.jefpat.org

Commodore Joshua Barney, a Revolutionary War hero, was described as a "flamboyant ex-privateer" who assembled eighteen small gunboats, barges, and sloops that formed the U.S. Chesapeake Flotilla and clashed

> **Did You Know?** Local tradition claims that after the British bought a horse from the Canter family farm, near Benedict, 19-year-old Henry Canter was able to sneak up on the enemy encampment during the night, whistle for his horse, and proudly ride it back home.

with a larger British squadron on waters bordering today's Jefferson Patterson Park and Museum. The naval engagement got support from American army, marine, and militia units who assembled and operated a gun battery on park property. Archaeological evidence has been found in the form of cannonballs, musket shot, and other military artifacts.

Leonardtown Public Wharf Park
End of South Washington Street, Leonardtown
www.leonardtown.somd.com/attractions/attractions
.html

A British force landed in barges at the Leonardtown Wharf, which is now part of a public park that is perfect for an evening stroll or a kayak trip. Signage along the wharf speaks to Leonardtown's maritime heritage along the waterfront.

Leonardtown Public Wharf Park

Lower Marlboro Steamboat Wharf
End of Lower Marlboro Road, Lower Marlboro
www.calvert-county.com/communities/lowermarlboro/
lowermarlboro.html

A British raid resulted in damage to several structures along the Lower Marlboro wharf, but one of the survivors was the Harbor Master's House, which became the general store and post office. The Lower Marlboro Steamboat Wharf, created in 1859, is one of twenty steamboat landing sites identified in Calvert County.

Did You Know? A tale is told of some young boys in Lower Marlboro who offered a "bird's nest" to the British, telling them that by opening the plug in the nest once at sea, a small bird would serenade them during their voyage home. The nest was actually a wasp nest.

Sotterley Plantation
44300 Sotterley Lane, Hollywood
301-373-2280, 1-800-681-0850
www.sotterley.com

The only remaining Tidewater plantation in Maryland, Sotterley is a circa-1703 National Historic Landmark that was raided by British troops during the War of 1812. Today, Sotterley offers a full range of visitor activities and educational programs representing eighteenth-century plantation life, set amidst 95 acres of fields, gardens, and riverfront.

St. Ignatius Catholic Church–St. Thomas Manor
8855 Chapel Point Road, Port Tobacco
301-934-8245
www.chapelpoint.org

Utilized by the U.S. Navy during the War of 1812 as an observation point, the present church was erected in 1798 and blessed by John Carroll, the first bishop of Baltimore. The interiors of both the church and manor house were scarred by fire in 1866, but restoration work was completed in less than two years.

For More Info

Calvert County Tourism Office
Courthouse Square, 205 Main Street, Prince Frederick
1-800-331-9771
www.co.cal.md.us/visitors

Charles County Tourism Office
200 Baltimore Street, La Plata
301-259-2500
www.charlescounty.org/tourism

Crain Memorial Information Center
12480 Crain Highway (U.S. Route 301), Newburg
301-259-2500
www.charlescounty.org.tourism

Fairview Information Center
8120 Southern Maryland Boulevard (MD Route 4),
Owings
410-257-5381

Solomons Visitor Information Center
14175 Solomons Island Road South (MD Route 2),
Solomons
410-326-6027
www.baygateways.net/general.cfm?id=30

Southern Maryland Heritage Area Consortium
P.O. Box 745, Hughesville
301-274-4083
www.destinationsouthernmaryland.com

St. Mary's County Tourism Office
23115 Leonard Hall Drive, Leonardtown
301-475-4200
www.visitstmarysmd.com

St. Mary's County Welcome Center
37575 Charlotte Hall School Road (MD Route 5),
Charlotte Hall
301-884-7059, 1-800-327-9023

What Else You'll Find

Maryland's colonial roots were planted by English settlers nearly four centuries ago, meaning visitors to the area have a lot of history to cover. In addition, the three counties that make up Southern Maryland also offer outdoor recreational opportunities that range from fishing to fossil hunting and biking in the countryside to camping beside the Chesapeake Bay.

St. Mary's County is where Maryland's story begins. On the east shore of the Potomac River, the St. Clement's Island Museum tells of those first settlers who arrived in 1634. A short while later, the fourth permanent settlement in British North America was established at what is now Historic St. Mary's City, a large living-history complex populated with costumed interpreters that toil around a colonial plantation, tall ship, brick chapel, and Indian hamlet.

At the core of the Charlotte Hall Historic District is a former military academy founded in 1774. During the War of 1812, the county's militia was headquartered at the academy. Notable alumni included Robert Bowie, who was governor of Maryland for the first few months of the war, and William B. Rochester, an aide-de-camp to General George McClure.

More than a century's worth of naval aviation history is explored in Lexington Park at the Patuxent River Naval Air Museum. Displays include aircraft, engines, unmanned aerial vehicles, and other items.

In the surrounding countryside of St. Mary's County, scenic bike routes and hiking paths give way to water trails that are suitable for a relaxing afternoon kayak trip or a multiday paddling adventure. Check out the Greenwell and St. Mary's River State Park properties for some of the best options, as well as a canoe/kayak launch at the Piney Point Lighthouse, Museum, and Historic Park that puts paddlers right out on the Captain John Smith Chesapeake National Historic Trail.

Farther up the Potomac, Charles County promises more outdoor adventure found surprisingly close to Washington, D.C. Smallwood State Park has often been tapped to host national fishing tournaments, while Purse State Park is a favorite spot to hunt for fossilized shark's teeth at the water's edge. Mallows Bay has a first-class canoe and kayak launch facility from which paddlers can head for the "ghost fleet," a collection of abandoned ships submerged in the cove off the Potomac River. But those in the know travel up the creek to leave civilization behind and commune with bald eagles, herons, and other wildlife.

A prime location on the Potomac Heritage National Scenic Trail is the Thomas Stone National Historic Site, which celebrates one of Maryland's signers of the Declaration of Independence. Situated near Port Tobacco, this property invites visitors to stroll the 322 acres surrounding Haberdeventure, a restored plantation home that has ranger-led tours.

After hiking, biking, paddling, or sightseeing at heritage sites, visitors are bound to find a waterfront restaurant close by, offering seafood for sure and maybe a few Southern Maryland specialties cooked with fresh local produce.

Sandwiched between the Chesapeake Bay and Patuxent River, Calvert County takes recreational activities to a whole other level. In such a water-laced location, it's no wonder that the county has long challenged such destinations as Annapolis and Ocean City as the charter-fishing capital of Maryland. In addition, there are canoe trails at Kings Landing Park and hiking trails at Parker's Creek Preserve (managed by the American Chestnut Land Trust), beaches and bayfront campgrounds around Breezy Point, historic oyster buyboat cruises from the Calvert Marine Museum, fossil-hunting expeditions inside both Calvert Cliffs State Park and Flag Ponds Nature Park, and even an elevated boardwalk through the Battle Creek Cypress Swamp Sanctuary.

Throughout the region, romantic getaways range from a quaint cottage in Charlotte Hall to a vineyard-based bed and breakfast in the town of Ridge, and even an early-1800s manor house in the town of Scotland.

Rounding out the allure of Southern Maryland are lighthouse tours and wine trails, as well as a year-round schedule of festivals that often concentrate on an exploration of maritime traditions or a sampling of local seafood.

By the Way . . .

America's roots of religious freedom run deep amid the centuries-old churches that contribute to Southern Maryland's peaceful, small-town charm. Officially designated an "America's Byway," the Religious Freedom Byway covers nearly two hundred miles from Port Tobacco to Point Lookout, visiting a Jesuit residence and quaint parishes that predate the Revolutionary War. A key site on the tour is Historic St. Mary's City, often recognized as "the birthplace of religious tolerance in North America."

Another famous bit of history is covered by the "Booth's Escape" Maryland Scenic Byway. Taking visitors back to April 1865, the byway moves through Clinton, Waldorf, and other towns while tracing the southerly route taken by John Wilkes Booth as he fled Washington, D.C., following the assassination of President Abraham Lincoln.

The Indian Head Rail Trail is an exciting new recreational route through some of the region's most undeveloped natural areas—including wetlands and mature forests—as well as occasional farmland. The trail covers thirteen miles connecting the town of Indian Head to U.S. Route 301 in White Plains.

Other land-based trails in Southern Maryland have been collected under the heading "Earth, Art, Imagination!" Routes with names like the "Fossils and Farmscapes Ramble" and "Barnwood and Beach Glass Loop" cover large chunks of the region, showing off shops and markets that tout authentic, handmade, and homegrown goodies. Check the Destination Southern Maryland website (www.destinationsouthernmaryland.com) for byways, trails, suggested itineraries, and information about the Southern Maryland Heritage Area.

On the water, exceptional kayak and canoe trails venture along the lower Potomac, middle Patuxent, Port Tobacco, Wicomico and St. Mary's Rivers, as well as Herring, Mattawoman, and Nanjemoy Creeks. Check with the Maryland Department of Natural Resources (www.dnr.state.md.us/boating/mdwatertrails) for public-access paddling opportunities.

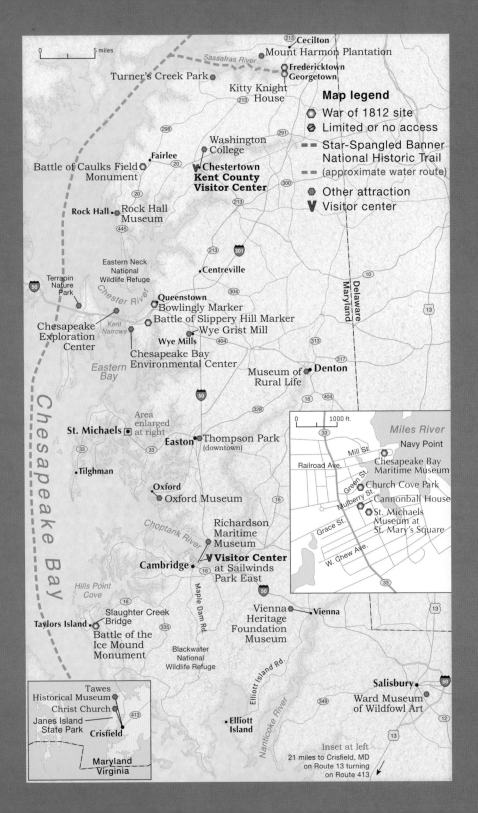

Map legend

⬡ War of 1812 site
⊘ Limited or no access
- - - Star-Spangled Banner National Historic Trail (approximate water route)
⬠ Other attraction
V Visitor center

Considering that Washington, D.C., Baltimore, and other prominent venues targeted by the British are largely located along the western shore of the Chesapeake Bay, it's no wonder that War of 1812 sites on Maryland's Eastern Shore sometimes get overshadowed.

The Eastern Shore played an important role in the War of 1812. Two battles, seven skirmishes, and at least fourteen raids occurred here, at places with names like Slippery Hill and Slaughter Creek. Twice the town of St. Michaels successfully fended off British attacks. One of the best-preserved War of 1812 battlefields in the mid-Atlantic region is Caulks Field, located near Fairlee. And the nearly forgotten Battle of the Ice Mound unfolded near Taylors Island about a month *after* the much more famous Battle of New Orleans, which is often listed last on War of 1812 timelines.

So, let this be a wake-up call for visitors interested in getting a complete picture of the War of 1812 in the Chesapeake region. Among the vibrant waterside towns, the many antiques and collectibles shops, the fine restaurants, and the miles of winding back roads waiting to be explored, Maryland's Eastern Shore delivers several must-see, history-related destinations.

The former shipbuilding center of St. Michaels is a good place to begin. It offers a nice

4 Maryland's Eastern Shore Region

St. Michaels harbor

Cannon at St. Michaels waterfront

variety of lodging choices, ranging from water-view bed and breakfasts to a luxury golf and spa resort, but it's also near Easton, which gives visitors additional options for filling their nights with live theater, musical entertainment, or an unforgettable dining experience.

St. Michaels has also been numbered among the nation's top ten "romantic escapes" by *Coastal Living* magazine, so excuse us if we start this tour with a tale that might be slightly romanticized. When the town faced its first attack under a twilight sky in August 1813, townspeople were said to have hung lanterns from the tops of houses, trees, and ships' masts so that the British would be fooled into overshooting their targets. Though it's more correct to say that the British force was driven off by American cannon placed at strategic points around the harbor, St. Michaels's nickname—"the town that fooled the British"—though not based in fact, still holds a certain amount of charm.

The British returned with a larger force two weeks after the first attack but withdrew after a short exchange of fire. A small exhibit with references to both operations is found inside the **Chesapeake Bay Maritime Museum,** which is most popular for its lighthouse, working boatyard, and hands-on activities.

Among exhibits at the **St. Michaels Museum** at St. Mary's Square—which consists of three nineteenth-century structures moved from their original locations—is a model depicting the town as it appeared during the war. On the edge of the square is the **Cannonball House,** built circa 1805 by shipwright William Merchant. Still a private residence, it is said that it was struck by a cannonball that penetrated the roof, continued

> **Did You Know?** After the death of Sir Peter Parker at Caulks Field, his body was shipped back to London via Bermuda in a cask filled with spirits and buried at St. Margaret's Church next to Westminster Abbey.

Farmers Market, Chestertown

across the attic, and rolled down the inner staircase.

After journeying about forty miles east and then north out of St. Michaels, visitors travel through Queenstown. Here a marker on the south side of MD Route 8 in the Slippery Hill area speaks of a skirmish where about twenty local militiamen successfully delayed superior British troops, allowing the main American force to safely withdraw toward nearby Centreville. Today, both town centers retain their rural atmosphere and include many historic homes and buildings. In Queenstown, a private estate commonly known as **Bowlingly** features an eighteenth-century manor house that was damaged by British forces; and the attractive Centreville courthouse, completed in 1792, features a coffered tin ceiling supported by cast iron columns.

Certainly one of the highlights of an Eastern Shore War of 1812 tour is found farther up MD Route 213, amid the cornfields near Fairlee just northwest of Chestertown. In August 1814, a battle unfolded at Caulks Field that left fifteen British soldiers dead, including the promising young captain, Sir Peter Parker, who was eulogized at a public funeral by his first cousin, the poet Lord Byron. The Americans, whose casualties amounted to just three wounded, viewed the engagement as a victory, helping to buoy American morale and confidence prior to the Battle for Baltimore less than two weeks later. Today, a simple battle monument stands at the field. Lieutenant Colonel Philip Reed, who led the American militiamen defending the field, is buried at **Christ Episcopal Church,** a short drive to the north in Worton.

> **Did You Know?** Henry Waller engaged Francis Scott Key as his attorney to secure reimbursement from the federal government for losses sustained when his bayside farmhouse in Kent County was burnt by the British. Seventeen years later, after several petitions, Congress awarded Waller $7,000 in compensation.

More than a year earlier in the war, British forces attacked and burned the villages of Fredericktown and Georgetown on the banks of the Sassafras River. Among several residences that survived is the **Kitty Knight House,** which "Miss Kitty" is credited with having saved by pleading that an elderly lady occupied it. The Kitty Knight House is now an inn and restaurant that contains a rocking chair said to have belonged to Miss Kitty and a twentieth-century mural depicting the attacks on Fredericktown and Georgetown.

A little farther north in the town of Cecilton, there is a private residence where U.S. Navy hero Jacob Jones once lived. Jones commanded the U.S. sloop-of-war *Wasp,* which early in October 1812 captured the H.M. brig *Frolic* off Chesapeake Bay after a vicious fight that left both vessels disabled.

To see the site of one of the final engagements of the war, head back on the Eastern Shore toward the **Slaughter Creek Bridge** on Taylors Island. Here, a monument to participants in the Battle of the Ice Mound consists of a carronade captured from a British tender to H.M. sloop *Dauntless* after it became stuck in ice at nearby James Island.

This battle—actually more of a skirmish—took place on February 7, 1815, a month *after* the Battle of New Orleans and just ten days prior to ratification of the Treaty of Ghent in Washington, D.C. The Battle of the Ice Mound was the last engagement of the war in Maryland.

Boardwalk at Chestertown waterfront

1812 Destinations

Battle of the Ice Mound Monument, Taylors Island

Battle of the Ice Mound Monument

North side of Taylors Island Road (Route 16), west side of Slaughter Creek Bridge, Taylors Island

The monument's 12-pounder carronade, mounted around 1950 and refurbished in 1999, is nicknamed "Becky Phipps," in recognition of both a cook and commander on the British tender from which the carronade was taken. But the cook's name was actually Becca, not Becky, and the commander was Lieutenant Matthew Phibbs, not Phipps.

> **Did You Know?** A slave named Nathan, belonging to Robert Gardner of Kent Island, having a "pert and lively look," was suspected of serving as a pilot for the British in their attack on Queenstown. He was arrested and put in the Centreville jail but escaped in February 1814.

Caulks Field Monument

North side of Caulks Field Road, northwest of intersection with Tolchester Beach Road (Route 21), Fairlee

The dedication of the monument in 1902 was attended by guests who arrived from Baltimore on the steamboat *Kitty Knight*. The monument commemorates "the patriotism and fortitude of the victor and vanquished."

Church Cove Park

Foot of Green Street, St. Michaels

Cannon are an unusual gift to give as a peace offering, but the two 6-pounders overlooking St. Michaels harbor were donated by Jacob Gibson, who, in 1813, disguised his boat as a British naval vessel as a prank to frighten St. Michaels residents. In remembrance, replica cannon were mounted in the park in 1975.

Kitty Knight House, Georgetown

Kitty Knight House Inn and Restaurant

14028 Augustine-Herman Highway (Route 213), Georgetown
410-648-5200
www.kittyknight.com

The inn was actually created by the joining of two houses, the William Henry House and Archibald Wright House. It was the Wright house that Kitty Knight allegedly saved from destruction by the British and in which she lived until her death in 1855.

Cross Island Trail, Kent Island

St. Michaels Museum at St. Mary's Square

St. Michaels
www.stmichaelsmuseum.com

The museum contains mementos from the centennial commemoration of the Battle of St. Michaels. A model of the town shows the location of the Parrott Point gun battery, which was hastily abandoned by the militia.

> **Did You Know?** With the British encamped on Kent Island, a small force of American cavalry crossed from the mainland to Eastern Neck Island via a ferry, in full view of the British lookout boats stationed at the mouth of the Chester River. By counter-marching and continually re-crossing the river, the Americans hoped to make the British believe they had a much larger force.

For More Info

Dorchester County Office of Tourism*

2 Rose Hill Place, Cambridge

410-228-1000

www.tourdorchester.org

*The Dorchester County Visitor Center is also at this location.

Heart of Chesapeake Country Heritage Area

410-228-1000

www.tourchesapeakecountry.com

Kent County Office of Tourism

400 High Street, 2nd Floor, Chestertown

410-778-0416

www.kentcounty.com

Kent County Visitors Center

118 N. Cross Street, Chestertown

410-778-0500

www.chestertown.com/visitor_center.php

Lower Eastern Shore Heritage Council

410-651-4420

http://skipjacknews.net/index.php/LESHeritage/

Queen Anne's County Office of Tourism

425 Piney Narrows Road, Chester

410-604-2100

www.discoverqueenannes.com

Stories of the Chesapeake Heritage Area

410-778-1460

www.storiesofthechesapeake.org

Talbot County Office of Tourism

11 S. Harrison Street, Easton

410-770-8000

www.tourtalbot.org

What Else You'll Find

We've already learned that Maryland's Eastern Shore weathered its share of agitation at the hands of the British. But even if the region hadn't been touched directly by the War of 1812, certainly nobody would blame today's travelers for wanting to cross the Chesapeake Bay Bridge from the Bay's western shore and hang out for a while.

Waterfront communities with walkable town centers have helped earn the area a reputation as a warm and friendly place to kick back and relax any time of the year. Dozens of locations are convenient links in the officially designated Chesapeake Bay Gateways and Watertrails Network, offering easy access to boating, bird watching, fishing, and sightseeing opportunities. These include Janes Island State Park, which offers kayakers more than thirty miles of water trails near Crisfield, and the Wye Grist Mill, which is still operating more than two centuries since it ground flour for General George Washington's Continental Army.

Around the Kent Narrows, in an area that was seized by British troops before their planned attack on nearby Queenstown, two other Bay Gateways offer an intimate look at the region's diverse nature and cultural history. The Chester-based Chesapeake Exploration Center features an interactive exhibit called "Our Chesapeake Legacy," and the Chesapeake Bay Environmental Center, located in Grasonville, fifteen minutes from the Bay Bridge, is a 500-acre preserve visited throughout the year by more than two hundred species of birds. The Environmental Center is also a site along the Star-Spangled Banner Geotrail.

Farther inland, the Eastern Shore delivers bike trails, visitor-friendly vineyards, and quaint shops. And when art aficionados say that the region's cultural destinations have gone to the birds, they mean it as a compliment. Wildfowl decoy carving is a traditional craft celebrated during several annual festivals and at sites such as Salisbury's Ward Museum of Wildfowl Art and Crisfield's Tawes Historical Museum (both of which are also official Bay Gateways).

To help travelers get their bearings, the Cambridge-based visitor center at Sailwinds Park

Kayakers on Maryland's Eastern Shore

Visitor Center at Sailwinds Park East, Cambridge

Along with the Harriet Tubman Underground Railroad route that begins in Cambridge there is another national scenic byway encompassing much of the Eastern Shore. The Chesapeake Country National Scenic Byway extends for 419 miles from Chesapeake City to Elliott Island and invites travelers to pursue a little biking, kayaking, gallery hopping, and seafood dining. The route's mid-Shore section—with stops in Wye Mills, Easton, St. Michaels, and Oxford—shows off exceptional Eastern Shore history and a very active arts community.

Some of these towns are also a key part of the Stories of the Chesapeake Heritage Area, which lists more than forty heritage sites that not only crisscross the colonial landscape but also celebrate the arts, maritime traditions, and recreational opportunities of the region. The Eastern Shore is home to two more Maryland heritage areas: The Heart of Chesapeake Country explores the American Indian, colonial, and nautical heritage of an area surrounding the waterfowl-friendly Blackwater National Wildlife Refuge; and the Lower Eastern Shore Heritage Area, nestled between the Bay and the Atlantic Ocean, incorporates museums, parks, historic mansions, and discovery centers around a recreationally rich region.

On Kent Island, a popular hiking and biking route is the Cross Island Trail, which covers six miles from the Terrapin Nature Park to Kent Narrows. Natural vistas make for nice wildlife viewing, and the well-maintained trail also incorporates family-friendly public parks.

East—recognizable by its giant, sail-shaped canopy that dwarfs the actual building—is positioned just off U.S. Route 50, a major entryway to the Lower Eastern Shore. It offers plenty of tourist information as well as exhibits related to local Bay ecology and history. As a bonus, the visitor center also provides access to historic Cambridge and serves as the starting point for a 125-mile national byway dedicated to Underground Railroad history and famous, locally born "conductor" Harriet Tubman. In addition to exposing an abundance of African-American heritage, the byway follows landscapes that have changed little in the one hundred fifty years since Tubman and others risked their lives for freedom.

In and around Cambridge, look for opportunities to enjoy shopping, shows, art, and adventure. Northward toward St. Michaels and Easton—both of which are located in an area that promotes itself as "The Hamptons of the Chesapeake"—picturesque hamlets are hugged by acres of natural beauty.

Colonial history is a key ingredient of Maryland's Eastern Shore. Towns that successfully avoided capturing the attention of British troops during the War of 1812 have hung on to many eighteenth-century structures. Chestertown, for instance, still features a number of red-brick merchants' houses, not to mention a replica 1768 schooner, the *Sultana*, docked nearby.

With all of this history and heritage related to bayside destinations, it's sometimes easy to forget that the Atlantic Ocean is just around the corner. Much of the region is an hour's drive from the oceanfront boardwalk, seaside amusements, and white-sand beaches of Ocean City, a favorite family destination.

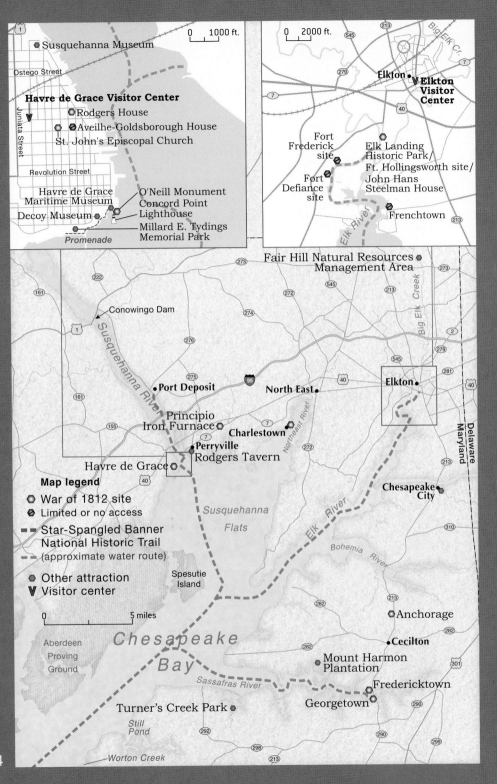

In early 1813, the British were threatening the upper Chesapeake Bay, which had only local militia and no naval protection to prevent British troops from raiding. Given this advantage, Frenchtown, Elk Landing, and Havre de Grace were hit and the Principio Iron Works was destroyed. Fear ran rampant that the important du Pont gunpowder mill near Wilmington, Delaware, would be the next to fall.

Still, America's defenders had their moments: Elk Landing (present-day Elkton) twice turned back British assaults, and from the attack on Havre de Grace came a local hero, John O'Neill.

Today's travelers will find engaging small towns with charming main streets that complement the history preserved throughout the region. Among the most handsome destinations, and the most hard-hit during the war, is Havre de Grace, Maryland's "harbor of grace" situated on the west side of the Susquehanna River. In May 1813, it was the site of a savage British attack after a brief exchange of gunfire with local militia. A force of four hundred British troops, supported by a rocket-vessel, landed and then set most of the town ablaze.

Of the sixty-two private homes in Havre de Grace, approximately forty were burned. But a couple that survived the attack—the **Aveilhe-**

5 The Upper Bay Region

Susquehanna Lockhouse Museum reenactment event, Havre de Grace

Goldsborough House, built in 1810, and the 1788 **Rodgers House**—are still standing today. Amazingly, the Rodgers House, recognized as the town's oldest documented structure, was set on fire three times by the British. The 1809 **St. John's Episcopal Church** also survived these attacks.

The centennial **Monument to John O'Neill,** located at the foot of Lafayette Street, was erected in 1914 near where tradition claims O'Neill manned a cannon to ward off the British onslaught before being taken prisoner. This gun battery was actually farther north, near the end of Bourbon and Fountain Streets. But just behind

the monument is the **Concord Point Lighthouse,** which was built in 1827 and is the oldest beacon in continuous use on the Bay. O'Neill was named the first lighthouse keeper here in recognition of his war service. Across the street is the lighthouse keeper's house, one of O'Neill's former residences.

Crossing over to the east side of the Susquehanna River, near Perryville, one finds the **Principio Furnace,** an important colonial-period iron company and home to Maryland's first blast furnace. The British destroyed the Principio complex during a raid, but it was quickly rebuilt and remained an active iron-manufacturing location well into the twentieth century. The ruins visible today are believed to date from after its run-in with the British.

Next on the tour is Charlestown, which earned some ignominy as the only jurisdiction in Maryland to officially capitulate to the British rather than possibly face a more searing fate. But as a result, the **Charlestown Historic District** has pedestrian- and bicycle-friendly streets lined with over a hundred charming historic homes and inns that evoke a time predating the War of 1812 by as many as seventy years. One such historical structure, the **107 House / Tory House,** is described as a federal-period home with a colonial basement kitchen.

Former Principio Office

In 1813 and again in 1814, British troops attempted to take Elkton by ascending Big Elk Creek. Both times they were repulsed, earning Elkton a position alongside St. Michaels as one of only two towns in the Chesapeake region known to have successfully fended off a pair of British attacks.

Elk Landing Historic Park is the site of **Fort Hollingsworth,** one of three forts (actually earthworks) to defend the town. Located today near the **John Hans Steelman House,** Fort Hollingsworth is where citizens gathered to celebrate in February 1815 when word reached Elkton that the Treaty of Ghent had been signed.

> **Did You Know?** After destroying the Principio Iron Works, British Rear Admiral George Cockburn is reputed to have said the Americans knew better how to make guns than to use them.

1812 Destinations

O'Neill Monument

Access at Commerce Street, Havre de Grace
A monument to War of 1812 town hero John O'Neill is located near the Concord Point Lighthouse.

www.concordpointlighthouse.org

Elk Landing Historic Park

590 Landing Lane off Pulaski Highway (U.S. Route 40), Elkton
410-620-6400
www.elklanding.org

The park is the site of Fort Hollingsworth, which helped to defend the town. It was also where citizens gathered to celebrate the signing of the Treaty of Ghent. In 1999, the town of Elkton acquired the property from descendants of the Hollingsworth family.

Did You Know? **During the British attack on Havre de Grace, at least six Americans were captured. Three were quickly released, but the remaining prisoners, including local hero John O'Neill, were carried onboard one of the British warships. They were set free when, under a flag of truce, a group of prominent citizens and Matilda O'Neill, the hero's teen-aged daughter, successfully pleaded for their release.**

Concord Point Lighthouse, Havre de Grace

Principio Iron Furnace

South side of Principio Furnace Road just west of Principio Creek, Perryville
410-642-2358

Principio fueled the growth of the eighteenth-century iron industry, providing pig and bar iron to Great Britain between 1718 and 1755. The furnace supplied cannon to American navy and Maryland privateers during the War of 1812.

Indian Queen Tavern/Red Lyon Tavern (in background), Charlestown

For More Info

Cecil County Tourism Office
Perryville Outlet Center, 68 Heather Lane, Suite #43, Perryville
410-996-6299, 1-800-CECIL-95
www.SeeCecil.org

Elkton Visitor Center
101 East Main Street, Elkton
410-398-5076

Fair Hill Natural Resources Management Area

Harford County Tourism Office
220 South Main Street, Bel Air
410-638-3059, 1-888-544-4695
www.harfordmd.com

Havre de Grace Visitor Center
450 Pennington Avenue, Havre de Grace
1-800-851-7756
www.hdgtourism.com

Lower Susquehanna Heritage Greenway
410-457-2482
www.hitourtrails.com

What Else You'll Find

There aren't many places that are as seemingly far removed from fast-paced city life and yet as easy to access as Maryland's Upper Bay region. It's a relatively quick commute from anywhere via I-95, but worlds away from the hustle and bustle. Visitors can take in the natural beauty and nautical history and even kayak on the mighty Susquehanna River. They can also enjoy strolls across quiet main streets with window-shopping for local crafts and keepsakes.

At Havre de Grace don't miss the boardwalk promenade along the waterfront that runs a half-mile between Concord Point and the 8-acre Millard E. Tydings Memorial Park. The park contains the community's largest playground, overlooks the City Yacht Basin,

Did You Know? During the attack on Havre de Grace, a militiaman named Webster (possibly Ensign Richard Webster, Jr.), was killed by a Congreve rocket as he retreated from a gun battery. He is one of only three persons known to be killed by rockets in the Chesapeake during the war.

and hosts a variety of events throughout the year. The promenade also connects the park to other popular attractions, such as the Havre de Grace Maritime Museum and Havre de Grace Decoy Museum, the latter of which houses a large and impressive collection of wooden waterfowl carvings. On the north side of town is the Susquehanna Museum housed in a lock keepers house. Just outside is the first lock of the Susquehanna and Tidewater Canal.

At Perryville is a new addition to the Lower Susquehanna Heritage Greenway, the 315-year-old Rodgers Tavern. This Revolutionary War hero's property was frequented by George Washington on his trips between Virginia and New York. The owner's son, Commodore

Did You Know? After Captain Oliver Hazard Perry's victory on Lake Erie, the citizens of Elkton celebrated by roasting a fine fat ox decorated with flags and ribbons that was consumed with accompanying music and merriment.

John Rodgers, has been called the "Father of the American Navy" and is credited with firing the first shot of the War of 1812 from aboard the U.S. frigate *President*. The tavern offers nice views of the Susquehanna River and provides a public boat launch.

The Upper Bay enchantment is found amid the picturesque harbor town of Havre de Grace, along the C&D Canal in tranquil Chesapeake City, within the antiques shops and specialty boutiques of North East, and throughout the 5,600 acres of protected wilderness at the Fair Hill Natural Resources Management Area. A former du Pont property with a covered bridge and eighty miles of trails, Fair Hill is also known for a turf course where horse races are held during Memorial Day weekend.

Moving away from the Chesapeake Bay along the Susquehanna River, fishing and bird watching are available below the Conowingo Dam. When completed in 1928, the dam was second only to Niagara Falls for providing hydroelectric power output in the United States. As water levels rise and fall, the dam also provides a feast of fish for winged hunters. Migrating hawks stop by each autumn, bald eagle sightings increase from November through February, and gulls come by in large numbers well into March.

Bass fishing is also a popular pursuit at the dam, as well as around the Susquehanna Flats, which are accessible from launch ramps in Havre de Grace, North East, and Port Deposit.

By the Way . . .

Along a 33-mile driving route from Havre de Grace to Perryville, numerous opportunities for outdoor recreational activities present themselves. This is Maryland's officially designated Lower Susquehanna Scenic Byway, and one of its primary destinations is Susquehanna State Park, where heavy forest cover and massive rock outcrops set the stage for camping, mountain biking, fishing, and touring historical sites such as a working grist mill and former toll house. The owner of the grist mill was said to have sold grain to the British during the War of 1812.

The byway also hooks up with a 2.2-mile Lower Susquehanna Heritage Greenway, which links land and water trails for optimum hiking, biking, and kayaking enjoyment. Outdoors enthusiasts who prefer "passive activities" enjoy keeping an eye out for local wildlife such as bald eagles, great blue heron, and migratory waterfowl that arrive seasonally while winging their way along the Atlantic Flyway. Various species of unique plants, flowers, and trees are also widespread.

The chance to explore hidden creeks and coves is available along a Sassafras River water trail, with tours coordinated by Sultana Projects, Inc., that connect to the Captain John Smith Chesapeake National Historic Trail. On their Sassafras River journey, canoeists and kayakers just might spy muskrats, osprey, crabs, and other Bay creatures.

Did You Know? Rear Admiral Cockburn coveted an elegant brass-trimmed coach he saw during the attack on Havre de Grace and ordered it hauled aboard his vessel as a gift for his wife.

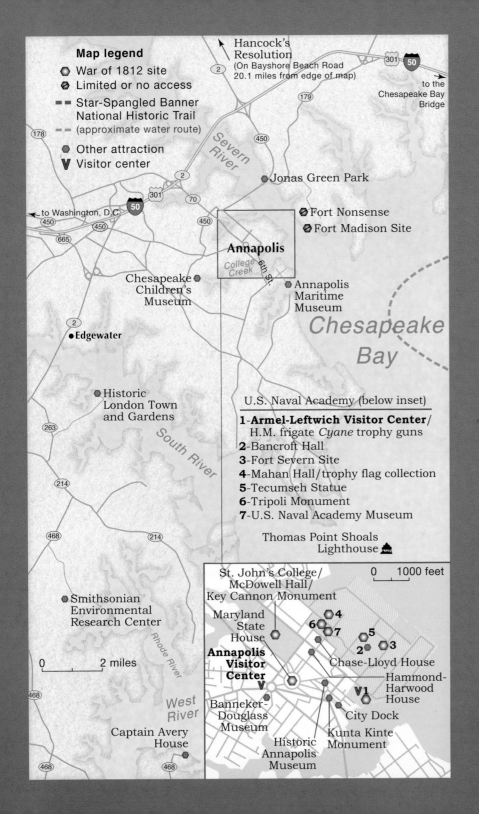

Map legend
- ⬡ War of 1812 site
- ⊘ Limited or no access
- ▬ ▬ Star-Spangled Banner National Historic Trail
- ─ ─ (approximate water route)
- ⬣ Other attraction
- **V** Visitor center

to Washington, D.C.

Annapolis

College Creek

6th St.

Severn River

Hancock's Resolution
(On Bayshore Beach Road 20.1 miles from edge of map)

to the Chesapeake Bay Bridge

Jonas Green Park

⊘ Fort Nonsense
⊘ Fort Madison Site

● Chesapeake Children's Museum

● Edgewater

Annapolis Maritime Museum

Chesapeake Bay

● Historic London Town and Gardens

South River

U.S. Naval Academy (below inset)

1-**Armel-Leftwich Visitor Center**/ H.M. frigate *Cyane* trophy guns
2-Bancroft Hall
3-Fort Severn Site
4-Mahan Hall/trophy flag collection
5-Tecumseh Statue
6-Tripoli Monument
7-U.S. Naval Academy Museum

Thomas Point Shoals Lighthouse

● Smithsonian Environmental Research Center

Rhode River

0   2 miles

West River

Captain Avery House

St. John's College/ McDowell Hall/ Key Cannon Monument

Maryland State House

Annapolis Visitor Center

Banneker-Douglass Museum

Historic Annapolis Museum

0   1000 feet

4
6 **7**
5
2 **3**

Chase-Lloyd House

Hammond-Harwood House

V1

City Dock

Kunta Kinte Monument

It shouldn't take much effort for today's traveler to imagine what Maryland's capital city must have been like when British troops threatened her boundaries in the early 1800s. Its charming tree-shaded streets, lined with brick walkways, contain the largest collection of eighteenth-century buildings in the United States. Many of these historical structures now house cafés, contemporary clubs, pubs, and chic boutiques all vying for the attention of visitors. And the **City Dock**—symbolic focal point of an area often acknowledged as the Chesapeake's sailing capital—is bustling with sleek, fiberglass sailboats and motor yachts.

Many of the historic homes and their well-manicured grounds are open to the public, with self-guided and docent-led tours showing off grand gardens and elegant chambers where important events took place and grave issues were debated during the years leading up to the War of 1812.

Getting to Annapolis means leaving the spine of the Star-Spangled Banner National Historic Trail, which extends from Southern Maryland north into Baltimore, and heading east to where the Bay mingles with the Severn River. In addition to the town's waterfront appeal, what makes Annapolis particularly charming from a traveler's perspective is the historic district's pedestrian-

6 The Annapolis Region

Maryland State House

friendliness. Several key sites are within walking distance of each other, accessible along streets where residents and visitors have gathered since colonial times.

Homes linked to four signers of the Declaration of Independence—Charles Carroll, Samuel Chase, Thomas Stone, and William Paca—are still prominent features on the Annapolis cityscape. At Samuel Chase's residence, known as the **Chase-Lloyd House,** visitors looking for a tie to the War of 1812 will be interested to know that Francis Scott Key, author of the "Star-Spangled Banner," held his wedding here. Key and Mary Tayloe Lloyd tied the knot in January 1802.

Key spent several years in Annapolis beginning at the age of ten when he attended one of the nation's oldest institutions of higher learning, **St. John's College**. Founded in 1696 as King William's preparatory school, St. John's received its collegiate charter in 1784. The campus occupied just a few acres at the time of Key's graduation in 1786, but has since expanded to cover 32 acres

> **Did You Know?** Lieutenant Colonel H.A. Fay, commander of Annapolis Forts Madison and Severn, complained that on several occasions he could row across the river at night, scale the walls of Fort Madison, and surprise the men on duty. In fact, two British officers walked around the fort to ascertain troop and armament strength, reportedly without detection.

on the edge of College Creek, near the confluence of the Severn River and Chesapeake Bay. Today, students can often be seen participating in sailing and rowing activities, and the popular annual rivalry croquet game between the college and the U.S. Naval Academy takes place in late April.

Just a couple of blocks from campus stands the **Maryland State House.** Completed in 1779,

the state house is recognized as America's oldest state capitol that has remained in continuous legislative use. During the War of 1812, it was from the structure's distinctive wooden dome—the largest in the United States—that British ship movements could be observed on the Chesapeake Bay.

Serving not only as the legislative center of state government but also the location of a military camp, Annapolis was the best-fortified city in Maryland until Baltimore was threatened in late 1814. Protection was provided by at least four forts, the last remnant of these being Fort

Chase-Lloyd House

Nonsense, an 80-foot, circular earthwork built circa 1810. Legend has it that the fort was so named because it was ineffectively constructed too far inland for its artillery to reach Annapolis harbor. Nevertheless, it actually helped to defend against a land attack on nearby Fort Madison, no longer extant.

One other harbor fortification was destined to become the future home of the **U.S. Naval Academy.** Established in 1845 on the 10-acre site of Fort Severn, the Academy was originally called the Naval School when it welcomed its first fifty midshipmen. Over the years, the campus swelled in size beyond 300 acres, and enrollment has climbed to four thousand. Even though the Academy didn't exist during the war, it features a superb museum with relevant paintings, exhibits, and artifacts. Among the museum's most valued possessions is the original "Dont Give Up the Ship" flag flown by Captain Oliver Hazard Perry during his victorious engagement with

Tecumseh statue

Did You Know? After the British occupation of Washington, D.C., Judge Jeremiah T. Chase, chairman of the Annapolis Committee of Safety, endorsed a resolution to surrender the state capital if threatened by the British. The resolution did not pass.

the British on September 10, 1813, at the Battle of Lake Erie. At one time, all midshipmen who entered the Academy stood below this flag to take their oath. The museum collection also includes a British Royal Standard taken at Fort York in Toronto.

The beautiful grounds of the Academy also show off numerous war trophies, such as two carronades placed just outside the **Armel-Leftwich Visitor Center.** These short, cast iron cannon are from the H.M. frigate *Cyane*, captured on February 20, 1815, by the U.S. frigate *Constitution*.

The **"Tecumseh Statue,"** located in front of the Academy's huge Bancroft Hall dormitory building, dates to 1891 and is the only monument in the Chesapeake region that commemorates the role of American Indians during the War of 1812. As a tribute to Tecumseh and in hope of good fortune, the bronze figure is transformed with washable paint before every home football game, the week that Navy plays Army, and during the commissioning ceremony for midshipmen. Pennies are also traditionally placed on the monument for good luck before exams.

Luck was apparently on the side of Annapolitans during the War of 1812. Though threatened on several occasions, the city was ultimately spared from attack.

1812 Destinations

Maryland State House
100 State Circle, Annapolis
410-974-3400, 1-800-235-4045
www.statehouse.md.gov

America's first peacetime capitol, the State House was the 1783 site of George Washington's resignation as commander in chief of the Continental Army. It was also the location of the ratification of the Treaty of Paris in January 1784, officially ending the Revolution.

St. John's College
60 College Avenue, Annapolis
410-263-2371
www.sjca.edu

Attended by Francis Scott Key, the college dates to 1696 and contains several historic buildings that can be viewed on a walking tour of the campus. Among these is the circa 1724 Carroll Barrister House and the circa 1720 Chancellor Johnson House, both of which were moved from town in the 1900s. McDowell Hall, the oldest original building on campus, has a plaque dedicated to Key, one of its more famous students.

U.S. Naval Academy Museum
Preble Hall, 118 Maryland Avenue, Annapolis
410-293-2108
www.usna.edu/Museum

Welcoming more than a hundred thousand visitors each year, the museum offers two floors of exhibit space, with uniforms, swords, ship models, paintings, prints, and more. The United States Navy Trophy Flag Collection totals more than six hundred American and captured foreign flags, thirty-four from the War of 1812 alone, that are exhibited at nearby Mahan Hall. Also on the Academy grounds, visitors can see a typical midshipman's dormitory room in Bancroft Hall and the crypt of naval hero John Paul Jones in the Naval Academy Chapel.

For More Info

Annapolis and Anne Arundel County Conference and Visitors Bureau*
26 West Street, Annapolis
410-280-0445, 1-888-302-2852
www.visitannapolis.org
*The Annapolis Visitor Center is located at 26 West Street, with a satellite visitor center booth at the Annapolis City Dock.

Four Rivers: The Heritage Area of Annapolis, London Town and South County
The Arundel Center, 44 Calvert Street, Annapolis
410-222-1805
www.fourriversheritage.org

City of Annapolis

What Else You'll Find

There are more than five hundred miles of shoreline in Anne Arundel County, with well-traveled waterways serving as scenic avenues for narrated boat tours, charter fishing trips, and relaxing getaways. Many of the 4 million annual visitors arrive by pleasure craft.

On the Severn River, Jonas Green Park has a sandy beach for canoe and kayak launching and offers a nice view of the U.S. Naval Academy and Chesapeake Bay. At the mouth of the South River, the Thomas Point Shoal Lighthouse has survived for more than one hundred twenty-five years. Accessible by boat, it is one of two offshore, screwpile-style lighthouses still being used by the U.S. Coast Guard. The Chesapeake Chapter of the U.S. Lighthouse Society conducts tours of the lighthouse from the Annapolis Maritime Museum in the summer.

In the heart of Annapolis, opportunities abound to sightsee among colonial-era buildings, grab a stool at a waterfront pub, browse around upscale boutiques, dine on delectable seafood, and enjoy a flourishing visual and performing arts scene. The historic City Dock is where Kunta Kinte, famous ancestor of *Roots* author Alex Haley, was led ashore as a slave, and where both men are now immortalized with a plaque and bronze statue, respectively. Annapolis is also home to one of the state's leading repositories of African-American history, the Banneker-Douglass Museum.

For young visitors, the Chesapeake Children's Museum has hands-on activities in a quiet woodland setting.

Farms, small towns, and watermen's villages surround Annapolis. To the south, at Historic London Town and Gardens in Edgewater, you can tour a Georgian house, stroll through woodland gardens, and investigate archaeological digs. To the north, Hancock's Resolution in Pasadena is an authentic, late-eighteenth-/early-nineteenth century farmstead that hosts an annual War of 1812 reenactment commemorating the burning of the American schooner *The Lion* in nearby Bodkin Creek.

By the Way . . .

While traveling to Annapolis, look for roadside signs identifying the officially designated "Roots & Tides" Maryland Scenic Byway. This forty-seven mile route digs into the timeless traditions of bayside towns nestled between the state capital and Southern Maryland's Chesapeake Beach. Many sites along the way are part of the Chesapeake Bay Gateways and Watertrails Network, an assortment of waterside parks, historic ports, museums, and wildlife refuges that offer convenient access to Bay-based recreation. Examples are the hiker-friendly 2,800-acre Smithsonian Environmental Research Center in Edgewater, which includes the ruins of a former captain's house from the 1812 era. In Shady Side, the Captain Avery Museum is a restored, nineteenth-century waterman's cottage that hosts a museum.

The byway is part of a larger Four Rivers Heritage Area that extends from Sandy Point State Park at the Chesapeake Bay Bridge down through southern Anne Arundel County to the small community of Rose Haven. Along the way, visitors get an appreciation of Maryland's rich historic, cultural, and natural legacy while following the shoreline, rivers, and creeks of the Bay. For boaters and paddlers on the Captain John Smith Chesapeake National Historic Trail, "smart buoys" found along the route provide historical information and near-real-time climate and environmental data. The closest smart buoy to Annapolis is bobbing at the mouth of the Severn River.

> **Did You Know?** As the British fleet sailed up the Chesapeake Bay toward Baltimore during the second week of September 1814, people in Annapolis, fearing an attack of their own, fled the city in wagons loaded with their possessions.

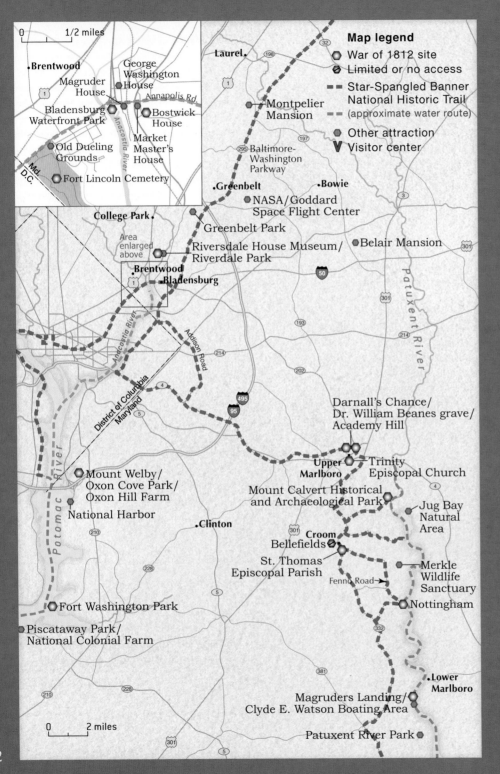

Map legend

- ⬡ War of 1812 site
- ⊘ Limited or no access
- ▬ ▬ Star-Spangled Banner National Historic Trail
- ▬ ▬ (approximate water route)
- ⬡ Other attraction
- V Visitor center

0   1/2 miles

Brentwood
George Washington House
Magruder House
Annapolis Rd.
Bladensburg Waterfront Park
Bostwick House
Market Master's House
Old Dueling Grounds
Fort Lincoln Cemetery
Md. D.C.

Laurel
Montpelier Mansion
Baltimore-Washington Parkway
Greenbelt
Bowie
NASA/Goddard Space Flight Center
College Park
Greenbelt Park
Area enlarged above
Riversdale House Museum/ Riverdale Park
Belair Mansion
Brentwood
Bladensburg
Anacostia River
Addison Road
District of Columbia Maryland
Darnall's Chance/ Dr. William Beanes grave/ Academy Hill
Upper Marlboro
Trinity Episcopal Church
Mount Welby/ Oxon Cove Park/ Oxon Hill Farm
National Harbor
Mount Calvert Historical and Archaeological Park
Jug Bay Natural Area
Clinton
Croom
Bellefields
St. Thomas Episcopal Parish
Fenno Road
Merkle Wildlife Sanctuary
Patuxent River
Potomac River
Fort Washington Park
Nottingham
Piscataway Park/ National Colonial Farm
Lower Marlboro
Magruders Landing/ Clyde E. Watson Boating Area
0   2 miles
Patuxent River Park

The area of Maryland directly south and east of America's capital city offers travelers many options beyond its easy access to Washington, D.C. Here, within Prince George's County, entertainment possibilities are as plentiful as the pleasing views to be found along the recreationally and historically rich Potomac River, a federally protected American Heritage River.

The southern portion of this region also offers pastoral settings surrounding country roads that, in some cases, were the very ones used by British troops on their northward march toward Washington. Their route, now featured around the midway point of the **Star-Spangled Banner National Historic Trail,** took them through such towns as Upper Marlboro and, of course, Bladensburg, scene of one of America's greatest defeats during the war.

Now a modern suburb of Washington, Bladensburg was founded in the mid-eighteenth century and quickly became a major port for shipping tobacco. In 1814 it was the location of a decisive battle that lasted just a few hours but cleared the final obstacle preventing a British invasion of the nation's capital.

A good place to begin a tour through this region is at the **Bladensburg Waterfront Park.** The park not only overlooks the battlefield site, but also has a public boat ramp, fishing pier, 1812

7 The Bladensburg Region

Darnall's Chance, Upper Marlboro

U.S. naval hero Commodore Joshua Barney was wounded and captured after he and his men had provided a rare bright spot for the American side of the battle. Though British forces were actually outnumbered, they had little difficulty routing the raw militia that filled most of the American lines. While other troops ran, Barney led a group of U.S. Chesapeake Flotillamen and U.S. Marines that put up the only serious resistance to the British advance.

The right flank of the thin American line was positioned on what is now Fort Lincoln Cemetery, chartered in 1912 and located in present-day Brentwood. The entrance to the cemetery is about one mile west of Bladensburg Waterfront Park. This peaceful ground once reverberated with the sounds of muskets, rifles, cannon, Congreve rockets, bugles, officers calling out orders, and the cries of fighting men. Look near the

George Washington House, Bladensburg

mausoleum for a historical marker and monument commemorating Barney and his troops. Between here and the Anacostia River was also the site of the **Old Dueling Grounds,** where 41-year-old naval hero Stephen Decatur received a mortal wound in 1820.

Several blocks east of Bladensburg Waterfront Park is **Bostwick**, a historic home built in 1746 for Christopher Lowndes, a local shipyard owner and merchant whose trading company imported spices, building materials, dry goods, and slaves. Colonel Thomas Barclay, British prisoner-of-war agent during the war, resided at Bostwick and warmly welcomed the British as they marched into Bladensburg.

trail orientation center, and other features. Free, naturalist-led pontoon boat tours are often available, as well as canoe, kayak, and rowboat rentals in the spring, summer, and fall.

From within the park, a pedestrian/bike bridge crosses the Anacostia River near the location of a former bridge used by the British to attack the American defenders on the opposite side. Farther to the west, President James Madison and Secretary of State James Monroe watched the action on the heights in the distance.

> **Did You Know?** African-American Frederick Hall was a slave who escaped from the Oden farm at Bellefields (present-day Croom) in 1814, changed his name to William Williams, enlisted in the U.S. Army at age twenty-one, and was mortally wounded during the bombardment of Fort McHenry.

Kayaker at Jug Bay Natural Area

Three other pre–Revolutionary War structures still standing in town are the **Magruder House** (also known as the William Hilleary House), built between 1742 and 1764; the **George Washington House,** completed in 1765 and now occupied by the Anacostia Watershed Society; and the circa-1765 **Market Master's House,** which may have been used to oversee tobacco activity at the busy shipping port. British troops passed the Magruder House as they marched toward the bridge and battlefield. Local tradition holds that cannonballs fired during the conflict scarred the brick walls of the George Washington House, though no evidence of this can be seen today.

Residing a couple of miles upriver in what has become known as Riverdale Park, Rosalie Stier Calvert claimed to be a witness to the Battle of Bladensburg. From her bedroom window, she reported observing "several cannonballs with my own eyes." (The cannonballs were probably actually Congreve rockets.)

Rosalie was married to George Calvert, grandson of the fifth Lord Baltimore, and they lived in a stucco-covered, five-part, brick, federal-style mansion called Riversdale. Henry Clay, a War of 1812 War Hawk, was a frequent visitor, and the Calverts were known to have become friends with some of the wounded British officers left behind after the Battle of Bladensburg. Rosalie's husband and slaves helped to bury the dead. The history of the site during the War of 1812 is the subject of an interpretive panel in the **Riversdale House Museum** visitor center. In addition, a Battle of Bladensburg reenactment, complete with demonstrations, drills, and representations of military camp life, is held there each August.

To the south, numerous sites have ties to the progress of the war leading up to the action in Bladensburg.

In June 1814, the British raided Magruders Landing and burned the Moil and Magruder warehouse. All that remain today are pilings from a post–War of 1812 steamboat-era wharf (fishing and boating are available nearby at the Clyde E. Watson Boating Area in Brandywine).

The town of Nottingham was used as a base for the U.S. Chesapeake Flotilla during July and August 1814, but the site was abandoned after British expeditionary forces applied pressure to a small group of dragoons under Secretary of State James Monroe. The townspeople were said to have fled so quickly that they left bread baking in their ovens. Interpretive signage is found around the historic **Nottingham School.**

Extending northward from Nottingham, Fenno Road still looks much as it did in 1814, when large trees provided cool shade for the woolen-clad British soldiers marching in the summer heat. A few miles northwest is **Mattaponi,** a home formerly belonging to Governor Robert Bowie. Bowie assisted in rounding up British soldiers as they looted Upper Marlboro following the burning of Washington. A few miles west is **St. Thomas Episcopal Parish,** formerly Page's Chapel, the home church of Anglican Bishop Thomas John Claggett and the supposed burial spot for seven British soldiers. The location of the graves is marked by flat, concrete squares alongside the Berry family plot.

> **Did You Know?** Benjamin Ogle II, governor of Maryland from 1798 to 1801, lived at Belair Mansion near Bowie during the War of 1812. On August 27, 1814, the family negotiated the sale of their horses to the British. In 1822, Henrietta Ogle successfully won compensation in the amount of $3,401 for slaves carried off by the British.

At the **Mount Calvert Historical and Archaeological Park** in Croom, a federal-style plantation house built circa 1790 offers dramatic views of the Patuxent River, as well as boat access. Laden with artillery, a contingent of Royal Marines and seamen disembarked from boats here to join the British Army at Upper Marlboro for their march on Washington.

In Upper Marlboro, where the British Army and Navy linked up about sixteen miles from Washington, an eighteenth-century residence known as **Darnall's Chance** was the home of John Hodges, who reluctantly released some captured British stragglers following the enemy occupation of Washington. For his actions, Hodges became the only person known to be tried for treason during the war.

On Academy Hill in Upper Marlboro, next to where his house was once located overlooking Schoolhouse Pond, is the grave of **Dr. William Beanes,** an American prisoner of war whose release was negotiated by Francis Scott Key and John Stuart Skinner several days prior to the bombardment of Fort McHenry.

Upper Marlboro is also the location of **Trinity Episcopal Church.** British soldiers entered the church and ripped pages from the parish register book. The oldest portion of the present church structure dates only to the mid-1840s.

Mount Welby, the circa-1811 home of Dr. Samuel DeButts, is operated by the National Park Service as part of Oxon Cove Park / Oxon Hill Farm. Here, Mary Welby DeButts wrote letters describing the British squadron advancing up the Potomac River in August 1814, firing Congreve rockets, three of which landed near her home. Visitors to Oxon Cove Park can experience the evolution of two centuries of farming through hands-on activities and living-history programs.

Fort Washington, built on a high bluff of the Potomac River in 1808, was blown up by the Americans without firing a shot when threatened by a British squadron in 1814. As a result, Captain Samuel Dyson, the fort's commander, was relieved of his command, found guilty of abandoning his post and destroying government property, and ultimately dismissed from service. A new fort, completed in 1824, underwent major remodeling prior to playing an important role in the protection of Washington during the Civil War.

Operated today by the National Park Service, Fort Washington offers great views of the Potomac River and the distant Washington skyline. But it's quite a different image from the one that British forces saw after fighting their way through Bladensburg and marching toward America's capital.

1812 Destinations

Dr. William Beanes's Grave
Academy Hill
14518 Elm Street and Governor Oden Bowie Drive, Upper Marlboro

Dr. Beanes was a respected Maryland doctor who helped apprehend British deserters and stragglers after the burning of Washington. When the British, in turn, took Beanes prisoner, a chain of events was set into motion that ultimately led to lawyer Francis Scott Key's witnessing the Battle for Baltimore at Fort McHenry. The grave of Dr. Beanes rests next to his former home site on Academy Hill.

Bladensburg Waterfront Park
4601 Annapolis Road, Bladensburg
301-779-0371
www.pgparks.com/Things_To_Do/Nature/Bladensburg_Waterfront_Park.htm

The park, which overlooks the battlefield site, offers an 1812 trail orientation center. Although Bladensburg was once a vital colonial port, today the park is used for recreational fishing, bicycling, walking, boating, and paddling.

Bostwick
3901 48th Street, Bladensburg
301-927-7048
www.townofbladensburg.com/cms/bostwick

Built in 1746, Bostwick is one of just four pre-Revolutionary structures still standing at Bladensburg. The Georgian brick house was constructed for Christopher Lowndes, a local shipyard owner. During the War of 1812, Colonel Thomas Barclay, a British prisoner-of-war agent who lived there, welcomed the British.

Fort Washington Park

Darnall's Chance

14800 Governor Oden Bowie Drive, Upper Marlboro
301-952-8010
www.pgparks.com/places/eleganthistoric/darnalls_
intro.html

Now a house museum, Darnall's Chance was built in the 1740s and included outbuildings and an ornamental garden. The only person tried for treason during the War of 1812 lived here. An eighteenth-century underground burial vault was discovered in 1987 and found to be filled with eighteenth- and nineteenth-century household trash, beneath which were the remains of nine people.

Fort Lincoln Cemetery

3401 Bladensburg Road, Bladensburg
www.hmdb.org/marker.asp?marker=3614

The right flank of the American line waged a battle here against the British on August 24, 1814. In the Civil War, the grounds were the site of Battery Jameson; the battery's remains can still be seen beside the old springhouse.

Fort Washington

1355 Fort Washington Road, Fort Washington
301-763-4600
www.nps.gov/fowa

American troops blew up the 1808 fort when threatened by a British squadron in 1814. The fort's commander, Captain Samuel Dyson, was found guilty of destroying government property. Now a national park, the site boasts sweeping views of the Potomac.

Mount Calvert Historical and Archaeological Park

16302 Mount Calvert Road, Upper Marlboro
301-627-1286
www.pgparks.com/places/parks/mtca;vert/html

Before the British marched on Washington, they were joined by a contingent of Royal Marines that landed at this 1790 tobacco plantation on the Patuxent River. Ongoing archaeological research is being conducted on the property, which also has an interpretive trail, restored plantation house with exhibits, and boat access.

Oxon Cove Park/Oxon Hill Farm (Mount Welby)

6411 Oxon Hill Road, Oxon Hill
301-839-1176
www.nps.gov/oxhi/index.htm

From her home, Mary Welby DeButts wrote letters describing the British advancing up the Potomac River in August 1814. Now a national park, Oxon Cove Park/Oxon Hill Farm has living-history programs and hands-on activities that let visitors experience colonial farm life.

Riversdale House Museum

4811 Riverdale Road, Riverdale Park
301-864-0420
www.riversdale.org

The Battle of Bladensburg echoes at Riversdale. Every August a reenactment is held on the mansion's grounds, complete with drills and demonstrations of military camp life. Built between 1801 and 1807, Riversdale is open to the public for docent-guided tours.

Did You Know? Unaware of how close he was to British troops, President James Madison was nearly captured at Bladensburg in his haste to find Brigadier General William Winder, commander of the American forces.

For More Info

Anacostia Trails Heritage Area

4310 Gallatin Street, Hyattsville
301-887-0777
www.anacostiatrails.org

Prince George's County Conference and Visitors Bureau

9200 Basil Court, Suite 101, Largo
301-925-8300
www.visitprincegeorges.com

What Else You'll Find

For a satisfying journey into the diverse past of Prince George's County, tour one of the many visitor-friendly plantation and manor houses that are now museums. Montpelier Mansion in Laurel welcomed guests such as George Washington and Abigail Adams; the Marietta House in Glenn Dale interprets three generations of nineteenth-century residents, including Supreme Court Justice Gabriel Duvall, who served during the War of 1812 era; and the eighteenth-century Belair Mansion in Bowie has had a long connection to thoroughbred horse racing.

The evolution of flight is investigated in College Park at the oldest continuously operating airfield, which was established in 1909 by none other than Wilbur Wright. Meanwhile, the future unfolds in Greenbelt at the NASA/Goddard Space Flight Center, which explores satellite control, spacecraft construction, and out-of-this-world communication operations.

One of the area's newest attractions is National Harbor, an urban-waterfront community with elegant shops and galleries, a variety of dining establishments, and water taxi service that extends across the Potomac River to Old Town Alexandria, Virginia.

Getting in touch with the outdoors in Prince George's County might involve observing hundreds of Canada geese at the Merkle Wildlife Sanctuary; fishing within the National Park Service's Fort Washington Park; utilizing a boat launch at Piscataway Park (which also features the National Colonial Farm living-history museum); or renting a canoe at Patuxent River Park. And keep in mind that all of these destinations—from the mansions and museums to the canoe launches and hiking trails—are just minutes from the nation's capital.

> **Did You Know?** An American battle flag recovered at the Bladensburg battlefield and taken to England as a war prize still survives at the Royal Hospital Chelsea in London.

By the Way . . .

Much of the land in the Bladensburg region is part of the Anacostia Trails Heritage Area and offers opportunities for pleasant walks across landscapes that have changed little since the War of 1812 era. At Darnall's Chance in Upper Marlboro, a walk of less than a half-mile takes visitors past a mill pond to the grave of Dr. William Beanes. Other recommended short strolls are along the river at Fort Washington and around Oxon Cove Park, site of Mount Welby.

> **Did You Know?** African-American Charles Ball, a flotillaman serving with Joshua Barney during the Battle of Bladensburg, described the American militia as "sheep being chased by dogs."

For bikers, skaters, runners, and walkers alike, the Anacostia Riverwalk Trail features a continuous sixteen miles of pleasant scenery and many historical sites. In addition, an Anacostia River Water Trail is also available, incorporating part of the Captain John Smith Chesapeake National Historic Trail. Beginning at the 32-acre Magruder Park in Hyattsville, the Anacostia trail soon passes Bladensburg Waterfront Park and continues on to include a variety of other land-based sites, including the National Arboretum and the Washington Navy Yard. Thus, a kayaking excursion can turn into a driving, biking, or hiking tour.

Last, but not least, there is an Anacostia River Trail that, at less than two miles, is perfect for a short bicycle outing. The trail hooks into the Colmar Manor Community Park (near the site of the Old Dueling Grounds) and is part of the Anacostia Tributary Trail System.

The Patuxent Water Trail, extending from lower Calvert County in Southern Maryland to the Tridelphia

Reservoir in Montgomery County, north of Washington, D.C., offers another opportunity for canoeists and kayakers. Among several Prince George's County–based launches providing access to approximately 80 miles of the 110-mile-long Patuxent River are the Cedar Haven Fishing Area in Eagle Harbor, Selby's Landing in the Jug Bay Natural Area (Upper Marlboro), and the Governor Bridge Natural Area in Bowie. In addition to the area's historical significance, the water trail boasts scenery that ranges from marshlands to thick forests and farm fields.

For visitors interested in extending their journey by driving an hour or more into the northern reaches of Maryland, downtown Frederick won't disappoint. Located about fifty miles northwest of Washington, D.C., Frederick is famous for its artsy streetscape and three centuries of American history. Francis Scott Key once lived, worshipped, and practiced law here, and his sister married local resident Roger Brooke Taney, a chief justice of the U.S. Supreme Court. Key and Taney practiced law together, and both are buried in Frederick. Near Key's gravesite at Mount Olivet Cemetery is a striking bronze statue erected in his honor in 1898, fifty-five years after his death.

Mount Welby, Oxon Cove Park

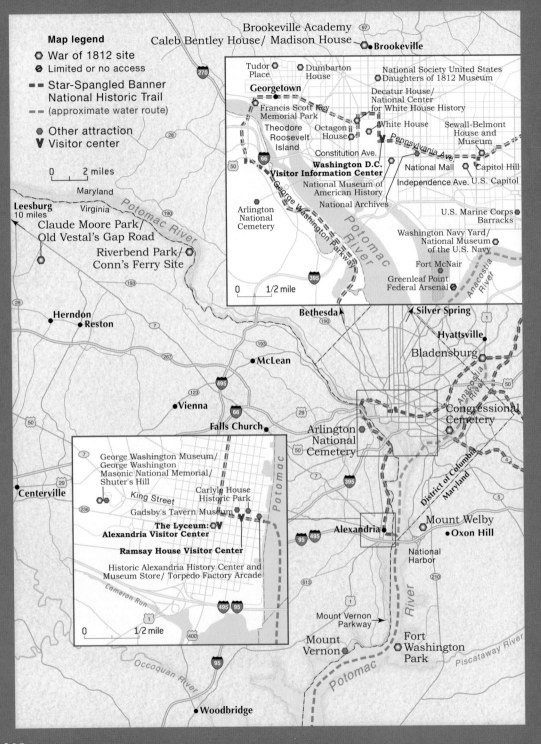

Map legend

- ◎ War of 1812 site
- ◎ Limited or no access
- ▪▪▪ Star-Spangled Banner National Historic Trail
- --- (approximate water route)
- ● Other attraction
- V Visitor center

0   2 miles

Maryland

Leesburg
10 miles   Virginia   Potomac River

**Claude Moore Park/
Old Vestal's Gap Road**

**Riverbend Park/
Conn's Ferry Site**

Herndon
Reston

McLean

Vienna

Falls Church

Centerville

George Washington Museum/
George Washington
Masonic National Memorial/
Shuter's Hill

King Street

Carlyle House
Historic Park

Gadsby's Tavern Museum

**The Lyceum:
Alexandria Visitor Center**

Ramsay House Visitor Center

Historic Alexandria History Center and
Museum Store/ Torpedo Factory Arcade

Cameron Run

0   1/2 mile

Brookeville Academy
Caleb Bentley House/ Madison House   Brookeville

Tudor
Place   Dumbarton
House

National Society United States
Daughters of 1812 Museum

Georgetown

Francis Scott Key
Memorial Park

Decatur House/
National Center
for White House History

Theodore
Roosevelt
Island

Octagon
House   White House

Sewall-Belmont
House and
Museum

Pennsylvania Ave.

Constitution Ave.

**Washington D.C.
Visitor Information Center**

National Mall   Capitol Hill

National Museum of
American History

Independence Ave.   U.S. Capitol

National Archives

Arlington
National
Cemetery

U.S. Marine Corps
Barracks

Washington Navy Yard/
National Museum
of the U.S. Navy

Fort McNair

Greenleaf Point
Federal Arsenal

0   1/2 mile

Bethesda   Silver Spring

Hyattsville

Bladensburg

McLean

Arlington
National
Cemetery

Congressional
Cemetery

District of Columbia
Maryland

Alexandria

Mount Welby

Oxon Hill

National
Harbor

Mount Vernon
Parkway

Mount
Vernon

Fort
Washington
Park

Piscataway River

Occoquan River

Woodbridge

208

Barely two decades before the start of the War of 1812, Washington, D.C., was just beginning to take shape in the mind of the man selected to design the new Federal City. As French engineer Pierre Charles L'Enfant formulated his plan, he looked toward Jenkins Hill—a knob of land that plateaus 88 feet above the nearby Potomac River—and made his famous pronouncement that this precious site was "a pedestal waiting for a monument."

Jenkins Hill became Capitol Hill, and on its crest was placed the **U.S. Capitol.** Since that time, Washington has become a fertile garden of tributes to people and events, with monuments, memorials, and museums sprouting up among the many government buildings. Visitors arrive every day by the tens of thousands to be inspired, educated, and enthralled.

During the War of 1812, the U.S. Capitol building—standing up there on its pedestal—must have looked to be a tantalizing target for British forces. Other public structures, including the White House, were also in the invaders' sights. Many of the buildings were burned.

Of course, Washington wasn't just the seat of the federal government in those days. It also contained important military resources, including the Washington Navy Yard, the U.S. Marine Barracks, and a federal arsenal. Yet, Secretary of War

8 The Washington, D.C., Region

White House

John Armstrong was convinced that Washington would not be a target of the enemy because of its relatively minor strategic value when compared to other cities such as Portsmouth and Baltimore. Thus, Washington was poorly defended. And as a result, during the month of August 1814, the capital was occupied by a foreign power for the first and only time in America's history—a stunning blow for the proud, young nation.

The U.S. Capitol was not complete in 1814. There was no central core with a dome, only a north and south wing connected by a wooden causeway that ran about the length of a football field. The scene in August must have been surreal, with the flag of Great Britain flying beside the

unfinished burning structure and British troops bivouacking on Capitol Hill.

An exhibition hall in the U.S. Capitol's underground visitor center features many items related to the war, including a model of what Capitol Hill looked like at the time. Artifacts include the plans submitted by British-born architect Benjamin Henry Latrobe for rebuilding the Capitol, as well as a letter written in September 1814 by Thomas Jefferson, offering his substantial personal collection of books to replace the congressional library lost in the fire. (Thanks to Jefferson's generosity, the course was set for establishment of the Library of Congress as it is known today, housed in its current location since 1897.)

Free tours of the U.S. Capitol reveal many original features, including the walls of the Old Supreme Court Chamber and six columns in the Old Senate Vestibule, each depicting cornstalks and ears of corn.

Did You Know? Henry Foxall, a Methodist minister and mayor of Georgetown, prayed that his iron foundry would be spared when the British invaded. When it survived, Foxall in return paid for the construction of a new Methodist Church.

Sewall-Belmont House

Two blocks northeast of the Capitol is the **Sewall-Belmont House and Museum,** one of the few private structures toward which British forces directed their wrath. Built in 1800, the house was partially burned in retaliation for an American sniper attack from its windows. After several renovations, it has served as the headquarters of the National Women's Party since 1929 and a museum of the women's suffrage and equal rights movements.

The White House—known as the "President's House" at the time of the war—stands several blocks northwest on Pennsylvania Avenue in the Lafayette Park area. First occupied fourteen years earlier by President John Adams, the White House was left a roofless shell by the British. Only a few objects remain in the rebuilt

Executive Mansion from before the time of the fire: one is a portrait of George Washington that hangs in the East Room (First Lady Dolley Madison is credited with saving the painting prior to British occupation), and another is a small wooden medicine chest in the Map Room.

Near the White House are several notable structures including the U.S. Department of State, **U.S. Treasury,** and the **Washington, D.C., Visitor Information Center.**

Octagon House, completed in 1801, is one of the oldest structures in Washington. After the burning of the White House, it served as a temporary Executive Mansion for President James Madison. The Treaty of Ghent, officially ending the war, was ratified here.

Back toward Capitol Hill is the **National Museum of American History,** part of the **Smithsonian Institution** complex. Some visitors to this museum might want to sneak a peek

U.S. National Archives

at pop culture icons like Dorothy's ruby slippers or Michael Jackson's hat; others will be excited to view a Vietnam War–era UH-1H Huey helicopter or the chairs used by Civil War Generals Grant and Lee during the surrender ceremony at Appomattox Court House, Virginia. But the centerpiece of the museum—one of the most sought-out artifacts in the Smithsonian collection—is the huge garrison flag that flew over Fort McHenry as the British departed Baltimore. Within a climate-controlled gallery that re-creates "dawn's early light," the tattered banner is dramatically displayed behind a 35-foot-long, floor-to-ceiling glass wall.

The **National Society United States Daughters of 1812** has its national headquarters in Washington, complete with an 1812 museum. Among various relics is a vintage twelve-star

---

Did You Know? With many of Washington's public buildings in ruins, Congress debated moving the capital to Philadelphia, but intense lobbying from the administration coupled with the offer of construction loans from the Bank of the Metropolis helped tip the balance for remaining in Washington, D.C.

American flag carried during the war. There is also a War of 1812 walking tour available at the **Congressional Cemetery,** with stops at the burial sites of such notables as Attorney General William Pinkney, Commodore Joseph Smoot, and Major General Jacob Brown. Another walking tour, entitled "The Burning of Washington,"

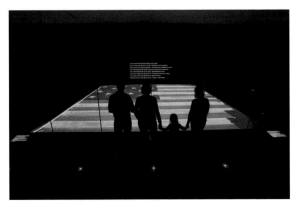
Family viewing the Star-Spangled Banner

incorporates the public vault where Dolley Madison was temporarily interred.

At the **Washington Navy Yard** in southeast D.C., the main gate, constructed in 1806, is one of the few structures that survived the burning of the Navy Yard to keep it out of the hands of the British. In the 1880s, the gate was incorporated into a larger Victorian structure, losing its original appearance. But the **National Museum of the U.S. Navy,** located on site, features among its many exhibits such items as a replica of the U.S. frigate *Constitution*'s gun deck and artifacts from Commodore Joshua Barney's Chesapeake Flotilla.

In the opposite corner of the District of Columbia, the 260-year-old neighborhood of Georgetown is an international community of embassies, upscale shops, and eclectic eateries. Here Martha Washington's granddaughter, Martha Peter, watched from her bedroom window at **Tudor Place** as the nation's capital burned. Tudor Place and its nearly six-acre garden are open to the public. Tours are also available of the **Dumbarton House,** to which First Lady Dolley Madison fled when British troops threatened the White House. In addition, there is a **Francis Scott Key Memorial Park,** paying tribute to the "Star-Spangled Banner" writer while noting the former location of Key's residence when he lived on M Street. The park is located next to Francis Scott Key Bridge.

An interesting sidetrack is available eighteen miles north of Washington in Brookeville, Maryland. This Montgomery County town earned the nickname "United States Capital for a Day" after President Madison and members of his cabinet, seeking refuge following the occupation of Washington, spent one night and part of the next morning at the residence of Caleb Bentley

Lanesville Ordinary, Claude Moore Park

(subsequently renamed the Madison House). Brookeville boasts several other historical buildings, including the **Brookeville Academy,** which is where U.S. Senate records were kept during the British occupation of Washington.

Other documents, including the Declaration of Independence, had been packed in twenty-two carts that traveled along a portion of Old Vestal's Gap Road (roughly following present-day Route 7) and into Leesburg, Virginia, for safekeeping. Along the way, the caravan traveled through the present site of **Claude Moore Park,** which encompasses 357 acres in Sterling. George Washington frequently passed this way en route from Mount Vernon to the western frontier, and General Edward Braddock's troops, including Daniel Boone, moved through here during the French and Indian War nearly sixty years earlier.

Another site with significance to President Madison and his flight from Washington is the 400-acre **Riverbend Park** in Great Falls, Virginia. This was the location of Conn's Ferry, which the president used to cross the Potomac River from Virginia into Maryland, heading toward Brookeville. A boat ramp exists near where the ferry used to land on the Virginia side, and the park is especially popular for hiking, fishing, and kayaking.

Following the destruction inflicted upon Washington, officials in nearby Alexandria, Virginia, didn't want to risk igniting British ire and suffering a similar fate. Thus, the city meekly capitulated to a British naval squadron and survived a weeklong enemy occupation (August 28 to September 3, 1814) without major incident.

News of Alexandria's quick surrender wasn't well received among many neighboring towns, and even Dolley Madison considered the terms of

the city's capitulation to have been humiliating. However, one could argue that the Alexandria of today might not otherwise exist. Perhaps there would be no compelling reason to walk along present-day King Street and other avenues in Old Town Alexandria, admiring the merchants' houses, warehouses, and churches, and perhaps ducking into a quaint shop or restaurant along the waterfront.

Alexandria's history museum is located in an 1839 Greek Revival structure called **The Lyceum**. A small exhibit on the War of 1812 includes a carronade recovered from the shoreline of the Potomac River. Another war artifact, this one a banner carried by the Alexandria Independent Blues, is exhibited inside a museum linked to the **George Washington Masonic National Memorial.** The memorial is prominently located on Shuter's Hill (the spot Thomas Jefferson proposed for the site of the U.S. Capitol) and is worth a visit just for the view. Late afternoon or early evening is best, as the setting sun casts its last rays of the day toward old Alexandria and the Potomac.

1812 Destinations

Claude Moore Park
21544 Old Vestal's Gap Road, Sterling
571-258-3700
www.loudoun.gov

Within the 357-acre, multi-use park, a house built in the late 1700s was used as an ordinary by travelers on the Vestal's Gap Road. Many of America's most important documents traveled down this road for safekeeping when Washington was threatened by British troops.

Congressional Cemetery
1801 E Street, S.E., Washington, D.C.
202-543-0539
www.congressionalcemetery.org

The cemetery covers more than 35 acres and features fourteen thousand headstones, with burial places for

Table on which the Treaty of Ghent was signed by James Madison, Octagon House

more than fifty-five thousand people. Two walking tours are specifically related to the War of 1812, while others cover topics such as the Civil War, Men of Adventure, and Women of Arts and Letters.

Francis Scott Key Memorial Park
M Street at Francis Scott Key Bridge, Washington, D.C.

Popular for bikers, the park has signage noting where the former house of "Star-Spangled Banner" writer Francis Scott Key was located when he lived in Georgetown.

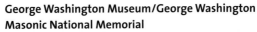

Did You Know? On February 16, 1815, at 7 p.m., a gun salute was fired and Washington was illuminated by the synchronized lighting of candles and oil lamps in the homes. The war was officially over.

George Washington Museum/George Washington Masonic National Memorial
101 Callahan Drive, Alexandria
703-682-2007
www.gwmemorial.org

The design of the memorial was inspired by the Egyptian Lighthouse of Alexandria. Guided tours are available to learn about American Freemasons, including George Washington. On this hill American officers contemplated how to attack the British fleet then occupying Alexandria.

The Lyceum
201 South Washington Street, Alexandria
703-838-4994
www.alexandriava.gov/lyceum

Before becoming Alexandria's history museum, the building was used as a private home, Civil War hospital,

Georgetown waterfront

office building, and the nation's first bicentennial center. A carronade from the War of 1812 is exhibited here.

National Museum of American History
National Mall, 14th Street and Constitution Avenue, N.W., Washington, D.C.
202-633-1000
www.gosmithsonian.com

The original Star-Spangled Banner from Fort McHenry is displayed in a climate-controlled room at the museum. One of the flag's fifteen stars was cut out and apparently given away in the 1800s. An "A" was reportedly sewn onto one of the flag's white stripes by Louisa Armistead, widow of the War of 1812 commander at Fort McHenry.

National Museum of the U.S. Navy
Washington Navy Yard, 805 Kidder Breese Street, S.E., Washington, D.C.
202-433-4882
www.history.navy.mil/branches/org8-1.htm

Among War of 1812 artifacts at the museum are a model of the U.S. frigate *Constitution* ("Old Ironsides") and the desk of Commodore Thomas Macdonough, hero of the Lake Champlain Campaign.

National Society United States Daughters of 1812 Museum

1463 Rhode Island Avenue, N.W., Washington, D.C.
202-745-1804
www.usdaughters1812.org/museum.html

The facility is dedicated to history from 1784 to 1815. The Andrew Jackson Room has artifacts from the Battle of New Orleans. The flagpole in front of the national headquarters is crafted from the topgallant mast from the U.S. frigate *Constitution*. Museum is open Tuesdays and Thursdays only.

Octagon House

1799 New York Avenue, N.W., Washington, D.C.
202-626-7312
www.nps.gov/nr/travel/wash/dc22.htm

When James and Dolley Madison used the house as a temporary "Executive Mansion," the president utilized the circular room above the entrance as his study and signed the Treaty of Ghent here. Prearranged tours are available by appointment.

Riverbend Park

8700 Potomac Hills Street, Great Falls, Virginia
703-759-9018
www.fairfaxcounty.gov/parks/riverbend

The park, located at the site of President Madison's ferry crossing as he fled Washington, features a 2.5-mile portion of the Potomac Heritage Trail, which links national and regional parkland.

U.S. Capitol

Intersection between Maryland and Pennsylvania Avenues, and Constitution and Independence Avenues, Washington, D.C.
202-226-8000
www.visitthecapitol.gov

Guided tours of the Capitol, which must be reserved in advance, begin with a thirteen-minute orientation film, followed by stops at the Crypt of the Capitol, the Rotunda, and the National Statuary Hall. The U.S. Capitol

Did You Know? Concerned that an attack was imminent, officials imposed a 10 p.m. curfew on the citizens of Washington on August 20, 1814. All unauthorized persons had to be off the streets or risk getting arrested. The British arrived four days later.

Visitor Center, the main public entrance, is located underground on the east side of the building at First and East Capitol Streets.

White House

1600 Pennsylvania Avenue, N.W., Washington, D.C.
202-456-7041
www.whitehouse.gov/about/tours-and-events

The first residents of the White House were John and Abigail Adams in 1800. Only the shell of the building survived the fire during the War of 1812; there was a second fire (in the West Wing) in 1929, when Herbert Hoover was president.

U.S. Capitol

For More Info

Alexandria Convention and Visitor Association

421 King Street, Suite 300, Alexandria
703-746-3300, 1-800-388-9119
www.visitalexandriava.com

Alexandria Visitor Center

1724 Ramsay House, 221 King Street, Alexandria
1-800-388-9119

Cultural Tourism DC

1250 H Street, N.W., Washington, D.C.
202-661-7581
www.culturaltourismdc.org

Destination DC

901 7th Street, N.W., 4th Floor, Washington, D.C.
202-789-7000
www.washington.org

Heritage Tourism Alliance of Montgomery County

12535 Milestone Manor Lane, Germantown
301-515-0753
www.heritagemontgomery.org

Historic Alexandria History Center and Museum Store

101 N. Union Street, Alexandria, Viriginia
703-746-4760
www.alexandriava.gov/historic

Washington, D.C., Visitor Information Center

Ronald Reagan Building, 1300 Pennsylvania Avenue, N.W., Washington, D.C.
202-312-1300
www.washington.org

What Else You'll Find

Washington, D.C., hardly needs any introduction. Tourism is a way of life here, as evidenced by the regular flow of foot traffic and tour buses all around the National Mall area. We're talking somewhere in the neighborhood of 16 million domestic and international visitors each year.

Monuments and memorials are around virtually every corner, honoring poets and civil rights leaders, inventors and war veterans, past presidents and other celebrated patriots. There's even a graceful granite statue dedicated to "the brave men who perished in the wreck of the Titanic," erected somewhat ambiguously by the "Women of America."

National Park Service staff members are on hand to offer daily interpretive programs as well as bicycle tours based on the War of 1812 and other themes. Programs are held at several of the most popular sites, including the Thomas Jefferson Memorial, Lincoln Memorial, Franklin Delano Roosevelt Memorial, World War II Memorial, Korean War Veterans Memorial, and Vietnam Veterans Memorial. Also within walking distance is the Washington Monument; shaped like an Egyptian obelisk and towering over the surrounding city at more than 555 feet tall, it stands 1.4 miles from the U.S. Capitol, separated by the long, narrow Capitol Reflecting Pool.

Carlyle House, Alexandria

Riverbend Park on the Potomac Heritage National Scenic Trail

Spring is a particularly picturesque time to visit the area, with cherry blossoms blooming and nearby gardens creating their own colorful statements.

For many tourists, a trip to D.C. isn't complete without a stop at one or more of the properties associated with the Smithsonian Institution, the largest museum and research complex on the planet. Collectively, the nineteen Smithsonian museums and galleries, ranging from the National Air and Space Museum to the National Portrait Gallery, contain more than 136 million objects. This includes seventeen properties in Washington and two in New York City, but what we don't know is whether all of the animals at the National Zoological Park got factored into the total! One thing's for sure: zoo admission is absolutely free, just like the other D.C.-based Smithsonian properties.

Without a doubt, Washington prides itself on catering to many interests. There's something for families and foodies, Civil War buffs and sports enthusiasts, urban explorers and those interested in African-American heritage. Performing arts are another pleasing diversion at a variety of theaters and other entertainment venues throughout town. In operation since 1971, the Kennedy

Center is one of the most popular places in the nation to enjoy a full schedule of ballet, classical music, dance, jazz, opera, vocal concerts, and more.

Much of D.C.'s commuter traffic comes through Union Station, located at the north end of Capitol Hill. Not only Washington's main Amtrak rail terminal, it also has retail stores, a food court, sit-down restaurants, and a seasonal outdoor market. In the northwest quadrant of D.C., the neighborhood of Georgetown offers a commercial corridor dominated by high-end shops and fine restaurants.

Across the Potomac River into Virginia, visitors have plenty of options for seeing the historical surroundings and interesting colonial structures of Old Town Alexandria. Among a variety of guided tours are river cruises, horse-drawn carriage rides, and walking tours along the cobblestone streets. Historical reenactments occur outside the Carlyle House Historic Park, which is best known for interpreting the lifestyle of an eighteenth-century Virginia family. Also, the Carlyle House, like the Congressional Cemetery in D.C. and the Dumbarton House in Georgetown, is part of the Star-Spangled Banner Geotrail, providing a fun opportunity for heritage-minded geocaching. Old Town Alexandria is a popular tourist area with convenient parking, as well as access via metro and DASH bus. (A free King Street trolley travels between the metro and waterfront.) Plan on starting out at the Ramsay House Visitor Center or Historic Alexandria History Center to get a map and brochures, and then spending several hours exploring, dining, and shopping throughout the area.

Another popular attraction is the Torpedo Factory, where, true to its name, torpedoes were manufactured during World War I and II. The building now houses studios for dozens of artists; visitors are welcome to watch printmakers, jewelry makers, painters, and potters at work. It's also a great place to find unique gifts and decorative items.

Fireworks on the National Mall

By the Way . . .

For self-guided walking tours in Washington, D.C., Neighborhood Heritage Trails have been mapped out by Cultural Tourism DC. Trail signs combine stories and photos that fit a certain theme, such as the diverse population of the Adams Morgan neighborhood or Civil War ties to the Brightwood community. Free audio commentaries can be downloaded for certain routes, such as the "Civil War to Civil Rights" Downtown Heritage Trail and the "City within a City: Greater U Street" Heritage Trail.

Just across the Potomac River from downtown Washington is a multi-use trail nearly eighteen miles in length and offering terrific views of the capital city. It is called the Mount Vernon Trail because the path follows the river's Virginia shoreline from Theodore Roosevelt Island to George Washington's Mount Vernon estate. Points of interest along the way include Old Town Alexandria and Arlington National Cemetery. Rangers lead bicycle and kayak tours.

Of course, paddlers will prefer a trip along the Potomac River Water Trail, which reaches more than a hundred miles toward the Chesapeake Bay. A tidal stretch of the river passes through landscapes rich with Revolutionary War, War of 1812, and Civil War history. The Potomac Heritage National Scenic Trail offers access to biking, hiking, and other recreation on this corridor between the Chesapeake Bay and the Allegheny Highlands.

Alongside the nation's capital, magical destinations are found throughout a Maryland heritage area known as Heritage Montgomery. Surrounding the bustling arts and entertainment districts of Bethesda and Silver Spring, heritage highlights in Montgomery County include eighteenth-century plantation homes, nineteenth-century railroad communities, historic White's Ferry, and a national trolley museum.

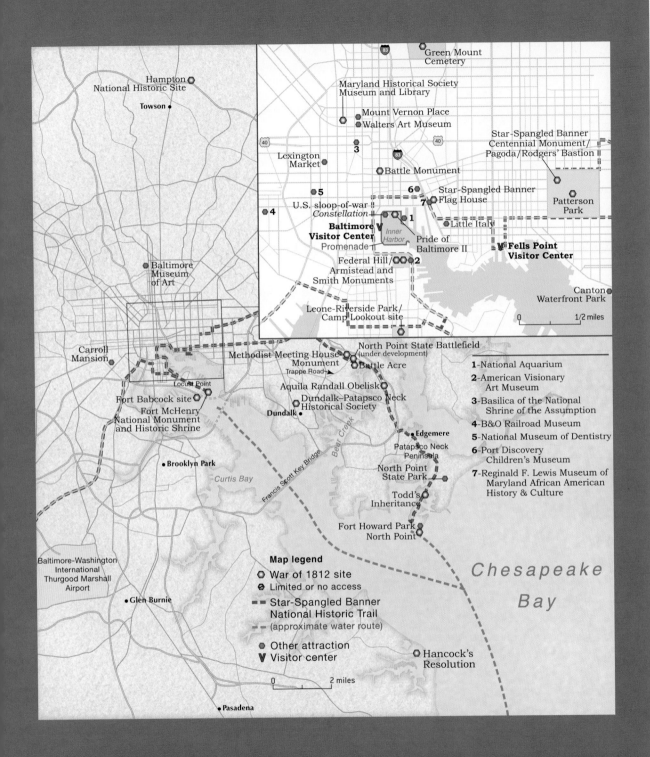

Green Mount Cemetery

Maryland Historical Society Museum and Library

Mount Vernon Place
Walters Art Museum

Star-Spangled Banner Centennial Monument/ Pagoda/Rodgers' Bastion

Lexington Market

3

Battle Monument

5

U.S. sloop-of-war *Constellation*

6

Star-Spangled Banner Flag House

7

Patterson Park

4

1

Baltimore Visitor Center
Promenade

Inner Harbor

Pride of Baltimore II

Little Italy

Fells Point Visitor Center

Federal Hill/ Armistead and Smith Monuments

2

Canton Waterfront Park

Leone-Riverside Park/ Camp Lookout site

0   1/2 miles

Hampton National Historic Site

Towson

Baltimore Museum of Art

Carroll Mansion

Locust Point

Fort Babcock site

Fort McHenry National Monument and Historic Shrine

Brooklyn Park

Curtis Bay

Baltimore-Washington International Thurgood Marshall Airport

Glen Burnie

Pasadena

North Point State Battlefield (under development)

Methodist Meeting House
Monument
Trappe Road
Battle Acre

Aquila Randall Obelisk

Dundalk–Patapsco Neck Historical Society

Dundalk

Bear Creek

Edgemere

Patapsco Neck Peninsula

North Point State Park

Todd's Inheritance

Fort Howard Park North Point

Francis Scott Key Bridge

1-National Aquarium

2-American Visionary Art Museum

3-Basilica of the National Shrine of the Assumption

4-B&O Railroad Museum

5-National Museum of Dentistry

6-Port Discovery Children's Museum

7-Reginald F. Lewis Museum of Maryland African American History & Culture

Map legend

◉ War of 1812 site
⊘ Limited or no access
▬ ▬ Star-Spangled Banner National Historic Trail
– – (approximate water route)
● Other attraction
V Visitor center

0   2 miles

Chesapeake Bay

Hancock's Resolution

216

When you hear those five simple words—"Oh say, can you see"—what comes to mind? Do you think of a point of land protecting the passage into Baltimore's Inner Harbor, a star-shaped fort perched on the Patapsco River; and fifteen broad red and white stripes and fifteen white stars on a blue field flag rippling high on a flagpole in dawn's early light?

This is what Francis Scott Key probably saw on the morning of September 14, 1814, piquing his national pride and moving him to write new lyrics to a popular song that would become the national anthem of the United States. Two centuries later, visitors can still be inspired by the fort, which has remained relatively similar to its War of 1812 appearance.

Fort McHenry National Monument and Historic Shrine, located at the tip of Locust Point in Baltimore, symbolizes the United States experience in the war. It is the most-visited War of 1812 site in the United States or Canada, with more than seven hundred thousand visitors in a year. And it represents the climactic conclusion of a trip along the Star-Spangled Banner National Historic Trail.

Of course, the beautifully maintained fort can also be a great starting point for a deeper exploration of the war as experienced around the

9 The Baltimore Region

Baltimore area. Museums, mansions, and former battlegrounds are all found within a short drive.

Any trip to Fort McHenry should begin with a stop inside the park's visitor and education center, which opened in March 2011. The center features exhibits, touch-screen panels, interactive displays, and a life-sized bronze sculpture of Key. The giant screen on which an orientation film is shown has been designed so that it slowly rises like a curtain at the film's conclusion, dramatically revealing a broad view of the fort and, when weather permits, a full-sized replica of the Star-Spangled Banner flying over the ramparts.

Baltimore skyline

Among items on display at the center are an officer's uniform worn during an 1814 battle, a book of poems written by Key, and a cape worn by a Baltimore City school student during the centennial commemoration of the writing of "The Star-Spangled Banner." The student had donned the cape while forming one small part of

> **Did You Know?** The Basilica of the Assumption, America's first Roman Catholic cathedral, was still under construction in 1814 when it was suggested as a good second line of defense if the first line could not hold against a British attack on Baltimore.

a "Living American Flag"—a tradition that has endured as an annual activity.

The fort's "flagship" event is Defenders Day—The Star-Spangled Banner Weekend. This three-day "encampment and extravaganza" celebrates Maryland's oldest holiday, commemorating the defense of the city and the penning of America's national anthem. The event is held each September and features reenactors, parades, music, musket-firing, fireworks, and a symbolic ship-to-shore bombardment.

Ranger program at Fort McHenry

Plan on spending up to two hours to complete a self-guided tour of the fort. During summer months, consider participating in one of the daily ranger talks to learn how the fort performed its military duty for one more century following the War of 1812, serving during the Mexican War, Civil War (as a prison camp for Southern sympathizers and Confederate prisoners of war), Spanish-American War, and finally World War I (as a three thousand–bed U.S. Army receiving hospital). The fort was made a national park in 1925, and then, fourteen years later, became the only place in the country to be designated both a national monument and historic shrine.

Constructed between 1799 and 1802, Fort McHenry is shaped like a five-pointed star, built primarily of brick and surrounded by a dry moat.

War of 1812 reenactment at Fort McHenry

From behind the cannon that point down the Patapsco River, visitors can imagine they are standing among the thousand Americans who participated in the "perilous fight" that commenced on a gray and wet day in September 1814. From atop the walls of the fort, visitors can see the anchorage site of the British fleet that, for twenty-five straight hours, sent rockets and bombs hurtling toward the structure with destructive intent.

By "dawn's early light," the British fury was spent. As enemy ships withdrew, a 17- by 25-foot "storm flag" flying within the fort was lowered and replaced by a grand garrison banner measuring 30 feet wide by 42 feet long. It is this flag that Key saw while under British guard onboard a truce ship in the Patapsco River. Fort McHenry still stood. The city was safe.

Having already created some lyrics during the bombardment, Key completed his work later in a Baltimore hotel room. Set to the tune of a popular British song, "The Star-Spangled Banner" was born, destined in 1931 to officially become the national anthem.

Key's original manuscript hasn't traveled far from its point of origin. The oldest known version is showcased in the Star-Spangled Banner Gallery at the **Maryland Historical Society Museum,** which is located in the same Mount Vernon neighborhood as The Walters Art Museum, the Enoch Pratt Free Library, and the Peabody Institute of The Johns Hopkins University. The Historical Society has the largest collection of War of 1812 memorabilia in Maryland, everything from portraits of Baltimore's famous Defenders and vivid scenes of local battles to an unexploded "bomb" that fell at the feet of a Fort McHenry

> **Did You Know?** **Thomas Kemp of Fells Point built the privateers** *Rossie, Rolla, Comet, Patapsco, Midas,* **and** *Chasseur,* **the last made famous under the command of Captain Thomas Boyle and referred to as the "Pride of Baltimore." Kemp also built the 5-gun U.S. sloop** *Erie* **and U.S. sloop** *Ontario,* **both launched in 1813, as well as gun barges for the Baltimore Flotilla and U.S. Chesapeake Flotilla.**

soldier and a cane made from the wood of a poplar tree under which British Major General Robert Ross was killed during the Battle of North Point. Among the seven million documents in the library is the log of the "Pride of Baltimore," the celebrated privateer *Chasseur.* Almost 170 years old, the Society is truly "Maryland's attic." It documents Maryland's colorful past with an entire city block of exhibits, living history, and year-round engaging programs for every age.

And what of the tattered Star-Spangled Banner that so inspired Key? It is displayed in Washington, D.C., at the Smithsonian Institution's National Museum of American History (see the Washington, D.C., Region travel section). Meanwhile, a full-sized glass replica adorns the exterior of the **Star-Spangled Banner Flag House** near Baltimore's Inner Harbor area. This museum and historic house is a tribute to Mary Pickersgill, the woman commissioned to sew the flag. Already a well-known flag maker at the time, Pickersgill was able to produce the heavy, woolen banner in less than two months with the assistance of her daughter, two nieces, and two servants. Pickersgill's house, built in 1793 and doubling as her place of business, contains numerous authentic, early-nineteenth-century artifacts and has a hands-on Discovery Gallery where children can design their own flag.

Just a day before the British naval attack on Fort McHenry, a land battle occurred southeast of Baltimore in the Dundalk and Edgemere

Jean and Lillian Hofmeister Museum at the Star-Spangled Banner Flag House

Meeting House Monument, Dundalk

areas. Approximately forty-five hundred British troops rowed ashore at the tip of the North Point (Patapsco Neck) peninsula, but more than three thousand American militia troops blocked North Point Road and put up a stubborn resistance during what has become remembered as the Battle of North Point.

Enemy troops landed near the present-day remnants of **Fort Howard,** a portion of which is now a county park. Fort Howard, which was actually constructed decades after the war, hosts a Defenders Day at North Point celebration that always occurs the weekend before Fort McHenry's annual event. There is an encampment, a flag-raising ceremony, a reenactment, and various living-history displays and interpretive sessions.

A short distance inland is **North Point State Park.** Part of the **Star-Spangled Banner National Historic Trail,** it features a visitor center, fishing areas, and flat-water paddling. Located between Fort Howard and the state park,

the **Todd House,** also called Todd's Inheritance, served as a horse courier station to report British movements to American troops. The British set the residence ablaze in retaliation, but another house was built on the original foundations. This still-rural section of North Point Road provides a glimpse of what the area might have looked like during the war.

Did You Know? U.S. Navy hero Joshua Barney was born on Bear Creek, near where, forty-five years later, the American right flank was located during the Battle of North Point. His home during the War of 1812 is now a bed and breakfast: www.joshuabarneyhouse.com

Though the British scored a tactical victory during the Battle of North Point, advancing troops suffered a greater number of casualties, including the death of Major General Robert Ross, "the man who captured Washington."

There are two surviving traces of the actual North Point battlefield. **North Point State Battlefield,** a 9-acre parcel currently under development by the Maryland Department of Natural Resources, will feature a commemorative walking trail, interpretation, native plantings, and public art. Across the street, **Battle Acre Park** was dedicated in 1839 to those who fought at North Point; a cannon-topped granite monument was added during the centennial celebration in 1914.

Visitors who like a challenge will enjoy finding the **Aquila Randall Obelisk,** which is a bit "off the beaten path." Surrounded by private

property, the monument is along North Point Road, which offers only narrow shoulder parking nearby. One of the first monuments ever erected on a battlefield, the obelisk was placed in 1817 to honor a 24-year-old private who was the only member of his Maryland militia unit to be killed in the battle.

At a museum operated by the **Dundalk Patapsco Neck Historical Society** are exhibits that feature historical prints and artifacts related to the Battle of North Point.

The key position of the American defense on the eastern edge of Baltimore is still partially visible inside **Patterson Park,** at the site of an 1891 Pagoda. When open on select days, the Pagoda offers excellent views of the British positions on the outskirts of Baltimore, not to mention the Francis Scott Key Bridge and even Fort McHenry. Directly in front of the pagoda, at the terrace of Commodore John Rodgers's Bastion, a bronze and granite **Star-Spangled Banner Centennial Monument** was erected in 1914. Created by J. Maxwell Miller, it depicts two children who, on their way home from school, apocryphally find

Patterson Park

Fells Point waterfront

a scroll telling the story of how the national anthem came to be written. Pupils of the Baltimore school system donated funds for the monument.

Major General Samuel Smith, who was in charge of the defense of Baltimore, and Lieutenant Colonel George Armistead, commander of Fort McHenry, are both honored with monuments atop **Federal Hill,** which offers perhaps the best view of the city's Inner Harbor area. On September 11, 1814, cannon fired three shots from the Hill to inform Baltimoreans that the British had landed on North Point. Suggestions for a walking tour in the Federal Hill District are available at www.federalhillonline.com.

Just to the south, **Leone-Riverside Park** is the former site of Camp Lookout, which was a key observation point and played a supporting role in repulsing a British nighttime flanking maneuver directed at nearby Fort McHenry.

Baltimore was the third largest city in the United States during the War of 1812 and among the young nation's most important seaports. In addition, here were built the swift-sailing Baltimore clipper ships that were so successfully

employed as privateers to harass British vessels. A working example of one such topsail schooner is the 157-foot-long **Pride of Baltimore II,** launched in 1988. Though the *Pride II* has visited more than two hundred ports in forty countries while serving as the official Goodwill Ambassador of the State of Maryland, she can often be seen at her home port in Baltimore.

Many privateering vessels were constructed in what is now the **Fells Point National Register Historic District.** This Baltimore neighborhood features cobblestone streets and great waterfront views but has become more popular for its shops, restaurants, and more than a hundred pubs. The former shipbuilding community celebrates Privateer Day each April, with activities that include live music and an authentic living-history camp.

Cannon for War of 1812 privateers were often supplied by a foundry under the ownership of wealthy Towson resident Charles Carnan Ridgely. A member of the Baltimore County Troop of Cavalry, Ridgely also contributed a hundred barrels of flour to aid in the war effort. The foundry is in ruins, but Ridgely's nearby home, **Hampton Mansion,** is just nineteen miles from Fort McHenry and considered to be one of the finest and largest surviving examples of Georgian architecture in the United States. On the grounds of this national historic site, visitors will find gardens and original slave quarters. At the rear stair landing of the mansion, there are two unexploded 13-inch British shells, presumed to be from the bombardment of Fort McHenry.

Baltimore is aptly called the Monumental City, a nickname conferred by President John Quincy Adams when he visited in 1827, and one

is likely to find statues and artifacts commemorating the war of 1812 in many places around the city. The best-known example is the 52-foot-tall **Battle Monument,** standing in a square on Calvert Street between Fayette and Lexington Streets. Battle Monument, designed by J. Maximilian Godefroy, was the first substantial monument built in the United States to commemorate the war, and it is today part of the official seal of the City of Baltimore as well as incorporated into Baltimore's flag.

At the Smithsonian-affiliated **National Museum of Dentistry,** there is a musket ball recovered from the North Point Battlefield. One theory of the ball's purpose is that, in an era before anesthetics, injured soldiers bit down on it to help them endure the pain of surgery—hence, the source of the phrase "to bite the bullet." More likely, the ball was chewed just to pass time and relieve stress.

Meanwhile, a somber reminder of the high price America paid to preserve this "land of the free" is found at **Green Mount Cemetery.** Among the approximately sixty-five thousand individuals buried here are the remains of more than three hundred War of 1812 veterans.

Did You Know? Fourteen-year-old Samuel Sands, a printer's assistant and later editor of the Baltimore *American Farmer,* printed as a handbill on September 17, 1814, the first copies of Francis Scott Key's lyrics "Defence of Fort M'Henry" (later renamed "The Star-Spangled Banner").

1812 Destinations

Battle Monument
Calvert Street between Fayette and Lexington Streets, Baltimore

The 52-foot-tall monument was the nation's first substantial monument commemorating the War of 1812. Composed mainly of locally quarried Cockeysville marble, the monument was designed by J. Maximilian M. Godefroy and completed in 1825.

Federal Hill
Covington Street, and Warren and Battery Avenues, Baltimore
www.baltimore.org/baltimore-neighborhoods/federal-hill

Best known for its views of the Inner Harbor, Federal Hill is also the home of a monument to War of 1812 heroes Major General Samuel Smith and Lieutenant Colonel George Armistead. It was from Federal Hill that three cannon shots were fired on September 11, 1814, warning that the British had landed at North Point.

Fort McHenry National Monument and Historic Shrine
2400 East Fort Avenue, Baltimore
410-962-4290
www.nps.gov/fomc

Built in 1799, the fort was named after Secretary of War James McHenry. Special events throughout the year include twilight tattoo ceremonies, a Living American Flag, National Flag Day, a Civil War Weekend, and Defenders Day—The Star-Spangled Banner Weekend.

Hampton National Historic Site
535 Hampton Estate Lane, Towson
410-823-1309
www.nps.gov/hamp

Now a national historic site, the Hampton Mansion, built after the Revolutionary War, once was surrounded by property as large as half of Baltimore City. Visitors today can learn about nearby Northampton Foundry where cannon were made for Baltimore privateers. Two British bombs ornament the mansion's south stairway overlooking the beautiful gardens.

Maryland Historical Society Museum and Library
201 West Monument Street, Baltimore
410-685-3750
www.mdhs.org

The museum and library houses Maryland treasures such as the original manuscript of the "Star-Spangled Banner" and a tortoise-shell box that British Rear Admiral George Cockburn gave to a teenaged girl whose father had been taken prisoner in Havre de Grace, Maryland. Cockburn was moved by the girl's courageous efforts to get her father released.

Patterson Park
East of Patterson Park Avenue between Baltimore and Gough Streets, Baltimore
www.pattersonpark.com

One of Baltimore's best-loved and most-used parks today, Patterson Park was also a key part of the city's

Battle Monument

defense strategy. The remnants of Commodore John Rodgers's Bastion are still partially visible near the 1891 Pagoda.

Pride of Baltimore II
1801 South Clinton Street, Baltimore
410-539-1151
www.pride2.org

The British invaded Baltimore because it was one of the nation's most important seaports and home to swift-sailing clipper ships that harassed British vessels. *Pride of Baltimore II* is a 157-foot near replica of a Baltimore privateer. As Baltimore's ambassador, *Pride* sails the seas of the world, so don't be surprised if you don't see her at her berth.

Star-Spangled Banner Flag House
844 East Pratt Street, Baltimore
410-837-1793
www.flaghouse.org

Learn the story behind the flag that flew over Fort McHenry after the Battle for Baltimore. Flag maker Mary Pickersgill lived in a tidy, brick 1793 home that is now an interactive museum.

Todd House (Todd's Inheritance)
9000 North Point Road, Edgemere
410-477-5000
www.toddsinheritance.org

This home served as a horse courier station, reporting on British movements. In retaliation, the British burned it, but another house was built on the original foundations. It is open to the public on Defenders Day, which commemorates the successful defense of the City of Baltimore during the War of 1812.

For More Info

Baltimore County Tourism Office
400 Washington Avenue, Towson
410-296-4886
www.enjoybaltimorecounty.com

Baltimore National Heritage Area
100 Light Street, 12th floor, Baltimore
443-878-6411
www.baltimoreheritagearea.org

Baltimore Visitor Center (Inner Harbor)
401 Light Street, Baltimore
1-877-225-8455 (call center)
www.baltimore.org/visitor-center

Visit Baltimore Tourism Office
100 Light Street, 12th Floor, Baltimore
1-877-225-8455 (call center)
www.baltimore.org

Hampton Mansion, Towson

What Else You'll Find

Built on humble maritime traditions, Baltimore—or "Charm City," as it's often called—is a bustling metropolis brimming with dynamic destinations.

Cultural attractions take center stage year-round, thanks largely to the rich and famous residents who settled centuries ago in the Mount Vernon area. Their legacy includes art museums, performing arts centers, and institutions of higher learning.

Elsewhere in town, visitors can emerge from a quaint Little Italy eatery or waterfront seafood restaurant to explore the Inner Harbor area. Featured destinations include the National Aquarium, Maryland Science Center, and American Visionary Art Museum, but there are also shops, paddle boats, water transportation provided by Baltimore Water Taxis, and even moonlight cruises. The U.S. sloop-of-war *Constellation,* which is docked at the Inner Harbor, is not the frigate that was pinned down by a British naval blockade for much of the War of 1812; that ship went on to travel the globe as part of an illustrious career that lasted until 1845, when she was laid up in Norfolk and then dismantled eight years later. The second *Constellation,* recognized as the last all-sail warship built by the U.S. Navy, was a Civil War–era vessel that achieved worldwide acclaim similar to her predecessor, helping to disrupt the African slave trade. Tours are provided.

Within easy walking distance of the *Constellation* is a collection of other historic vessels, including a U.S. Coast Guard cutter that saw action during Japan's attack on Pearl Harbor, a submarine that sank three Japanese ships near the end of World War II, and a mid-twentieth-century lightship that guided maritime traffic in and out of the Chesapeake Bay.

More history is ready to be discovered around town at such destinations as the B&O Railroad Museum, the Jewish Museum of Maryland, and the Reginald F. Lewis Museum of Maryland African American History and Culture.

Other corners of the city have antiques shops, art galleries, and the world-famous Lexington Market, a Baltimore tradition for more than two centuries.

Star-Spangled Banner Centennial Memorial, Patterson Park

Did You Know? On August 15, 1814–less than a month before the British assault on the city–Rembrandt Peale opened Peale's Baltimore Museum and Gallery of Fine Arts on North Holliday Street. An established member of the famous Peale family of artists, Rembrandt was later commissioned by the City of Baltimore to paint portraits of War of 1812 heroes. His renderings of Commodore Joshua Barney, Major General Samuel Smith, Brigadier General John Stricker, and Major George Armistead are now among the prized possessions of the Maryland Historical Society.

By the Way . . .

Sure, it's a long walk, but well worth the effort! Covering seven miles of shoreline, the nearly continuous Baltimore Waterfront Promenade connects historic communities such as Fells Point and Federal Hill to Harborplace and the city's modern downtown area. Opportunities for outdoor relaxation are offered at green spaces on both ends of the promenade—Canton Waterfront Park and Fort McHenry—while shopping and dining are recommended distractions around the Inner Harbor, in Little Italy, and in the new and vibrant Harbor East area. Along the way, glimpses of Baltimore's past and present are revealed through markers and plaques that explore a host of cultural, architectural, environmental, and social histories. A water taxi is also available to parallel the promenade route.

Baltimore's grandest and best-known thoroughfare, historic Charles Street, is the star attraction of a twelve-mile-long National Byway that incorporates world-renowned museums, impressive architecture, fine ethnic dining, and other cultural offerings. Attractions range from the Baltimore Museum of Art and Walters Art Museum to the Basilica of the National Shrine of the Assumption, built between 1806 and 1821 to become America's first Catholic cathedral.

Star-Spangled Trails, offered through the City of Baltimore's National Heritage Area office, are guided and self-guided walking, biking, and driving tours. Trail brochures and additional information are available at the Baltimore Visitor Center, which is also the starting point for a 3.2-mile Heritage Walk that connects twenty historic sites and museums. Some sites—such as Carroll Mansion, a merchant's townhouse linked to Declaration of Independence signer Charles Carroll—date back to the eighteenth century.

Other heritage experiences include a Baltimore Riot Trail that explores the first bloodshed of the Civil War; The Underground Railroad, Maryland's Network to Freedom; and a Mount Vernon Cultural Walk that spotlights Charles Street, once considered "the Fifth Avenue of the South."

By virtue of its important place historically and geographically in the settlement of the American continent, Baltimore is the intersection point of many organized trails and byways ready for guided or self-guided exploration. In addition to the Star-Spangled Banner National Historic Trail linking many War of 1812–related sites in the city, you'll also find the starting point of the multi-state Historic National Road (an America's Byway) at the Inner Harbor, the first miles of America's first railroad at the Smithsonian-affiliated B&O Museum, and the Jones Falls Byway and Trail which connect the Inner Harbor by car, bike, or foot to the quirky mill village of Hampden—once America's leading producer of cotton duck for sails. Baltimore and the Baltimore National Heritage Area are a treasure trove for those who want to explore American identity and have fun in the process.

Pride of Baltimore II in Baltimore's Inner Harbor

Sketch of the Battle of Caulks Field, August 31, 1814, as drawn by British Lieutenant Henry Crease within thirty-six hours of the action. American positions are represented in green and the British positions in blue and red. The American militia camp is depicted by tents in the upper left corner. The defile through which the British passed to reach the battlefield is located in the lower center. Note the detachment of American troops who fired on the British from the trees on right and withdrew to the main American line. The American official report claims the engagement took place on the north side of the road, not centered on the road as this sketch illustrates.

NOTES ON QUOTATIONS

Abbreviations

HSP	Historical Society of Pennsylvania
JHL	John Hay Library (Brown University)
LC	Library of Congress
MdHM	*Maryland Historical Magazine*
MdHS	Maryland Historical Society
NARA	National Archives and Records Administration
NAUK	National Archives United Kingdom
NLS	National Library of Scotland
WRHS	Western Reserve Historical Society

Chapter One. Drifting into War, 1807–1812

4 "Never since the Battle of Lexington . . ." Thomas Jefferson to James Bowdoin, July 10, 1807, Paul Leicester Ford, *The Writings of Thomas Jefferson,* 10 vols. (G. P. Putnam, 1892–1899), 9:105.

6 "We consider a neutral flag . . ." James Monroe, February 5, 1806, NARA, Calendar of Correspondence prepared from originals in the Department of State, 31.

9 "trying to convert this great agricultural country . . ." Thomas Jefferson quoted in Page Smith, *The Shaping of America,* 4 vols. (McGraw-Hill, 1980), 3:571.

9 "Here it is not felt, and in England . . ." American Minister in Paris, John Armstrong, quoted in Bradford Perkins,

Prologue to War, 1805–1812 (University of California Press, 1961), 166, and Donald R. Hickey, *The War of 1812: A Forgotten Conflict* (University of Illinois Press, 1995), 21.

12 "The time is come to humble the overgrown . . ." Republican A. McLane to Peter B. Porter, Feb. 28, 1812, Porter Papers, Buffalo and Erie County Historical Society, quoted in Hickey, *The War of 1812,* 27.

12 "no nation can preserve its freedom . . ." Madison, "Political Observations," April 20, 1795, *Letters and Writings of James Madison,* 4 vols. (J. P. Lippincott and Co., 1865), 4: 491.

14 "the blood of our murdered countrymen." London *Courier,* 1811, quoted in Perkins, *Prologue to War,* 273.

14 "By war we should be purified . . ." Vice President Elbridge Gerry to James Madison, May 19, 1812, quoted in Hickey, *The War of 1812,* 28.

14 "a well-regulated militia . . ." Madison, Section 13 of the Virginia Constitution of 1776, reprinted in *The Federal and State Constitutions, Colonial Charters, and Other Organic Laws,* ed. Francis Thorpe, 7 vols. (Washington, D.C.: Government Printing Office, 1909).

14 "When the regular troops of this House . . ." Henry Clay, February 22, 1810, a Speech proposing repeal of the Non-Intercourse Act delivered in the U.S. House of Representatives," *Papers of Henry Clay,* ed. James E. Hopkins, 10 vols. (University of Kentucky Press, 1959), 1:448.

17 "We'll feather and tar every d——d British Tory . . ." song of the Baltimore Mob, July 1812, Frank Cassell, "The Great Baltimore Riot of 1812," *MdHM* 70 (Fall 1970), 256.

19 "the worst of these parties . . ." John Quincy Adams, December 31, 1803, *Memoirs of John Quincy Adams, Comprising Portions of His Diary from 1795 to 1848,* ed. Charles Francis Adams, 12 vols. (J. P. Lippincott and Co., 1874), 1:282.

19 "more joyful at a dance, than they were at the abuse of the murdered." Narrative of John E. Hall, *Maryland Gazette,* Sept. 3, 1812.

20 "Since war is the word . . ." Boston *Republican Broadside,* June 1812, as quoted in *Channing* [William Ellery]: *The Reluctant Radical,* a biography by Jack Mendelsohn (Little, Brown & Co., 1971), 89.

20 "to quit the waters of the United States with all possible speed." Baltimore *Niles' Weekly Register,* August 29, 1812.

Chapter Two. A Red Terror Arrives on the Chesapeake, 1813

24 "The enemy robbed every house . . ." Baltimore *Niles' Weekly Register,* May 22, 1813.

24 "this of course gave to the Place an Importance . . ." Cockburn to Warren, May 3, 1813, LC, Papers of George Cockburn, Container 9, Letters Sent, 162–70.

25 "distressed people, women and children . . ." Baltimore *Niles' Weekly Register,* May 22, 1813.

25 "manly and open resistance . . ." Cockburn to Warren, May 3, 1813, LC, Papers of George Cockburn, Container 9, Letters Sent, 162–70.

25 "The grape-shot flew very thick . . ." Baltimore *Niles' Weekly Register,* May 15, 1813.

25 "shew[ed] their respect for religion . . ." [Rev. James Jones Wilmer], *Narrative Respecting the Conduct of the British from Their First Landing on Spesutia Island, Till Their Progress to Havre de Grace* (Baltimore: P. Mauro, 1813).

26 "wanton barbarity among civilized people." Baltimore *Niles' Weekly Register,* May 22, 1813.

27 "violator of all laws . . ." Baltimore *Niles' Weekly Register*, August 21, 1813.

28 "We do not intend this to be a mere paper blockade . . ." First Lord of the Admiralty Viscount Robert Saunders Dundas Melville to Warren, March 26, 1813, Indiana University, Lilly Library, War of 1812 manuscripts.

29 "with the most undaunted heroism . . ." Wilmington *American Watchman & Delaware Republican*, February 24, 1813.

29 "You must be content with blockading . . ." Croker to Warren, April 28, 1813, NARA, Adm. 2/1376, 320–22, and quoted in Stephen Budiansky, *Perilous Fight* (Alfred A. Knopf, 2010), 239.

29 "The more you ruin in a war, the more you hurt the nation at large . . ." Captain Frederick Chamier, *The Life of a Sailor* (London: Richard Bentley, 1850), 176–77.

30 "These People . . . have more to hope . . ." Cockburn quoted in James Ralfe, *The Naval Biography of Great Britain: Consisting of Historical Memoirs of Those Officers of the British Navy Who Distinguished Themselves During the Reign of His Majesty George III*, 4 vols. (London: Whitmore and Fenn, 1828), 3:289.

30 "warn their Countrymen against acting in the same rash manner . . ." Cockburn to Warren, May 6, 1813, LC, Papers of George Cockburn, Container 9, Letters Sent, 171–79.

33 "threw several rockets in the town . . ." Baltimore *American & Commercial Daily Advertiser*, May 14, 1813.

33 "The ruin complete, the savages . . ." Baltimore *Niles' Weekly Register*, May 22, 1813.

33 "leaving the People of this Place . . ." Cockburn quoted in "Admiral Cockburn's Despatches" (from a London newspaper) reprinted in Baltimore *Niles' Weekly Register*, October 16, 1813.

33 "is considered by them as at your Mercy . . ." Cockburn to Warren, May 6, 1813, NAUK, Adm. 1/503, fols. 679–85.

34 "She saved several families . . ." Knight's Obituary, November 22, 1855, quoted in the Baltimore *Sun*, August 10, 1913.

35 "Officers of the [U.S. Frigate] Constellation . . ." Cassin to Jones, June 23, 1813, NARA, RG45, Captain's Letters to the Secretary of Navy, 1813, vol. 4, no. 107 (M125, roll. 29).

35 "so much inured to villainy and destruction . . ." The Washington *Daily National Intelligencer*, May 14, 1813.

41 "was dying in his house in the arms of his wife . . ." Washington *Daily National Intelligencer*, July 2, 1813.

41 "Kirby, who for seven weeks or more had been confined to his bed . . ." Baltimore *Patriot*, July 23, 1813.

41 "With vengeful feelings, the soldiers chased . . ." Benson J. Lossing, *The Pictorial Field-Book of the War of 1812* (New York: Harper Bros., 1868), 687, footnote 2.

43 "From the face of things . . ." Neale, November 22, 1813, University of Georgetown Library, Archives of the Maryland Province of the Society of Jesus at Georgetown, box: 58, fold: 18, Correspondence (204 S1-9).

43 "The situation is extremely critical . . ." Captain James Forrest, Annapolis *Maryland Republican*, July 31, 1813.

43 "some of the finest and best stocked farms in the state." [Captain] Charles Gordon, August 7, 1813, reprinted in the Hartford *Connecticut Mirror*, August 16, 1813.

43 "beautiful spot resembling a gentleman's park." Captain James Scott, *Recollections of a Naval Life*, 3 vols. (London: Richard Bentley, 1834), 3: 160–61.

43 "evinced that we had fallen on the land of milk and honey." Ibid.

46 "the men, seeing the road suddenly lighted up . . ." Captain Frederick Robertson's account in H[ugh] Noel Williams, *The Life and Letters of Admiral Sir Charles Napier, K.C.B. (1786–1860)* (London: Hutchinson, 1917).

46 "Nothing was done with method . . ." Lieutenant Colonel Charles James Napier as quoted in Budiansky, *Perilous Fight*, 251.

Chapter Three. A Fateful Year Begins, 1814

50 "I then made the signal 'for Patuxent,' . . ." Barney to Jones, June 3, 1814, NARA, RG45, MLR, 1814, vol. 4, no. 86 (M124, roll no. 63).

51 "Your force is our principal shield, and all eyes will be upon you." Jones to Barney, Feb. 18, 1814, NARA, RG45, MLR, vol. 11, 219–20 (M149, roll no. 11).

51 "do any mischief on either side of the Potomac . . . within your power." Cockburn to Barrie, May 30, 1814, LC, Papers of George Cockburn, Container 10, vol. 25, fol. 12 (reel 7).

52 "vessel to carry provisions . . ." Barney to Jones, June 3, 1814, NARA, RG45, MLR, 1814, vol. 4, no. 86 (M124, roll no. 63).

53 "The enemy advanced a barge . . ." Barney to Jones, ibid.

53 "no man was ever killed at 200 yards . . ." Colonel George Hanger, Fourth Baron of Coleraine, *To All Sportsmen, and Particularly to Farmers, and Gamekeepers* (London, 1814).

54 "I have it much in my heart . . ." Vice Admiral Cochrane, 1814, Williams, *The Life & Letters of Admiral Sir Charles Napier*, 41.

55 "They return upon us as guides and soldiers and incendiaries . . ." Brigadier General John Hungerford to the Virginia Adjutant General, August 5, 1814, quote with no citation from Shomette, *Flotilla*, 211.

56 "I consider . . . that Tangier Island . . ." Cockburn to Cochrane, May 9, 1814, NLS, Cochrane Papers, MS 2333, fols. 53–59.

56 "though I have no doubt Moschettos [mosquitoes] . . ." Cockburn to Cochrane, ibid.

56 "readily found [drinking water] . . ." Cockburn to Warren, April 13, 1814, NLS, Cochrane Papers, MS 2333, fols. 18–23.

57 "This kind of fighting is much against us . . ." Barney to Jones, June 9, 1814, NARA, RG45, MLR, 1814, vol. 4, no. 105 (M124, roll no. 63).

59 "little to fear from an attack by boats, no matter how numerous." Barney to Jones, June 13, 1814, NARA, RG45, MLR, 1814, vol. 4, no. 111 (M124, roll no. 63).

59 "seemed determined to do something decisive." Barney to Jones, June 11, 1814, John Brannan, *Official Letters of the Military and Naval Officers of the United States, during the War with Great Britain in the Years 1812, 13, 14, & 15* (Washington, D.C.: Way & Gideon, 1823), 340.

59 "must have done them considerable damage." Barney to Jones, June 11, 1814, ibid.

60 "By destroying some of the tobacco stores . . ." Barrie to Cockburn, June 19, 1814, NLS, Cochrane Papers, MS 2333, fols. 106–10.

61 "If [the Americans] remained at home quietly . . ." Barney to Jones, June 13, 1814, NARA, RG45, MLR, 1814, vol. 4, no. 111 (M124, roll no. 63).

61 "I tell you the mischief the British . . ." Thomas B. King, July 14, 1814. Part of this letter is reproduced in Hulbert Footner, *Sailor of Fortune: The Life and Adventures of Commodore Barney, U.S.N.* (New York: Harper & Brothers Publishers, 1940), 276–77. A copy of the letter can be found in the Calvert Marine Museum archives, Solomons, MD. The location of the original is unknown.

63 "How sharply and unexpectedly [Brother] Jonathan [the U.S.] has exerted himself . . . " Cockburn to Cochrane, June 25, 1814, NLS, Cochrane Papers, MS 2574, fols. 135–39.

64 "I had the mortification to observe [the flotilla] rowing down the creek, and up the river." Brown to Cockburn, June 27, 1814, NLS, Cochrane Papers, MS 2333, fols. 146–47.

64 "The House had evidently been [the local militia] headquarters . . ." Captain James Scott, *Recollections of a Naval Life*, 3 vols. (London: Richard Bentley, 1834), 3: 243–44.

64 "he had drunk of the spirits . . ." Lieutenant Colonel Richard Elliott Parker, Baltimore *Niles' Weekly Register*, August 6, 1814.

65 "We marched to [Chaptico] and took possession . . ." Cockburn to Cochrane, July 31, 1814, NAUK, Adm. 1/507, fols. 110–11.

65 "They [the British] got about 30 hhds. [hogsheads] . . ." Baltimore *Niles' Weekly Register*, August 14, 1814.

66 "National honor is the national property . . ." James Monroe, First Inaugural Address, March 14, 1817.

67 "tall and well formed . . . quiet and dignified." Attributed to a Virginia lady who met President Monroe on New Year's Day, 1825; used in capsule biographies of the presidents such as www.whitehouse.gov/history/presidents/jm5.html [April 1, 2008].

67 "Monroe [is] so honest . . ." Attributed to Thomas Jefferson; used in capsule biographies of the presidents such as www.whitehouse.gov/history/presidents/jm5.html [April 1, 2008].

68 "more anxious to plunder . . ." Barney to Jones, July 8, 1814, NARA, RG45, MLR, vol. 5, no 43 (M124, roll no. 64).

69 "broke to pieces [and] only fit to stick frogs with." Annapolis *Maryland Gazette and Political Intelligencer*, August 4, 1814.

69 "black refugees increase so fast . . ." Nourse to Cockburn, August 4, 1814, LC, Papers of George Cockburn, Container 14, vol. 38, pp. 372–74 (reel 9).

69 "Altho Calvert [County] deserves nothing from us . . ." Barney to Jones, August 4, 1814, NARA, RG45, MLR, 1814, vol. 5, no. 111 (M124, roll no. 64).

69 "We gave them in all eleven guns . . ." Thomas Marsh Forman to his wife Martha Ogle Forman, July 12, 1814, MdHS, Forman Papers, MSS 403, 1732–1908.

69 "[t]his country is in general in a horrible state . . ." Cockburn to Cochrane, June 25, 1814, NLS, Cochrane Papers, MS 2574, fols. 135–39.

69 "[t]he general idea . . . is, that Washington is their objective." Monroe, Washington *Daily National Intelligencer*, August 22, 1814.

69 "There were forty six sail in the bay . . ." Annapolis *Maryland Republican*, August 20, 1814.

Chapter Four. Invasion! August 1814

72 "Your force on this occasion is of immense importance . . ." Jones to Barney, August 20, 1814, HSP, Papers of Joshua Barney.

72 "should [the British] advance upon you . . ." Jones to Barney, August 19, 1814, NARA, RG45, CLS, 1814, 181.

72 "in the event of the enemy advancing upon the flotilla . . ." Jones to Barney, August 20, 1814, HSP, Papers of Joshua Barney.

72 "[o]n nearing them we observed the Sloop . . ." Cockburn to Cochrane, August 22, 1814, NARA, RG45, MLR, 1814, vol. 6, no. 35 (M124, roll no. 65).

75 "lying at full length upon the grass . . ." Lieutenant George Robert Gleig, *A Subaltern in America: Comprising His Narrative of the Campaigns of the British Army, at Baltimore, Washington, &c. during the Late War* (Philadelphia and Baltimore: Carey, Hart & Co., 1833), 10–11.

75 "apparently, [there was] no enemy within many miles of the place." Lieutenant George Robert Gleig, *The Campaigns of the British Army at Washington and New Orleans* (E. Ardsley, Eng.: E. P. Publ. Ltd., 1972, reprint of 1847 ed.), 50.

75 "a most awful spectacle of a man named Calder . . ." Captain Harry Smith in *The Autobiography of Lieut. General Sir Harry Smith*, ed. G. C. Moore-Smith, 2 vols. (London: John Murray, 1902), 1:198.

75 "The effect of the lightning . . ." Gleig, 1972, reprint of 1847 ed., 53–55.

76 "Nine-tenths of tactics are certain and taught in books . . ." Lieutenant Colonel Thomas Edward Lawrence of Arabia, *The Evolution of a Revolt* (University Park: Pennsylvania State University Press, 1968), 9.

77 "We believe that Baron Steuben has made us soldiers . . ." The 1782 Creed of the 1st U.S. Army encamped at Verplanck's Point, New York. Quoted completely in *Army of the American Revolution and Its Organizer,* Rudolf Cronau (1923), 47. Quoted by Secretary of Defense Robert Gates at U.S. Army Military Academy Commencement, May 23, 2009.

78 ". . . detached bodies of [American] riflemen lay in ambush . . ." Gleig, 1972, reprint of 1847 ed., 55.

78 "I contrived to surround the spot . . ." Ibid., 56.

80 "an empty house was procured, in which the papers were safely placed . . ." Stephen Pleasonton to Brigadier General William H. Winder, August 7, 1814, NAUK, Adm. 1/507, fols. 110–11.

80 "you had better remove the records." James Monroe to President James Madison, August 22, 1814. Letter reprinted in Walter Lowrie Winder and Matthew St. Clair Clarke, *American State Papers, Documents, Legislative and Executive, of the Congress of The United States, From the First Session of the First to the Second Session of the Fifteenth Congress, Inclusive: Commencing March 3, 1789, and Ending March 3, 1819* (Washington: Gales and Seaton, 1832), 538.

81 "The enemy are in full march for Washington . . ." Secretary of State James Monroe to President James Madison, August 22, 1814, ibid.

81 "It seems indeed to be something . . ." Gleig, undated reprint of *The Campaigns of the British Army. . .* , 63.

81 "in these woods and cedar thickets . . ." Charles Ball, *A Narrative of the Life and Adventures of Charles Ball, A Black Man* (Lewistown, PA: John W. Shugert, 1836; reprinted in Yuval Taylor, ed. *I Was Born a Slave: An Anthology of Classic Slave Narrative*, vol. I, 1770–1849 [Chicago: Lawrence Hill Books, 1999], 467–68).

82 "hearty dinner undisturbed . . ." Gleig, August 22, 1814. Quoted in Charles R. B. Barrett, ed. *The 85th King's Light Infantry* (London: Spottiswoode, 1913), 137.

83 "A bright mulatto . . . fair enough to show freckles." Baltimore *American*, May 18, 1814.

84 "I made up my mind . . ." Brigadier General James Wilkinson, August 23, 1814, James Wilkinson, *Memoirs of My Own Times*, 4 vols. (Philadelphia: Abraham Small, 1816).

84 "in high spirits & [made] a good appearance." President James Madison to Dolley Madison, August 22, 1814, *Writings of James Madison,* ed. Gaillard Hunt, 9 vols. (New York, 1908), 8: 293–94.

85 "certain infallible, and irremediable disorder . . ." Winder and Clarke, eds., *American State Papers*, 556.

85 "smoking ashes, bundles of straw . . ." George Robert Gleig, *A Narrative of the Campaigns of the British Army at Washington, Baltimore and New Orleans under General Ross, Pakenham and Lambert in the Years 1814 and 1815* (London: John Murray, 1821), 112.

85 "men [falling] behind from absolute inability to keep up." Gleig, reprint of 1847 ed., 63.

86 "They ran like sheep chased by dogs." Ball, *A Narrative of the Life and Adventures of Charles Ball*, 404.

88 "great strength and commanding attitude . . ." Gleig, reprint of 1847 ed., 115.

88 "an entire company was swept away." Gleig, undated reprint of *The Campaigns of the British Army at Washington and New Orleans in the Years 1814–1815* (Champaign. IL: Book Jungle), 71.

88 "trampling on many of their dead and dying comrades." Gleig, ibid.

89 "in a few minutes the enemy again advanced" Barney to Jones, August 29, 1814, NARA, RG45, MLR, 1814, vol. 6, no. 57 (M124, roll no. 65).

91 "Barney now had the whole British army to fight . . ." Marine Captain Samuel Bacon in a September 16, 1814, letter, quoted in John Ockerbloom, "The Discovery of a U.S. Marine Officer's Account of Life, Honor and the Battle of Bladensburg, Washington and Maryland, 1814," *Military Collector & Historian* 61, no. 4 (Winter 2009), 260.

91 "They gave us the only fighting we have had." Quote without source in Mary Barney, *A Biographical Memoir of the Late Commodore Joshua Barney* (Boston: Gray and Bowen, 1832), 267.

91 "Good God! How have we been disgraced?" Joseph Hopper Nicholson to Secretary of Navy William Jones, August 28, 1814, HSP, William Jones Papers, Clarke Smith Collection, 1378A.

91 "[General] Wi[nder] ought to be hung and would b[e in] any other country." Marine Captain Samuel Bacon in a September 16, 1814, letter, quoted in Ockerbloom, "The Discovery of a U.S. Marine Officer's Account . . . ," 260.

92 "The precious portrait [was] placed in the hands of two gentlemen of New York for safekeeping." Dolley Madison (in an after-the-fact recreation) to her sister Lucy Payne Todd of an event that took place after 3 p.m., August 24, 1814, LC, Dolley Madison Papers, Manuscript Division.

92 "I must leave this [President's] house or the retreating [American] army will make me a prisoner in it . . ." Dolley Madison, ibid.

92 "the frame broken and the canvas taken out of it." Dolley Madison, ibid.

93 "My dearest . . . I have just received a line . . ." Madison to his wife from Bladensburg, August 24, 1814, LC, Manuscript Division, James Madison Papers.

Chapter Five. Washington Is Burning!
August 1814

96 "The spectators stood in awful silence . . ." Margaret Bayard Smith, quoted in Gaillard Hunt, ed., *The First Forty Years of Washington Society* (New York: Charles Scribner's Sons, 1906), 112.

96 "The British army . . . looked like flames of fier all red coats . . ." Michael Shiner, slave, recorded in his diary, LC, Manuscript Division.

96 "These modern republicans are led to flatter themselves . . ." George Robert Gleig, *A Narrative of the Campaigns of the British Army at Washington, Baltimore and New Orleans under General Ross, Pakenham and Lambert in the Years 1814 and 1815* (London: John Murray, 1821), 233–34.

96 "50 men, sailors and marines were marched . . ." Margaret Bayard Smith, Hunt, *The First Forty Years*, 112.

97 "infant towns," Gleig, 1821, 233–34.

98 "a melancholy spectacle . . ." Benjamin Henry Latrobe, *The Correspondence and Miscellaneous Papers of Benjamin Henry Latrobe*, ed. John C. Van Horne, 3 vols. (New Haven: Yale University Press, 1986), 2:32.

101 "Greater respect was certainly paid to private property . . ." Joseph Gales, Jr., Washington *Daily National Intelligencer*, August 31, 1814.

101 "[n]o houses were half as much plundered by the enemy . . ." Ibid.

101 "a rabble, taking advantage of the confusion. . ." Paul Jennings, *A Colored Man's Reminiscences of James Madison*, Bladensburg Series, Number Two (Brooklyn: George C. Beadle, 1865), Special Collections Library of James Madison University, reprinted in *White House History*, White House Historical Association, 1 (1981): 46–51.

101 "[It] is disgraceful to relate . . ." Captain Thomas Tingey to Jones, August 27, 1814, NARA, RG45, MLR, Captain's Letters, 1814, vol. 5, no. 18 (M125, roll no. 38).

101 "[It] was remarkable for nothing . . ." Gleig, 1821, 135.

102 "Never was nectar more grateful . . ." Captain James Scott, *Recollections of a Naval Life*, 3 vols. (London: Richard Bentley, 1834), 3, 303.

105 "to burn what would be useful to all mankind . . ." Dr. William Thornton, LC, Manuscript Division.

106 "The capture of Washington was more owing to the blindness . . ." Lieutenant George Robert Gleig, *The Campaigns of the British Army at Washington and New Orleans* (E. Ardsley, Eng.: E. P. Publ. Ltd., 1972, reprint of 1847 ed.), 84.

106 "One of the artillery-men most unfortunately dropped . . ." London *Morning Post*, October 7, 1814.

107 "Great God, Madam!" "Early Washington: An Old Resident's Recollections of the War of 1812," Washington *Evening Star*, March 31, 1888.

107 "The dead were still unburied . . ." Gleig, 1847, 78.

107 "The [American] troops were drawn up . . ." Ibid., 115.

107 "If it had not been for the flour . . ." Lt. Col. Harry Smith autobiography, circa 1824, reprinted as G. C. Moore-Smith, ed., *The Autobiography of Lieut. General Sir Harry Smith*, 2 vols. (London: John Murray, 1902).

108 "His heart is in the right place . . ." Captain Peter Parker, *A Biographical Memoir of the Late Sir Peter Parker, Baronet* (London, 1815), 3, 15.

109 "It was the height of madness . . ." Frederick Chamier, *The Life of a Sailor* (London: Richard Bentley, 1850), 185.

109 "captured a small boat and canoe . . ." Easton *Republican Star*, August 23, 1814.

110 "At five landed and set fire to the house . . ." Lieutenant Benjamin George Beynon journal, WRHS, Cleveland, OH, MS 1236, Microfilm Cabinet 40, Drawer 8.

110 "a great many [American] horsemen . . ." Ibid.

111 "A Tolerably good Diversion should . . ." Cockburn to Cochrane, July 17, 1814, NLS, Cochrane Papers, MS 2333, fols. 173–78.

112 "I believe each of the Ships . . ." Gordon to Cochrane, September 9, 1814, NAUK, Adm. 1/507, fols. 153–57.

112 "the retreat of the illustrious Washington . . ." Captain Charles Napier, August 26, 1814. Major General Elers Napier, *The Life and Correspondence of Admiral Sir Charles Napier, K.C.B., From Personal Recollections, Letters, and Official Documents* (London: Hurst and Blackett, 1862), 80.

112 "the bomb vessels [with mortars] at once . . ." Gordon, August 27, 1814, "Narrative of the Operations in the Potomac by the Squadron under the orders of Capt. Sir. James A. Gordon in 1814," *United Service Journal* 11 (1833):469–80.

114 "The town was providentially preserved . . ." Charles Simms. LC, Charles Simms Papers, vol. 6, Peter Force Collection, Series 8D, fols. 35428–29 (reel 66).

114 "this rash act excited the greatest alarm . . ." Simms, September 3, 1814, ibid.

114 "created a considerable alarm . . ." Napier, Quote in Charles G. Muller, "Fabulous Potomac Passage," *U.S. Naval Institute Proceedings* (1964):89.

114 "recommended that proper precautions should be taken . . ." Ibid.

115 "[i]t is impossible that men could behave better . . ." Charles Simms to his wife Nancy Simms, September 3, 1814, LC, Charles Simms Papers, vol. 6, Peter Force Collection, Series 8D, fols. 35428–29 (reel 66).

115 "surrender without resistance . . ." Washington *Daily National Intelligencer*, September 1, 1814.

116 "The most consummate artist in treason . . ." and "a general who never won a battle or lost a court martial." Historians Frederick Jackson Turner and Robert Leckie quoted in Wikipedia biography of James Wilkinson without attribution.

117 "too small a caliber . . ." Captain Oliver Hazard Perry to Jones, September 9, 1814, NARA, RG45, MLR Captain's Letters, 1814, vol. 6, no. 34 (M135, roll no. 39).

117 "Major General Ross and myself resolved . . ." Cochrane to Croker, September 17, 1814, Public Record Office, London, Adm. 1/507, fols. 171–75; Cochrane's letter book copy NLS, Cochrane Papers, MS 2348, pp. 74–79.

Chapter Six. The Battle for Baltimore, September 1814

120 "When little more than a hundred paces . . ." Lieutenant George Robert Gleig, *A Subaltern in America: Comprising His Narrative of the Campaigns of the British Army, at Baltimore, Washington, &c. during the Late War* (Philadelphia and Baltimore: Carey, Hart & Co., 1833), 132–33.

122 "In the varied scenes which have put to the test . . ." James Madison, April 22, 1815, LC, Manuscript Division, James Madison Papers, series 1, reel 17.

123 "Do not let me hear, my son . . ." John Pendleton Kennedy in Charles H. Bohner, *John Pendleton Kennedy, Gentleman from Baltimore* (Baltimore, 1961), 22.

123 "My friends I have but one life to lose . . ." Major General Samuel Smith to the Committee of Vigilance and Safety, August 25, 1814. William. D. Hoyt, ed., "Civilian Defense in Baltimore, 1814–1815," *MdHM* 39 (1944), 199–205, and W. M. Marine, *The British Invasion of Maryland, 1812–1815* (Baltimore, 1913), 133–45.

124 "We have a right to expect every master . . ." Captain George Stiles, Baltimore *American Commercial Daily Advertiser*, July 22, 1814.

124 "There remains no doubt . . ." Brigadier General William Winder to the Committee of Vigilance and Safety, August 1814, Hoyt, "Civilian Defense. . ."

125 "My wife, my children, my friends . . ." John Eager Howard, "Tell the members of your convention . . ." General Samuel Smith, Committee of Vigilance and Safety, August 25, 1814, Hoyt, "Civilian Defense . . ."

126 "All hearts and hands have cordially united . . ." Private George Douglas, August 30, 1814, Brown University, JHL, Henry Wheaton (1790–1870) Papers; copies of correspondence at library at Fort McHenry National Monument and Historic Shrine (SC 75).

127 ". . . a natural roughness, a polished diamond of the first order . . ." The Reverend Adam Wallace, *The Parson of the Islands: A Biography of The Rev. Joshua Thomas . . .* (1861 [reprinted by Tidewater Publishers, Cambridge, MD, 1961]).

128 "people now begin to show something like a patriotic spirit." Captain John Rodgers, August 28, 1814, LC, Rodgers Papers.

128 "all the [American] corps of every description . . ." Baltimore *American*, September 12, 1814.

129 "I give you joy, my dear friend . . ." Private George Douglas to a friend in Boston, September 30, 1814, Brown University, JHL, Henry Wheaton Papers, 1786–1899.

130 "The Lord Bless King George . . ." Reverend John Gruber, quoted without attribution in Walter Lord, *The Dawn's Early Light* (New York, 1972), 251.

131 "showed a considerable degree of science . . ." and "young gentlemen volunteers . . ." George Robert Gleig, *A Narrative of the Campaigns of the British Army at Washington, Baltimore and New Orleans under General Ross, Pakenham and Lambert in the Years 1814 and 1815* (London: John Murray, 1821), 171.

131 "I don't care if it rains militia." Quote from W. M. Marine, *The British Invasion of Maryland, 1812–1815* (Baltimore, 1913), 150.

132 "The temple of God . . ." Captain James Scott, *Recollections of a Naval Life*, 3 vols. (London: Richard Bentley, 1834), 3, 342.

134 "[o]ur advanced Guard . . . soon obliged the Enemy . . ." Cockburn to Cochrane, September 15, 1814, NLS, Cochrane Papers, MS 2332, fols. 20–27.

134 "[t]he General's horse, without its rider . . ." Lieutenant George Robert Gleig, *The Campaigns of the British Army at Washington and New Orleans* (E. Ardsley, Eng.: E. P. Publ. Ltd., 1972, reprint of 1847 ed.), 95.

135 "The British soldiers moved forward . . ." Gleig, 1833, 132–33.

135 "The accents of human woe floated upon the ear . . ." Scott, *Recollections*, vol. 3, 342.

135 "on not finding my father . . ." Dr. James Haines McCulloh, Jr., to General Samuel Smith, September 14, 1814, LC, Samuel Smith Papers.

137 "If I took the place, I should have been the greatest man in England . . ." Brooke, writing in his diary, September 1814. Quote from Christopher George, "Family Papers of Major General Ross, the Diary of Colonel Arthur Brooke, and the British Attacks on Washington and Baltimore of 1814," *MdHM* 88 (Fall 1993), 311.

137 "left was not so secure . . ." Quote from Brooke diary found in Christopher George, "The Family Papers of Major General Robert Ross, the Diary of Colonel Arthur Brooke, . . ." Ibid.

137 "He [the enemy] manoeuvred during the morning . . ." Smith to Monroe, September 19, 1814, NLS, Cochrane Papers, MS 2334, fols. 20–27.

137 "[p]ushing his advance to within a mile of us . . ." Smith to Monroe, September 19, 1814, NARA, RG107, MLR, Registered Series, S-141 (8) (M221, roll no. 66).

137 "To this movement . . ." Smith to Monroe, ibid.

139 "could hear the hogs squeal as [the British] killed them in their camp." 1st Lieutenant Jacob Crumbaker, September 2–13, 1814, Library at Fort McHenry National Monument and Historic Shrine, letters.

139 "down the bay as a signal for the [British] land forces . . ." Ibid.

139 "when the order was given to fall in . . ." Gleig to his wife, September 16, 1814, NLS, Gleig Papers, MS. 3869.

139 "the capture of the town . . ." Brooke to Secretary of State for War and the Colonies Henry Bathurst, 3rd Earl Bathurst, September 17, 1814, NAUK, WO 1/141, 75–89.

140 "We were like pigeons tied by the legs to be shot at." Captain Joseph Hopper Nicholson to Secretary of War James Monroe, September 21, 1814, LC, Joseph H. Nicholson Papers.

140 "[t]he defense of Fort McHenry was of no ordinary character . . ." James Wilkinson, *Memoirs of My Own Times*, 4 vols. (Philadelphia: Abraham Small, 1816).

144 ". . . a solitary report, accompanied by the ascension of a small bright spark into the sky." Gleig, 1833, 157.

144 "[t]he attack on Fort McHenry . . . was distinctly seen . . ." Salem [Massachusetts] *Gazette*, September 27, 1814.

144 "I do not feel able to paint out the distress . . ." Reverend James Stevens, "A Letter Describing the Attack on Fort McHenry, *MdHM* 51 (Dec. 1956), 356.

144 "During the firing of the enemy . . ." Sailing Master John Adams Webster account quoted in Marine, *The British Invasion of Maryland*, 177–81.

145 "the handsomest sight I ever saw . . ." Lieutenant John Harris to his brother William, September 27, 1814, MdHS, MS. 1846, War of 1812 Papers.

145 "A propitious omen." Sailors responding to a rooster in the rigging of the U.S. corvette *Saratoga* during the Battle of Plattsburgh, New York, September 11, 1814, Baltimore *Patriot*, November 24, 1814.

146 "I could hear a splashing in the water . . ." Sailing Master John Adams Webster, "Reminiscences of Captain John A. Webster to Mayor Brantz Mayer, July 22, 1853," MdHS Vertical Files, printed in Marine, *The British Invasion of Maryland*, 179.

146 "At the first dawn, every eye was directed towards the Fort . . ." Private John Leadley Dagg, "Autobiography by John L. Dagg," www.founders.org/library/dagg-bio.html.

146 "At dawn . . . our morning gun was fired . . ." Private Isaac Munroe, Baltimore Fencibles, Fort McHenry, to editor, Boston *Yankee*, September 30, 1814, "'Yankee Doodle Played': A Letter from Baltimore, 1814," *MdHM* 76 (1981), 381–82.

146 "In truth, it was a galling spectacle to behold . . ." Midshipman Robert J. Barrett, 1841, 464.

146 ". . . boats resorted in great number for water . . ." Gleig, 1847, 109.

147 "The Sacred Vestments thrown and dragged . . ." Jesuit Brother Joseph P. Mobberly to Reverend John Grassi, October 31, 1814, Georgetown University Maryland Jesuit archives; quoted in Edwin W. Beitzell, *The Jesuit Missions of St. Mary's County, Maryland* (Leonardtown, MD: St. Mary's County Historical Society, 1998), 107–10.

147 ". . . the Holy Altar stripped naked . . ." Ibid.

148 ". . . we commenced a fire . . ." Annapolis *Maryland Republican*, October 8, 1814.

148 "constantly on the alert . . ." Captain Robert Barrie, NAUK, Adm. 1/509, fols. 188–92.

148 "Three companies, of about 50 each, of negroes in uniform . . ." Brigadier General John Hartwell Cocke to Governor James Barbour, December 4, 1814, Virginia State Records, Governor's Office (RG3), Executive Papers, Governor James Barbour, 1812–1814.

148 "Court House [in Tappahannock] was consumed . . ." Captain Robert Barrie to Rear Admiral George Cockburn, December 7, 1814, NAUK, Adm. 1/509, fols. 188–92.

148 "While the Main Body of the Troops were halted at the Church . . ." Ibid.

148 "beastly Drunk . . ." Ibid.

Chapter Seven. Peace, Jubilation, and Memory, 1815

152 "I do therefore, by virtue of the power and authority in me . . ." Captain Thomas Boyle Proclamation, August 27, 1814, MdHS, manuscript copy.

153 "edged down upon one of them . . ." Quoted online on www.usmm.org, *The American Merchant Marine at War*,

"American Merchant Marine and Privateers in the War of 1812."

153 "a man whose patriotism, good sense and high moral character have won . . ." George Roberts's obituary quoted in Christopher George, *A Maritime Point of View*, "African-American Sailors Who Served in Our Nation's Private Navy," http://www.baltimoremd.com/monuments/blacks atsea.html.

154 "every exertion shall be used by myself . . ." Captain John Clavell to Rear Admiral George Cockburn, January 16, 1815, LC, Papers of George Cockburn, container 14, vol. 38, 502–4 (reel 9).

154 "People who handle dangerous weapons must expect wounds and Death." Commodore Edward Preble to William Bainbridge, March 12, 1804, quoted in Stephen Budiansky, *Perilous Fight* (Alfred A. Knopf, 2010), 3.

156 "among the members present were gentlemen of opposite politics . . ." Joseph Gales, Jr., written after the event, quote in Harold Donaldson Eberlein and Cortlandt Van Dyke Hubbard, *Historic Houses of George-Town & Washington City* (Richmond, VA: Dietz Press, Inc., 1958), 312.

157 "In the midst of this scene of light stood the State House . . ." Maryland *Gazette*, February 23, 1815.

160 "This heroic deed their fame evermore swells as martyrs of liberty!" local playwright Clifton W. Tayleure staged the play *The Boy Martyrs of Sept. 12, 1814, A Local Historical Drama in Three Acts* (Boston: Clifton W. Spencer, 1859). A complete text of the play is available at the Google free books website http://books.com.

161 "[i]t was here that the haughty General [Ross] . . ." Benjamin C. Howard, *Baltimore Patriot*, July 29, 1817.

162 "Then, in that hour of deliverance, and joyful triumph . . ." Edward S. Delaplaine, *Francis Scott Key: Life and Times* (New York: Biography Press, 1937), 379–80.

166 "The war has renewed and reinstated the national feeling and character . . ." Albert Gallatin to Matthew Lyon, May 7, 1815, quoted in Henry Adams, *The Life of Albert Gallatin* (Philadelphia, 1879), 560.

167 "[It] lies not in being more enlightened than any other Nation . . ." Alexis de Tocqueville, *Democracy in America*, Part I, Chapter 13.

Circa 1812 painted wooden barrel canteen inscribed "2nd Co. S.F. No. 48." The canteen belonged to Private Augustus Sadler, who served in Captain William H. Addison's 2nd company of U.S. Sea Fencibles. The "No. 48" refers to the soldier's numbered listing on the muster roll.

1814 British satirical cartoon speculating that President Madison has fled to Elba to join Napoleon
—to the amusement of the Federalists he abandoned.

Glossary

Many words have more than one meaning and the definitions of words change over time. This glossary defines words as used in context during the War of 1812.

Baltimore clipper. A colloquial name for fast-sailing two-masted schooners and brigantines built at Fells Point and other shipyards in Baltimore, Maryland. Similar ships used for privateering were also built in other locations of the Chesapeake Bay, such as St. Michaels, Maryland.

bivouac. A temporary encampment, often in an unsheltered area.

block sloop. Essentially a floating battery where speed was sacrificed to carry heavy guns. They typically had high bulwarks to provide protection to crew and to resist boarders. The Chesapeake Flotilla block sloop was approximately 50 feet in length, had an 18-foot beam, and was outfitted with one mast and two sails.

bomb (or bombshell). Hollow spherical cast iron projectile principally used in mortars. Gunpowder was inserted into a tapered filling fuse hole. The fuse was ignited by the gun blast. A thirteen-inch shell weighed 207 pounds when fully charged; a ten-inch shell weighed 96 pounds. Cast lug eyes next to the fuse hole enabled a tackle fitted with a special tong to hoist the shell from below deck to the gun's muzzle and deposit it in the gun bore.

bomb ship. A small, ship-rigged sloop-of-war primarily armed with one thirteen-inch and one ten-inch bore mortar placed in tandem directly upon separate massive wooden structures located just below the gun deck to absorb the massive shock of the mortars when fired.

brig. Type of sailing vessel with two square-rigged masts considered fast and maneuverable and used as both naval warships and merchant vessels.

broadside. The firing of all guns on one side of a vessel as nearly simultaneously as possible.

canister. Anti-personnel scatter-shot for cannon consisting of musket balls packed into a sheet metal cylinder closed at each end by a tight-fitting iron disc held in place by crimped tabs at the ends of the cylinder. Chain links, scraps of metal, shards of glass, rocks, etc. were also sometimes used. On firing, the balls spread out from the muzzle at high velocity, giving an effect similar to a shotgun, but scaled up to cannon size.

carronade. A type of short, light-weight cannon capable of firing a relatively heavy-caliber shot. Typically carried on the upper deck of a ship for short-range use. Named after Carron Ironworks, Scotland, where it was first made in the 1780s.

cartridge. Packaged powder charge: for cannon, contained in a flannel bag sized to fit snugly into the main bore or chamber; for portable firearms, wrapped in paper, which usually contained the ball and a felt wad.

Congreve rocket. Self-propelled projectile invented by William Congreve consisting of a cylindrical sheet-iron chamber filled with black powder, capped with a warhead, and strapped to a long wooden staff that helped to provide stability during flight. Propulsion gases were exhausted through a nozzle in the rear and could also ignite a fuse to detonate an optional explosive warhead, which could contain musket balls or combustible materials. Available in several sizes with ranges up to two miles. Launched from rocket ships or on land by portable copper tubes supported by a tripod.

corvette. A small, maneuverable, lightly armed warship smaller than a frigate and larger than a sloop-of-war, usually with a single gun deck. Used mostly for coastal patrol.

cossack. Lightly armored troops mounted on horses used primarily for reconnaissance, skirmishing, raiding, and, most importantly, communications. Usually armed with pistols and swords. The Old East Slavic origin of the word meant "itinerant laborer, vagabond, adventurer."

dragoon. Mounted infantry who were trained in horse riding as well as infantry fighting skills. Over time, dragoons evolved into conventional light cavalry units. The name is possibly derived from a type of firearm called a dragon carried by dragoons of the French Army.

earthworks. Fortifications constructed from soil that, when made thick enough, could provide adequate protection from weapons. Because soil was usually readily available in huge quantities it was often used to construct defenses such as gun emplacements, trenches, and bastions.

ensign. A flag to indicate nationality.

fagot. A bundle of twigs, sticks, or branches bound together.

feint. Maneuver or diversion designed to distract or mislead. Done by giving the impression that a certain action is planned, while in fact another, or even none, will take place.

fencibles. Generally mariners by trade who were employed for the defense of the ports and harbors of the United States. At Baltimore they manned the barges and guns at Fort McHenry's water batteries and stood guard duty.

fire globe. *See* globe match

firelock. The lock on the outside of a firearm is the system used to ignite the propellant (e.g., flintlock, matchlock, wheellock, and percussion lock). A complete firearm often consists of lock, stock, and barrel.

flank speed. A nautical term referring to a ship's maximum speed. Flank speed is usually reserved for situations in which a ship finds itself in imminent danger, such as when it is about to come under attack.

flatboat. A rectangular, flat-bottomed, shallow draft boat usually with square ends. It was generally poled or rowed to transport freight.

flotilla. A squadron of boats or small vessels.

frigate. A vessel of war, three-masted, fully rigged, in size between a corvette and a ship-of-the-line. Frigates had a full-length gun deck that, in the Chesapeake battles, typically carried 36 or 38 long guns in the Royal Navy and 38 or 44 in the U.S. Navy. When carronades were introduced, the 38-gun class frigates carried 44 or more large-caliber guns and the 44-gun class frigates carried 56 or more guns.

globe match (or fire globe). These portable fire makers were used to set fire to an enemy's town or defensive works, etc. They were created from paper mâché laid upon a wooden bowl and made perfectly round. The globe was then perforated in several places and filled with a flammable composition so that, when lit, a lively fire issued out of the several holes.

grapeshot. Grapeshot consisted of nine large metal balls, packed in tiers of three around a center post on a circular iron tray called a stool, and contained by a cinched canvas bag or netting, resembling a cluster of grapes (hence the name). Larger than canister shot, grapeshot had a greater range and penetration and was used to disable ships' sails and rigging.

gun barge. A new class of gunboat designed in 1812 with shallow draft and double-ended (sharp bow and stern) hulls somewhat resembling a large whaleboat. The 50-foot version carried one mast; the 75-foot version two masts, both lateen-rigged. They usually carried a long gun aft and carronade forward. Most of the vessels employed in the Chesapeake Flotilla were gun barges.

gunboat. A small vessel of shallow draft carrying one or more cannon of large caliber; or any small vessels fitted for carrying cannon. A total of 177 gunboats were built for the U.S. Navy prior to 1809. Two of these, *No. 137* and *No. 138*, each 60 feet 5 inches long and built in Baltimore, were part of the Chesapeake Flotilla.

hogshead. A tobacco hogshead was a large wooden cask used to transport and store tobacco. A standardized hogshead measured 48 inches long and 30 inches in diameter

at the head and was capable of holding approximately 1200 pounds of cured tobacco, worth about £12 or approximately $52.44.

hulled. A ship's hull pierced with a cannonball.

impressment. The act of taking men into a navy by force and without notice.

kedge anchor. A light anchor used for warping a vessel.

lateen-rig. A triangular sail set on a long yard mounted at an angle on the mast and running in a fore-and-aft direction.

Letter of Marque. A government license authorizing a privateer to attack and capture enemy vessels.

light infantry. Lightly armed and equipped mobile soldiers whose job was to provide a skirmishing screen ahead of the main body of infantry.

limber. A two-wheeled cart generally pulled by horses accommodating an ammunition chest and attachable in tandem to a carriage for field cannon.

long gun. In historical navy usage, a long gun was the standard type of cannon mounted by a sailing vessel, called such to distinguish it from the shorter carronade. In informal usage, the length was combined with the weight of shot, yielding terms like "long 9s," referring to full-length cannons firing a 9-pound round shot.

man-of-war. Three-masted warship up to 200 feet long with as many as 124 guns, requiring three cannon decks to hold them—one more than any earlier ship.

minute gun. A gun that is discharged once every minute, usually as part of a military funeral.

mosquito fleet. Squadron of small gunboats or barges.

packet ship. A vessel employed to carry mail packets to and from British embassies, colonies, and outposts. In sea transport, a packet service is a regular, scheduled service, carrying freight and passengers. The ships used for this service are called packet ships or packet boats.

portfire. A hand-held fuse used for firing cannons, rockets, igniting explosives, etc.

privateer. An armed private vessel possessing a Letter of Marque and operated to capture enemy vessels and profit from the sale of the vessels and their cargo.

Quasi-War. An undeclared war fought mostly at sea between the United States and the French Republic from 1798 to 1800.

razee. A sailing ship that has been cut down (razeed) to reduce the number of decks. The word is derived from the French *vaisseau rasé*, meaning a razeed (in the sense of shaved down) ship.

ropewalk. A long, straight, narrow building or covered pathway where long strands of material were laid before being twisted into rope.

schooner. Type of sailing vessel characterized by the use of fore-and-aft (as opposed to square) sails on two or more masts with the forward mast being no taller than the rear mast. During the War of 1812 era, schooners were two masted.

scion. A descendant of a notable family, usually a son or daughter.

ship-of-the-line. A type of naval warship constructed from the seventeenth through the mid-nineteenth centuries to take part in the naval tactic known as the line of battle, in which two columns of opposing warships would maneuver to bring the greatest weight of broadside guns to bear. Since these engagements were almost invariably won by the heaviest ships carrying the most powerful guns, the natural progression was to build sailing vessels that were the largest and most powerful of their time. Ships-of-the-line normally carried 74 guns but the number could range between 60 and 120.

sloop-of-war. A warship smaller than a frigate with a single gun deck that carried up to 18 guns.

Society of Cincinnati. A historical organization with branches in the United States and France founded in 1783 to preserve the ideals and fellowship of the Revolutionary War officers and to pressure the government to honor pledges it had made to officers who fought for American independence. The society is named after a Roman general who refused to become a dictator after a war and who, like George Washington, returned to his plow and life as a farmer. Members often proudly wore their Society medals when they had their portraits painted.

Now in its third century, the Society is a nonprofit historical and educational organization that promotes public interest in the American Revolution through its library and museum collections, exhibitions, programs, publications, and other activities.

squadron. A division of a fleet forming one body under the command of a flag officer. Also a detachment of warships on some special duty.

tar. A common English term used to refer to seamen of the Merchant or Royal Navy. In the days before the invention of waterproof fabrics, sailors would coat their clothes with tar to make them repel water. Later sailors frequently wore coats and hats made from a waterproof fabric called tarpaulin. This may have been shortened to "tar" at some point.

tender. A boat used to service a ship, generally by transporting people and/or supplies to and from shore or another ship.

torpedo. During the War of 1812, a floating device called a torpedo was used to attack ships with an explosive charge.

Treaty of Ghent. Signed on December 24, 1814, in Ghent (modern-day Belgium), this treaty ended the War of 1812 between the United States of America and the United Kingdom of Great Britain and Ireland. The terms of the treaty were called "status quo ante bellum," meaning everything was taken back to the same condition prior to war; there were no territorial gains by either side. The U.S. Senate unanimously approved the treaty on February 16, 1815, and President James Madison exchanged ratification papers with a British diplomat in Washington on February 17, officially ending the war. The treaty was proclaimed on February 18, 1815.

vedette. From Latin videre, meaning "to see," also spelled vidette, it refers to a mounted sentry or outpost with the function of bringing information, giving signals or warnings of danger, etc., to a main body of troops.

warp (or warping). To haul a vessel forward by using a boat to deploy a kedge anchor ahead and then taking in the line using the vessel's capstan or winch, thus moving the vessel in the desired direction, often against wind and/or currents but also sometimes over shallow waters.

Whiskey Rebellion. A resistance movement in the 1790s. It was rooted in western dissatisfaction with various policies of the eastern-based national government. The name of the uprising comes from a 1791 excise tax on whiskey that was a central grievance of the westerners. The tax was part of Treasury Secretary Alexander Hamilton's program to centralize and pay off the national debt.

Yankee. The first recorded use of the term by the British to refer to Americans in general appears in the 1780s, in a letter by Lord Horatio Nelson. Around the same time it began to be abbreviated to Yank. During the American Revolution, American soldiers adopted Yankee Doodle not as a term of derision but as an expression of national pride. The derisive use nonetheless remained alive and even intensified in the South during the Civil War, when it referred not to all Americans but to those loyal to the Union.

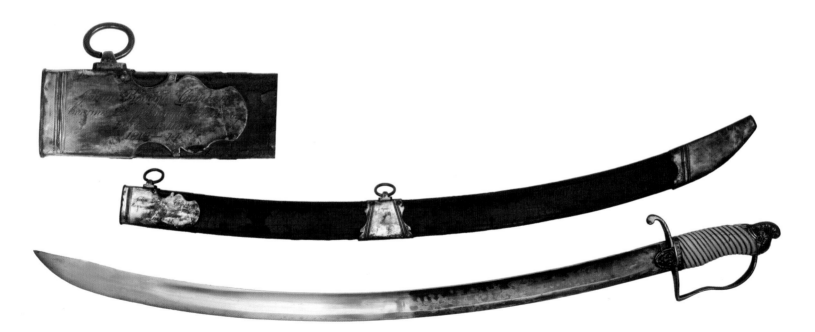

Captain John Berry's sabre and scabbard. Scabbard inscribed "John Berry Captain Commanding Washington Artillery Fort McHenry, 1812–1814."

SUGGESTIONS FOR FURTHER READING

Donald R. Hickey

For those interested in an overview of the War of 1812, a good place to start is *The War of 1812: A Forgotten Conflict*, rev. ed., by Donald R. Hickey (2011), which includes basic information on the political and diplomatic history of the war as well as the battles and campaigns. For the British/Canadian perspective, the best account is *The Incredible War of 1812: A Military History*, by J. Mackay Hitsman, updated by Donald E. Graves (1999). The most comprehensive military histories of the war, both of which have good treatments of operations in the Chesapeake, are *The War of 1812*, by John K. Mahon (1972) and *The U.S. Army in the War of 1812: An Operational and Command Study*, by Robert S. Quimby, 2 vols. (1997). For a classic antiquarian account

Pendant with musket ball that wounded Commodore Joshua Barney during the Battle of Bladensburg and ultimately took his life when the wound it inflicted flared up in 1818.

that is rich in detail and lore, see *The Pictorial Field-Book of the War of 1812*, by Benson J. Lossing (1868).

The best treatment of the war at sea is still *The Naval War of 1812*, 3rd ed., by Theodore Roosevelt (1883). For the role of privately armed vessels, many of which sailed from Baltimore, see *A History of American Privateers*, by Edgar Maclay (1899). No less important is *The Republic's Private Navy: The American Privateering Business as Practiced by Baltimore during the War of 1812*, by Jerome R. Garitee (1977), which is a superb account of the in-port side of privateering.

For works that focus on the war in the Chesapeake, *The Dawn's Early Light*, by Walter Lord (1972), is a lively account that is still serviceable. This should be supplemented with *Terror on the Chesapeake: The War of 1812 on the Bay*, by Christopher T. George (2000); *The Burning of Washington: The British Invasion of 1814*, by Anthony Pitch (1998); *The Battle for Baltimore, 1814*, by Joseph Whitehorne (1997); and *Flotilla: The Patuxent Naval Campaign in the War of 1812*, rev. ed., by Donald G. Shomette (2009).

There are several good biographies that shed light on the Chesapeake theater. For the president's role, see *James Madison: Commander-in-Chief, 1812–1836*, by Irving Brant (1961), or the more compact *The Presidency of James Madison*, by Robert Allen Rutland (1990). For information on those more immediately involved in the war in the Chesapeake, see *Merchant Congressman in the Young Republic: Samuel Smith of Maryland, 1752–1839*, by Frank A. Cassell (1971), and *Sailor of Fortune: The Life and Adventures of Commodore Barney, U.S.N.*, by Hulbert Footner (1940). For the view from the British perspective, there are two good biographies of the man in charge of many of the amphibious operations: *The Man Who Burned the White House: Admiral Sir George Cockburn, 1772–1853*, by James Pack (1987), and *Cockburn and the British Navy in Transition: Admiral Sir George Cockburn, 1772–1853*, by Roger Morriss (1997).

For primary sources bearing on the war in the Chesapeake see the indispensable *The Naval War of 1812: A Documentary History*, 4 vols., edited by William S. Dudley, Michael J. Crawford, and Others (1985–). See also the British memoirs by George R. Gleig, *A Narrative of the Campaigns of the British Army at Washington, Baltimore, and New Orleans* (1821), and James Scott, *Recollections of a Naval Life*, 3 vols. (1834).

The best guide to war-related sites in the Chesapeake is *The War of 1812 in the Chesapeake: A Reference Guide to Historic Sites in Maryland, Virginia, and the District of Columbia*, by Ralph Eshelman, Scott Sheads, and Donald R. Hickey (2010). For a more compact and portable version of this guide, see *A Travel Guide to the War of 1812 in the Chesapeake*, by Ralph Eshelman (2011).

Suggested websites include:

Library of Congress Guide to the War of 1812
www.loc.gov/rr/program/bib/1812

National Archives and Records Administration Military Resources: War of 1812
www.archives.gov/research/military/war-of-1812/index.html

U.S. Navy Naval History and Heritage Command
www.history.navy.mil/commemorations/1812/1812-index.htm

The Star-Spangled Banner: The Flag That Inspired the National Anthem
www.americanhistory.si.edu/starspangledbanner

War of 1812 in the Chesapeake Region: A Living History Clearinghouse
www.chesapeake1812.com

ILLUSTRATION CREDITS

Permission to use images in this book was granted specifically by the owner, copyright holder, or licensee of the image. Anyone seeking to reuse an image contained in this publication must contact the owner or copyright holder and obtain express permission to use the image. Such usage may require the payment of a fee. The list below contains information regarding the owner or copyright holder for all images.

Horseman's sabre used by Elijah Stansbury, Jr., of Captain Montgomery's Baltimore Union Artillery at the Battle of North Point. Elijah Stansbury, Jr., served as mayor of Baltimore from 1848 to 1850.

Abbreviations

CMM	Calvert Marine Museum, Solomons, Maryland
Embleton	Gerry Embleton
FMNMHS	Fort McHenry National Monument and Historic Shrine
GC	Granger Collection
LC-PPD	Library of Congress-Prints and Photographs Division
MdHS	Maryland Historical Society
MOTD	Maryland Office of Tourism Development
MSA	Maryland State Archives
NARA	National Archives and Records Administration
NGA	National Gallery of Art
NHHC	Naval History and Historical Command
NLS	National Library of Scotland
NMM	National Maritime Museum, Greenwich, England
NPS	National Park Service
O'Brien	Patrick O'Brien
Pratt	Robert E. Pratt
Schlecht	Richard Schlecht
USMC	U.S. Marine Corps Collection
USNAM	U.S. Naval Academy Museum
WHHA	White House Historical Association

Front Matter

iii: courtesy Jason Kopp, 2011; **vi:** (*left*), courtesy U.S. Geological Survey, Earth Resources Observation and Science Center; (*right*) © Pratt, commissioned 2011; **viii:** c. 1814 aquatint by John Bower, Hambleton Print Collection, item ID H89, courtesy MdHS; **x:** courtesy Clements Library, University of Michigan; **xiv:** 1813 oil painting by John Schetky, reference no. 1964.692, Mystic Seaport; **xvi–xvii:** © Pratt, commissioned 2011; **xviii–1:** © Embleton, commissioned 2011.

PART I. WAR IN THE CHESAPEAKE, 1812–1815

Chapter One. Drifting into War, 1807–1812

2-3: © Schlecht, commissioned 2011; **5:** (*left*) 1816 painting by Tomas Sully, USNAM; (*center*) image no. 0037544, GC; (*right*) etching, photograph no. NH 56817, NHHC; **6:** image no. 0009131, GC; **7:** image no. 836439, Library and Archives Canada; **8:** images no. 0032952 and 0035944, GC; **9:** 1813 etching with watercolor by William Charles, image no. LC-DIG-ppmsca-10756, LC, PPD; **10-11:** © Embleton, commissioned 2011; **13:** c. 1811 aquatint print, image no. 1937.1689.000001, Mariners' Museum; **14:** 1818 painting by Matthew Harris Jouett, courtesy Transylvania University; **15:** (*top*) *Escape of HMS* Belvidera, *23 June 1812*, painting by William John Huggins, image no. BHC0598, NMM; (*bottom*) *Explosion on the* President, from Willis J. Abbot, *The Naval History of the United States*, 1896, p. 294; **16:** Rodgers portrait, c. 1814 oil painting by John Wesley Jarvis, NGA; **17:** © Embleton, commissioned 2011; **18:** *Schooner Patapsco of Baltimore, Richard Moon, Com., Making her Escape from an 18 Gun Brig after receiving three Broad Sides off Lanzarote 21th September 1814*, watercolor by unknown artist, item ID

1986.88, courtesy MdHS; **21:** *Death of General Pike,* image no. 809023, New York Public Library.

Chapter Two. A Red Terror Arrives on the Chesapeake, 1813

22–23: *Attack on Havre de Grace. Admiral Cockburn Burning & Plundering Havre de Grace on the 1ˢᵗ of June 1813. Done from a Sketch Taken on the Spot at the Time,* c. 1813 print by William Charles, Hambleton Print Collection, item ID H151, courtesy MdHS; **24:** image no. BHC2619, NMM; **25:** © Embleton, commissioned 2011; **26:** © Embleton, commissioned 2011; **27:** (*top*) item ID 1931.4.1, courtesy MdHS; (*bottom*) item ID 1954.88.1, courtesy MdHS; **28:** © Embleton, commissioned 2011; **31:** *Rough sketch of French town, on Elk river, Cecil county Maryland,* by Benjamin Henry Latrobe, item ID 1960.108.1.9.3, courtesy MdHS; **32:** (*left*) © Embleton, commissioned 2011; (*right*) *Attack upon George & Frederick's towns by a detachment of boats from the R[ight] Honorable Sir. J.B. Warren's Squadron under Rear Admiral Cockburn in April 1813, Hon. Capt. Byng, Commanding,* LC-PPD; **33:** © Embleton, commissioned 2011; **34:** © Embleton, commissioned 2011; **35:** © Embleton, commissioned 2011; **37:** © Embleton, commissioned 2011; **38:** © Embleton, commissioned 2011; **39:** © Embleton, commissioned 2011; **40:** painting by H. Charles McBarron, Jr., courtesy Parks Canada; **41:** Benson J. Lossing, *Pictorial Field-Book of the War of 1812,* 1868, p. 688; **42:** © Embleton, commissioned 2011; **43:** detail of Mathew Carey, *Maryland* map, 1814; Huntingfield Corporation Map Collection, MSA SC 1399-1-40; **44:** © Embleton, commissioned 2011; **45:** © Embleton, commissioned 2011; **46–47:** © Embleton, commissioned 2011.

Chapter Three. A Fateful Year Begins, 1814

48–49: © Schlecht, commissioned 2011; **51:** (*left*) Model built by Jimmy Langley, image courtesy of CMM; (*right*) NARA; **52:** c. 1817 painting by Rembrandt Peale, Baltimore City Life Museum collection, image ID BCLM-CA.682, courtesy MdHS; **53:** (*top*) 2005 illustration, courtesy Carl E. Franklin; (*bottom*) from *A Treatise on the General Principals, Power and Facility of Application of the Congreve Rocket System . . . ,* London, 1827, plate 11, p. 81, Anne S. K. Brown Military Collection, Brown University Library; **55:** (*top*) © Embleton, commissioned 2011; (*bottom*) *Philanthropie moderne,* c. 1814 hand-colored engraving by Smith of New

York, image no. PolitCartP566 Bib ID: 153018, courtesy of American Antiquarian Society; **56:** c. 1814 water-colored pen-and-ink map, courtesy NLS; **57:** Ms 2326. ff 288A verso–288B recto, courtesy NLS; **58:** © Embleton, commissioned 2011; **60:** © Embleton, commissioned 2011; **61:** RG45, Misc. Letters Received, 1814, vol. 5, no. 111, M124, roll no. 64, NARA; **62:** © Embleton, commissioned 2012; **65:** © Embleton, commissioned 2011; **66:** c. 1819 oil portrait of James Monroe by Samuel Finley Breese Morse, image no. 965.587.1, courtesy WHHA; **66–67:** © Embleton, commissioned 2011; **68:** *Annapolis from Church Circle,* detail of 1794 watercolor by Cotton Milbourne, courtesy of the Hammond-Harwood House Association, image from MSA.

Chapter Four. Invasion! August 1814

70–71: © Schlecht, commissioned 2011; **73:** © Embleton, commissioned 2011; **74:** © Embleton, commissioned 2011; **76:** (*left*) unknown artist, portrait owned by Stephen Campbell, photograph courtesy of Christopher George; (*right*) 1804 engraving by C.B.J.F. de Saint-Memin, reproduction no. LC-USZ61-1899, LC-PPD, **77:** (*left*) courtesy of MSA; (*right*) Fort Covington Collection, MSS 35, Special Collections, St. Lawrence University Libraries, Canton, New York; **78–79:** © Embleton, commissioned 2011; **80:** (*left*) reproduction no. LC-USZ6-587, LC-PPD; (*top right*) © Ralph Eshelman, 2001 photograph; (*bottom right*) © Ralph Eshelman, 2011 photograph; **81:** © Ralph Eshelman, 2005 photograph; **82:** © Ralph Eshelman, 2011 photograph; **83:** (*top*) © Embleton, commissioned 2011; (*bottom*) Baltimore *American,* May 18, 1814, courtesy MSA; **84–85:** © Embleton, commissioned 2011; **86:** *Sketch of Bladensburg, looking northward,* by Benjamin Henry Latrobe, item ID 1960.108.1.9.7, courtesy MdHS; **87:** early 1980s painting by Charles Waterhouse, USMC Collection; **88:** © Embleton, commissioned 2011; **89:** © Embleton, commissioned 2011; **90:** Albert Small Collection, courtesy of Albert Small; **92:** © Embleton, commissioned 2011; **93:** © Embleton, commissioned 2011.

Chapter Five. Washington Is Burning! August 1814

94–95: *U.S. Capitol after burning by the British,* c. 1814 ink and watercolor by George Munger, reproduction no. LC-DIG-ppmsca-23076, LC-PPD; **97:** *A view of the Capitol of Washington before it was burnt down by the British,* c.

1800 watercolor by William Russell Birch, reproduction no. LC-DIG-ppmsca-07708 (digital file from original drawing), LC-PPD; **98:** (*left*) © Embleton, commissioned 2011; (*right*) © Ralph Eshelman, 2008 photograph; **99:** (*left*) detail, c. between 1803 and 1814, ink and watercolor wash by Benjamin Henry Latrobe, reproduction no. LC-USZC4-122, LC-PPD; (*right*) © Embleton, commissioned 2011; **100:** *From the Ashes,* painting by Peter Waddell, © 2005 Grand Lodge of the District of Columbia; **102:** © Embleton, commissioned 2011; **103:** 2004 painting by Tom Freeman, courtesy WHHA; **104:** (*top*) *U.S. White House after burning by the British,* c. 1814 ink and watercolor by George Munger, reproduction no.: LC-DIG-ppmsca-23076, LC-PPD; (*bottom*) ink and watercolor by Benjamin Henry Latrobe, item ID 1961.130.1, courtesy MdHS; **105:** © Embleton, commissioned 2011; **106:** © Embleton, commissioned 2011; **108:** image no. BHC2934, NMM; **109:** photograph by Gary Tarleton, NPS, courtesy of FMNMHS; **110:** (*left and right*) © Embleton, commissioned 2011; **112:** image no. BHC2717, NMM; **113:** (*top*) NARA; (*bottom*) © Embleton, commissioned 2011; **114:** © Embleton, commissioned 2011; **115:** © Embleton, commissioned 2011; **116:** (*left*) c. 1813 painting by Rembrandt Peale, item ID 1857.2.7, courtesy MdHS; (*top right*) painting by Charles Willson Peale, Independence National Park, courtesy NPS, Philadelphia; (*bottom right*) courtesy USNAM; **117:** © Embleton, commissioned 2011.

Chapter Six. The Battle for Baltimore, September 1814

118–19: © Schlecht, commissioned 2011; **121:** painting by Don Troiani, National Guard Heritage Series, © Troiani; **122:** *Baltimore, view from the Brickyard,* 1804 painting by Francis Guy, Baltimore City Life Museum Collections, item ID BCLM-MA.8148, courtesy MdHS; **124:** manuscript drawings, Captain Charles Gordon, USN, courtesy of MSA; **125:** 1817–18 painting by Rembrandt Peale, Baltimore City Life Museum, item ID BCLM-CA.681, courtesy MdHS; **126–27:** © Embleton, commissioned 2011; **127:** Adam Wallace, *The Parson of the Islands,* 1861, between p. 144–45; **128:** photograph of painting from Annie Leakin Sioussat, *Old Baltimore,* 1931, p. 187; **129:** (*left*) c. 1817–18 painting by Rembrandt Peale, Baltimore City Life Museum Collection, image ID BCLM-CA.683, courtesy MdHS; (*right*) detail of c. 1814 painting *Battle of North Point near Baltimore,* by Thomas Coke Ruckle, Sr., courtesy MdHS; **130:** © Embleton, commissioned 2011; **131:** © Embleton, commissioned 2011; **132:** *The death of General Ross, near Baltimore*, engraved by G. M. Brighty, published 1816 by T. Kinnersley, reproduction no. LC-USZ62-100670, LC-PPD; **133:** *View of the spot where General Ross fell Near Baltimore*, 1820 engraving by J. Hill based on painting by Joshua Shaw, published by M. Carey and Sons, Philadelphia, Hambleton Print Collection, item ID H92, courtesy MdHS; **134–35:** *Battle of North Point near Baltimore*, 1814 painting by Thomas Coke Ruckle, Sr., item ID 1939.11.1, courtesy MdHS; **136:** © Embleton, commissioned 2011; **138:** *The Gathering of the Troops on Hampstead Hill*, c. 1814 painting by Thomas Coke Ruckle, Sr., item ID 1979.2.1, courtesy MdHS; **139:** © Embleton, commissioned 2011; **140:** date and photographer unknown, courtesy Dundalk Patapsco Neck Historical Society; **141:** *An Eyewitness Sketch of the Bombardment of Ft. Mc Henry*, c. October 1814 watercolor sketch by Lieutenant Henry Fisher of the 27th Maryland regiment, Baltimore City Life Museum Collection, image ID BCLM-MA.480, courtesy MdHS; **142:** *The Battle of Fort McHenry*, painting attributed to Francis Guy, from the collection of Stiles T. Colwill, image courtesy of MSA; **143:** *Bombardment of Fort McHenry*, c. 1826–30 painting by Alfred Jacob Miller, item ID 1901.2.3, courtesy MdHS; **144:** courtesy Harford County Government; **145:** © Embleton, commissioned 2011; **147:** (*top*) painting attributed to Mary Cecilia Coad, Georgetown University Special Collections; (*bottom*) from *Early Manor Plantation Houses of Maryland*, by H. Chandlee Forman, 1934, p. 29; **149:** © Embleton, commissioned 2011.

Chapter Seven. Peace, Jubilation, and Memory, 1815

150–51: painting by Patrick O'Brien, © Patricia B. Kummerow Memorial Fund, 2011; **152:** photograph by unknown photographer of painting by unknown artist, City Life Museum Collections, item ID M.1975.3.3, courtesy MdHS; **153:** (*top*) undated albumen silver print photograph (prior to 1862) by Daniel Bendann and David Bendann, item ID PVF, courtesy MdHS; (*bottom*) Surprise *Capturing the Star, January 28, 1815*, pen and ink, watercolor and gouache painting by Murdock McPherson, image no. 1909.2.1, courtesy MdHS; **154:** *Battle between the Brig* Chasseur *and the schooner* St. Lawrence, *off Havana on the 26th Feb 1815*, tinted lithograph by A. Weingartner, image no.

PAD5856, NMM; **155:** © Embleton, commissioned 2011; **157:** © Embleton, commissioned 2011; **158:** (*left*) c. 1815 painting by Rembrandt Peale, MSA/Peabody Institute Library, copy courtesy MdHS; (*right*) 1828 engraving by B. Tanner, courtesy MdHS; **159:** Benson J. Lossing, *Pictorial Field-Book of the War of 1812*, 1868, p. 964; **160:** (*top*) 1858 photograph by unknown photographer, item MC2088, courtesy MdHS; (*bottom*) 1880 photograph by unknown photographer, item ID PP135.36, courtesy MdHS; **161:** c. 1876–80 photograph by W. Ashman, item ID GPVF, courtesy MdHS; **162:** © Embleton, commissioned 2011; **163:** © Embleton, commissioned 2011; **164:** Lester S. Levy Star-Spangled Banner Collection, Sheet Music Collection, Courtesy MdHS; **165:** photograph courtesy National Museum of American History, Smithsonian Institution; **167:** c. 1873 chromolithograph by George A. Crofutt after painting by John Gast, reproduction no. LC-DIG-ppmsca-09855, LC-PPD; **168–69:** © Embleton, commissioned 2012.

PART II. VISITING HISTORIC SITES AND OTHER ATTRACTIONS

170-71: courtesy Visit Baltimore; **174:** (*left*) courtesy Visit Baltimore; (*right*) Dietrich Ruehlmann, 2010, courtesy NPS; **175:** courtesy MOTD; **176:** © Pratt, commissioned 2011; **177:** (*left*) © Ralph Eshelman, 2011; (*right*) John H. Whitehead III, 2001, courtesy of Foundation for Historic Christ Church; **178:** Starke Jett, courtesy NPS; **179:** Matt Rath, 2011, courtesy NPS; **180:** (*left*) © Ralph Eshelman, 2007; (*right*) © Ralph Eshelman, 2011; **182:** (*left*) © Pratt, commissioned 2011; (*right*) © Ralph Eshelman, 2011; **183:** courtesy of Earl Robicheaux, 2006; **184:** © Ralph Eshelman, 2010; **185:** David Krankowski, 2006, courtesy Jefferson Patterson Park and Museum; **186:** courtesy St. Mary's County Tourism Office, 2009; **188:** © Pratt, commissioned 2011; **189:** (*left*) courtesy MOTD; (*right*) © Ralph Eshelman, 2010; **190:** (*left and right*) © Ralph Eshelman, 2010; **191:** (*left*) © Ralph Eshelman, 2008; (*center*) Kathi Ash, 2012; (*right*) © Middleton Evans, courtesy NPS; **192:** courtesy MOTD; **193:** courtesy Dorchester County Tourism; **194:** © Pratt, commissioned 2011; **195:** (*left*) Kathi Ash, 2012; (*right*) City of Havre de Grace; **196:** (*top center*) courtesy MOTD; (*bottom center*) © Ralph Eshelman, 2010; (*right*) © Ralph Eshelman, 2010; **198:** © Pratt, commissioned 2011; **199:** (*left*) © Ralph Eshelman, 2011; (*right*) © Ralph

Eshelman, 2011; **200:** © Ralph Eshelman, 2011; **201:** courtesy MOTD; **202:** © Pratt, commissioned 2011; **203:** (*left*) © Ralph Eshelman, 2010; (*right*) © Ralph Eshelman, 2011; **204:** © Middleton Evans, courtesy NPS; **206:** © Ralph Eshelman, 2011; **207:** Suzanne Copping, 2010, courtesy NPS; **208:** © Pratt, commissioned 2011; **209:** (*left*) Terry Adams, 2007, courtesy NPS; (*right*) © Ralph Eshelman, 2011; **210:** (*left*) Richard Schneider, 2011, courtesy U.S. National Archives; (*right*) courtesy National Museum of American History, Smithsonian Institution; **211:** © Ralph Eshelman, 2011; **212:** (*left*) courtesy Jane Kinsman, 2012; (*right*) courtesy NPS, 2008; **213:** © Ralph Eshelman, 2012; **214:** (*left*) Chris Spielmann, courtesy NPS; (*right*) Erik Kvalsvik, 2011, courtesy Carlyle House Historic Park; **215:** courtesy NPS, 2010; **216:** © Pratt, commissioned 2011; **217:** (*left*) courtesy MOTD; (*right*) Courtesy Visit Baltimore, 2012; **218:** (*left*) Dietrich Ruehlmann, courtesy NPS; (*right*) courtesy Visit Baltimore, 2012; **219:** (*left*) © Ralph Eshelman, 2009; (*right*) Kathi Ash, 2009; **220:** © Middleton Evans, courtesy NPS; **221:** Kathi Ash, 2012; **222:** (*left*) © Ralph Eshelman, 2004; (*right*) © Ralph Eshelman, 2009; **223:** © Middleton Evans, courtesy NPS.

BACK MATTER

224: courtesy National Archives United Kingdom, London; **231:** item ID 1923.8.2, MdHS; **232:** S.W. Fores, "The Fall of Washington or Maddy in full flight," LC-PPD; **235:** auction catalog, current location unknown, www.historicalimagebank.com/gallery/main.php/v/album02/album33/album82/WOa181d+Sword+of+Captain+John+Berry+commanding+the+Washington+Artillery+at+the+battle+of+Fort+Mc Henry+Baltimore+1814.html; **236:** DAR Museum, Gift of Mr. Richard H. Thompson; **237:** item ID 1897.3.1a, MdHS; **240:** (*top*) courtesy MSA; (*bottom*) Pulteney Malcolm Papers, William L. Clements Library, University of Michigan; **251:** item ID 1923.8.1, MdHS.

An unidentified individual made this entry in the minute book of Trinity Church some time after the British passed through Upper Marlboro, Maryland, in August 1814, noting that pages were removed by some of Major General Ross's men. The entry concludes, "to their eternal disgrace be it recorded."

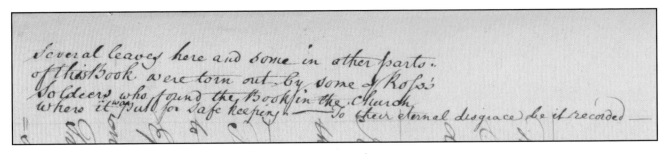

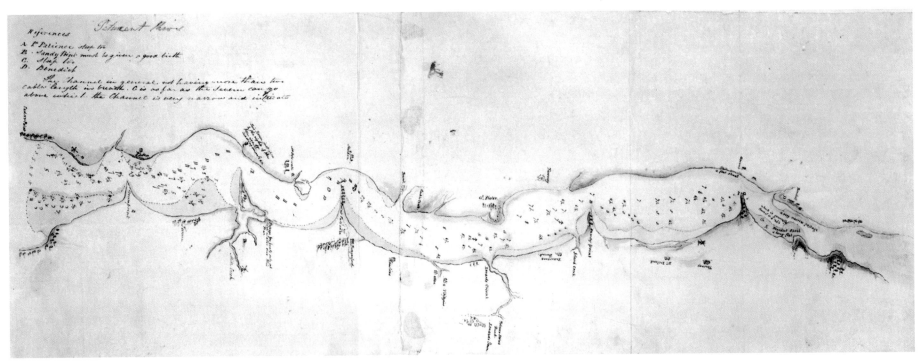

Circa 1814 British chart of the lower Patuxent River showing water depths, anchorages, and landmarks to help navigate the river. This chart was prepared in anticipation of the British fleet's ascending the river for the invasion of Maryland and the occupation of Washington, D.C.

Index

Page numbers in italics refer to illustrations

U.S. Army Model 1813 enlisted leather cap, copied from the British and known as a "tombstone" cap. The white paint on the edge imitates a cloth binding. The cap was originally decorated with tassels draped across the front. The leather flap could be folded down over the high coat collar during inclement weather.

About the Creative Team

Two historians, researchers, and writers—Ralph Eshelman and Burt Kummerow—conceived the idea for this book and led the creative team.

Ralph Eshelman has over thirty-five years of cultural resource management experience. Specific to the War of 1812, he was co-director of the Patuxent River Cultural Resources Survey, partially excavating an American 1812 military vessel. Eshelman conducted an extensive survey of Maryland 1812 sites for the National Park Service American Battlefield Protection Program and served as historian consultant on planning teams for the Star-Spangled Banner National Historic Trail Feasibility Study and Star-Spangled Banner National Historic Trail Comprehensive Management Plan. He has written or co-authored three War of 1812 books and, having personally visited and photographed nearly every 1812 site in the Chesapeake Bay region, is considered the leading expert on this resource base. Many of his photographs are included in this book.

Burt Kummerow began his career studying Rome and Greece and especially Pompeii, then went on to early America. He helped found the Living History Movement and has been a writer and popular speaker, public television producer, museum director, and rock musician. As the president of Historyworks, Inc., based in Maryland, he is a multi-faceted public historian who uses a wide range of skills and experience to bring history to the general public. He was a principal consultant to the French and Indian War 250th Anniversary Consortium. He is the author of three other books, *War for Empire, Heartland,* and *Pennsylvania's Forbes Trail*. At present, Kummerow is the president and CEO of the Maryland Historical Society.

Internationally recognized military and maritime artists Richard Schlecht, Gerry Embleton, and Patrick O'Brien have provided over fifty original drawings and paintings for *In Full Glory Reflected*.

Richard Schlecht has been a Maryland-based freelance illustrator since 1970. He has specialized in history, archaeology, and anthropology and is noted for his accurate and detailed illustrations, especially of military and maritime historical events. Clients have included the National Geographic Society, the United States Postal Service, the National Park Service, Colonial Williamsburg Foundation, and the Yorktown Museum.

Gerry Embleton is an Anglo-Swiss artist working both in Europe and the United States. He is well known as an illustrator of military subjects, specializing in highly detailed, accurate studies of costume with his specialty being military uniforms. His work has appeared in over forty titles by the military publisher *Osprey*.

Patrick O'Brien has been an acclaimed illustrator and painter since 1985. In 2003 he entered the marine art field and has been featured in *Naval History* and *Sea History* magazines as well as on the History Channel. O'Brien has had several one-man shows, the latest at the U.S. Naval Academy Museum in 2010.

Robert E. Pratt is a freelance mapmaker with twenty-eight years of experience at the National Geographic Society Map Department. A Virginian with a family that goes back centuries in the Old Dominion State, Pratt has produced several National Geographic Society maps on the region. His latest efforts chart U.S. Maritime Wrecks in the Chesapeake, the Civil War in the region, and the Journey Through Hallowed Ground between Charlottesville and Gettysburg.

Alex Castro, the book's designer, is an award-winning artist and architect who specializes in architectural, exhibition, and book design. He is the creative director of Baltimore's *Urbanite* magazine and is a lecturer in studio art at Washington College, Chestertown, Maryland. He is a member of the Maryland Public Art Commission.